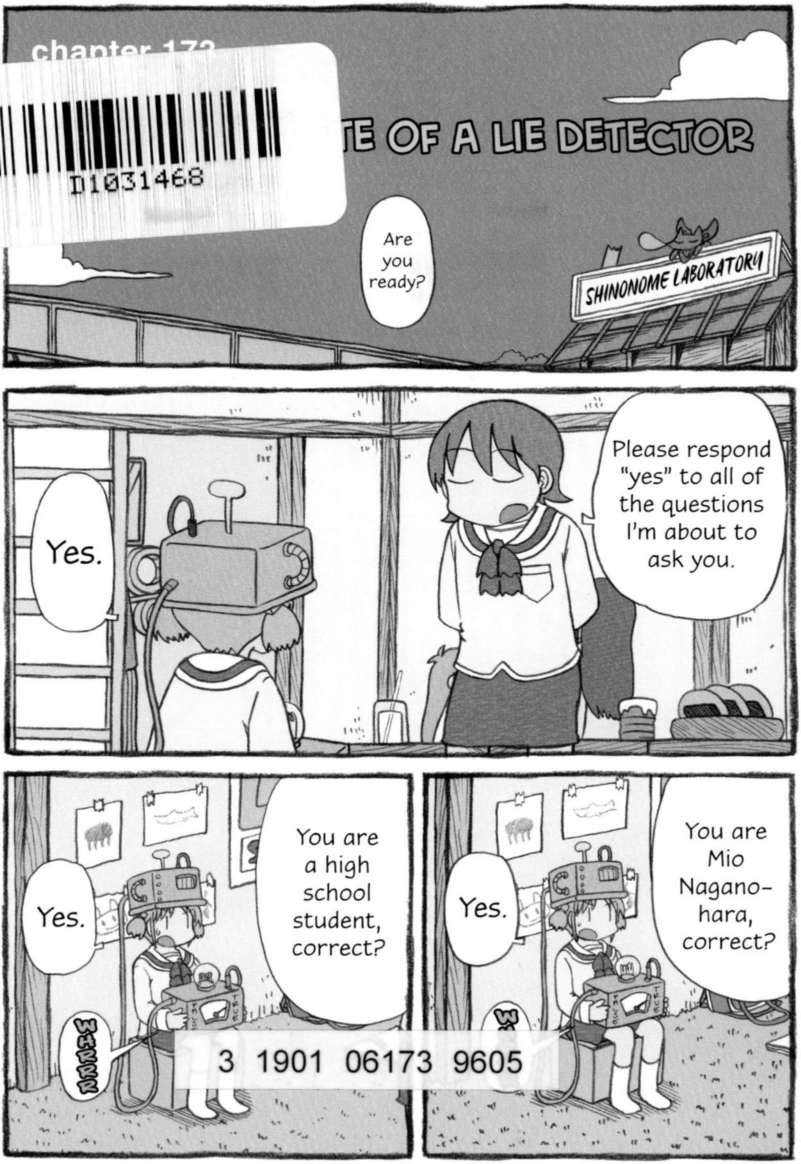
chapter 17
TE OF A LIE DETECTOR
Are you ready?
SHINONOME LABORATORY
Please respond "yes" to all of the questions I'm about to ask you.
Yes.
You are Mio Nagano-hara, correct?
Yes.
You are a high school student, correct?
Yes.
WHRRR

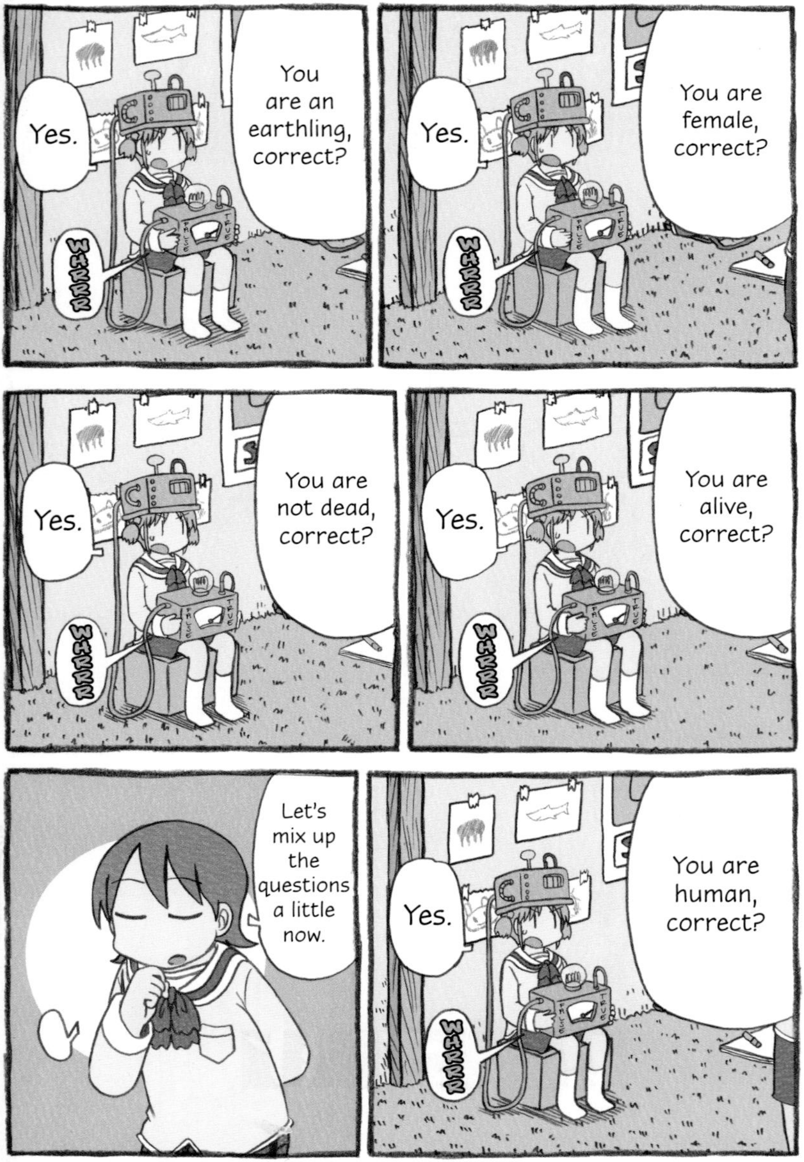
You are female, correct?
Yes.
WHRRR
You are an earthling, correct?
Yes.
WHRRR
You are alive, correct?
Yes.
WHRRR
You are not dead, correct?
Yes.
WHRRR
You are human, correct?
Yes.
WHRRR
Let's mix up the questions a little now.

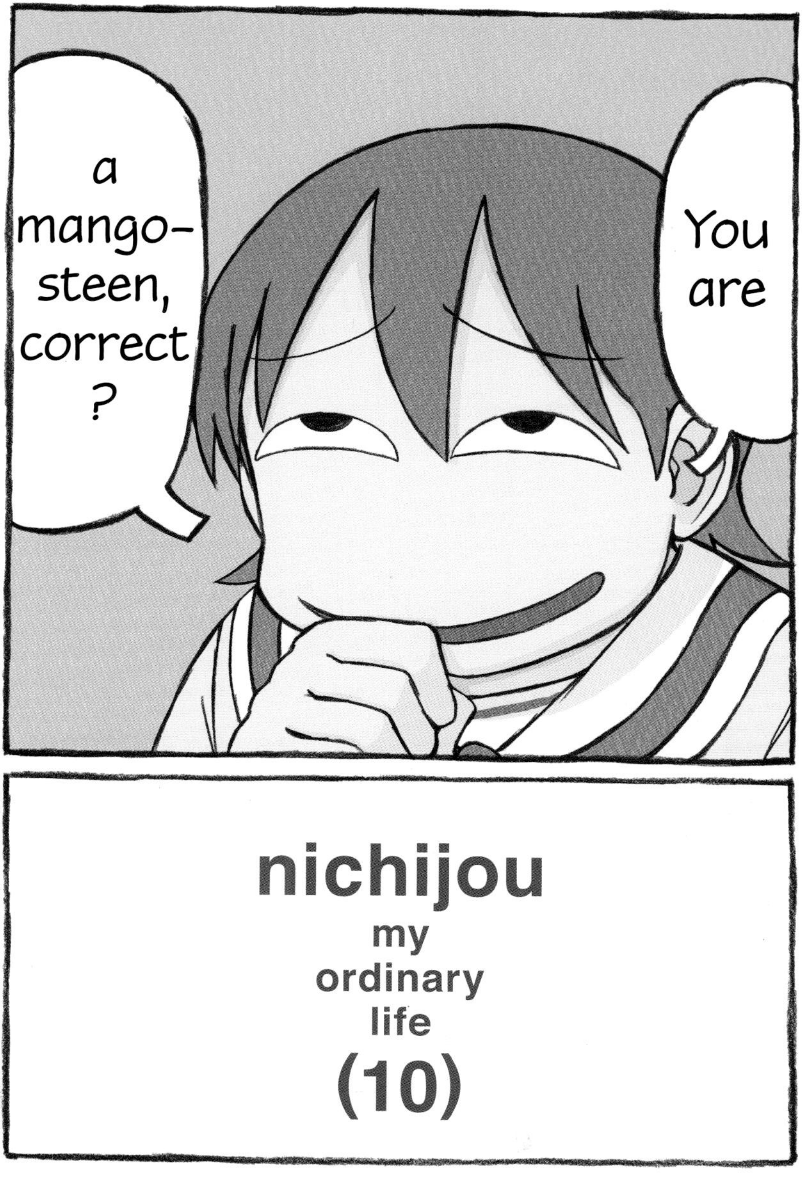
You are
a mango-steen, correct ?

nichijou
my ordinary life
(10)

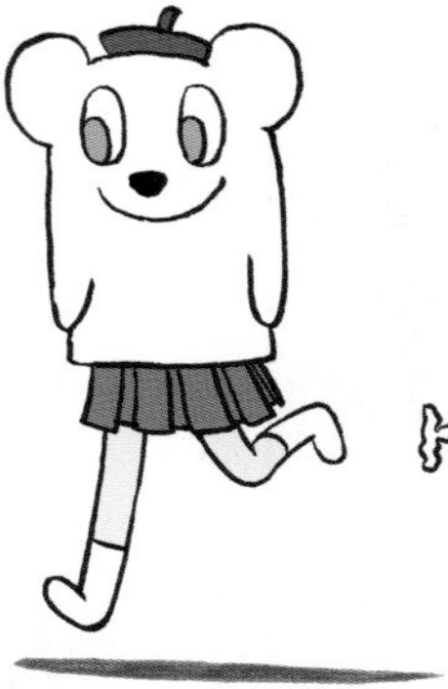

THE TOC

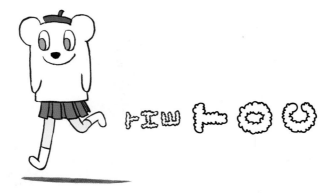

chapter 174

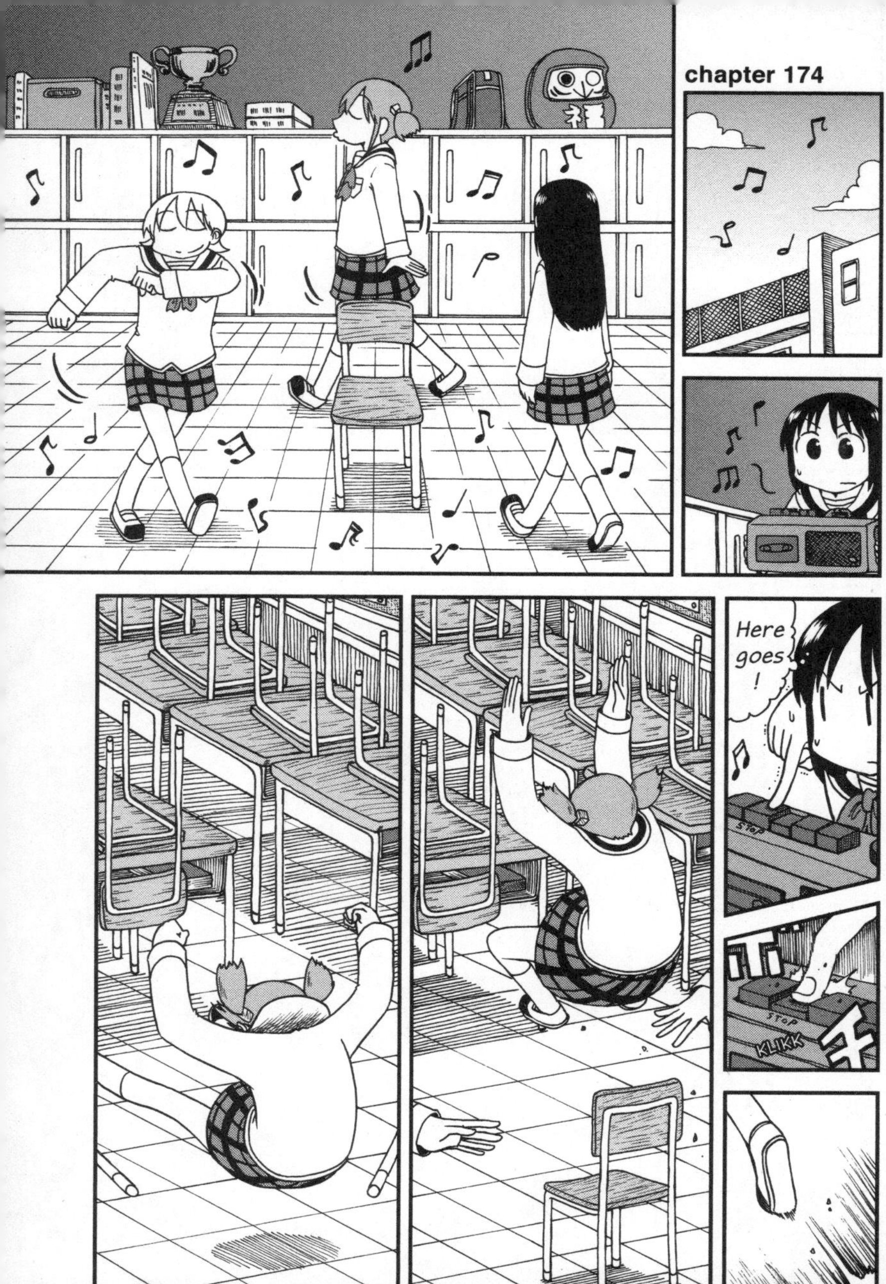
Here goes!
STOP
STOP
KLIKK

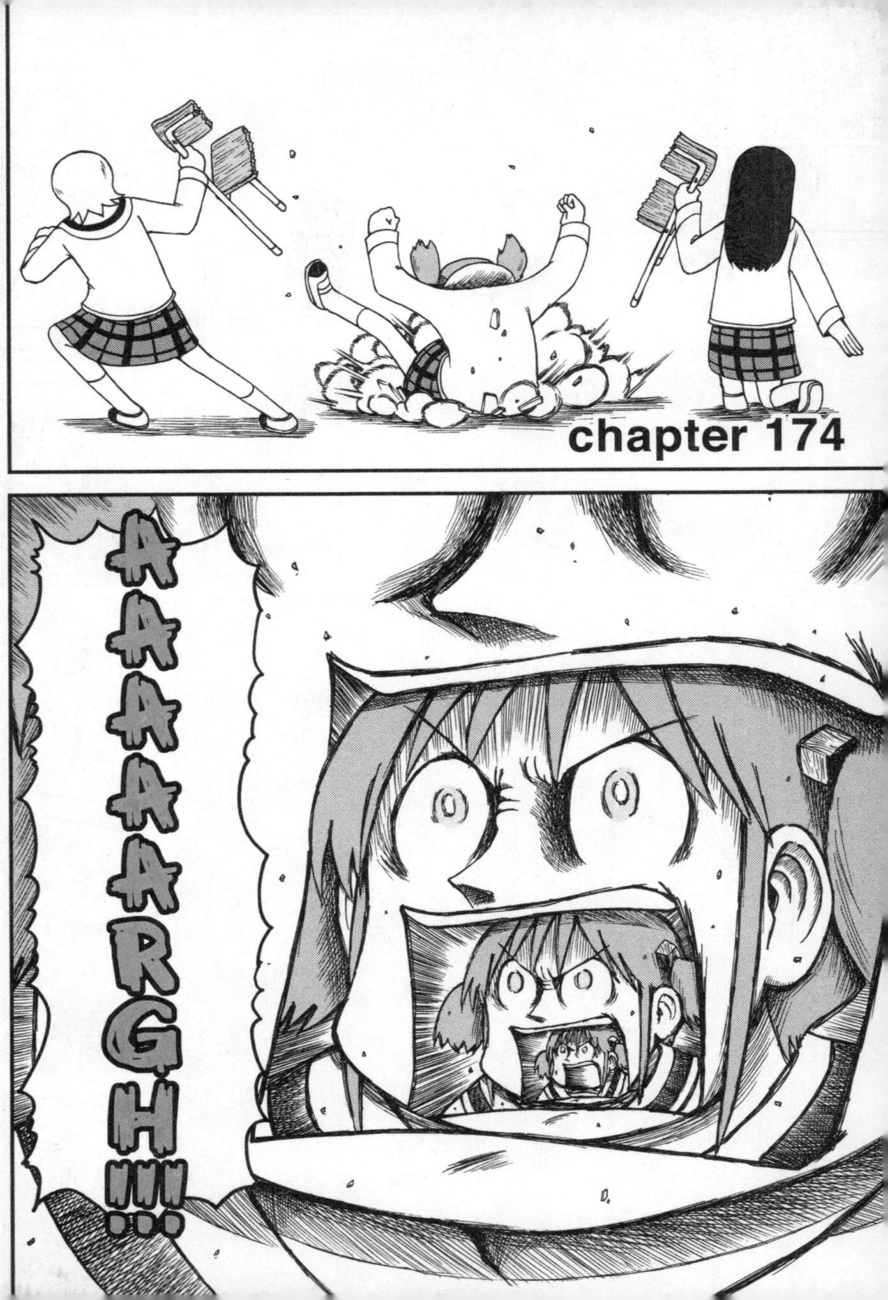
chapter 174
AAAAARGH!!!

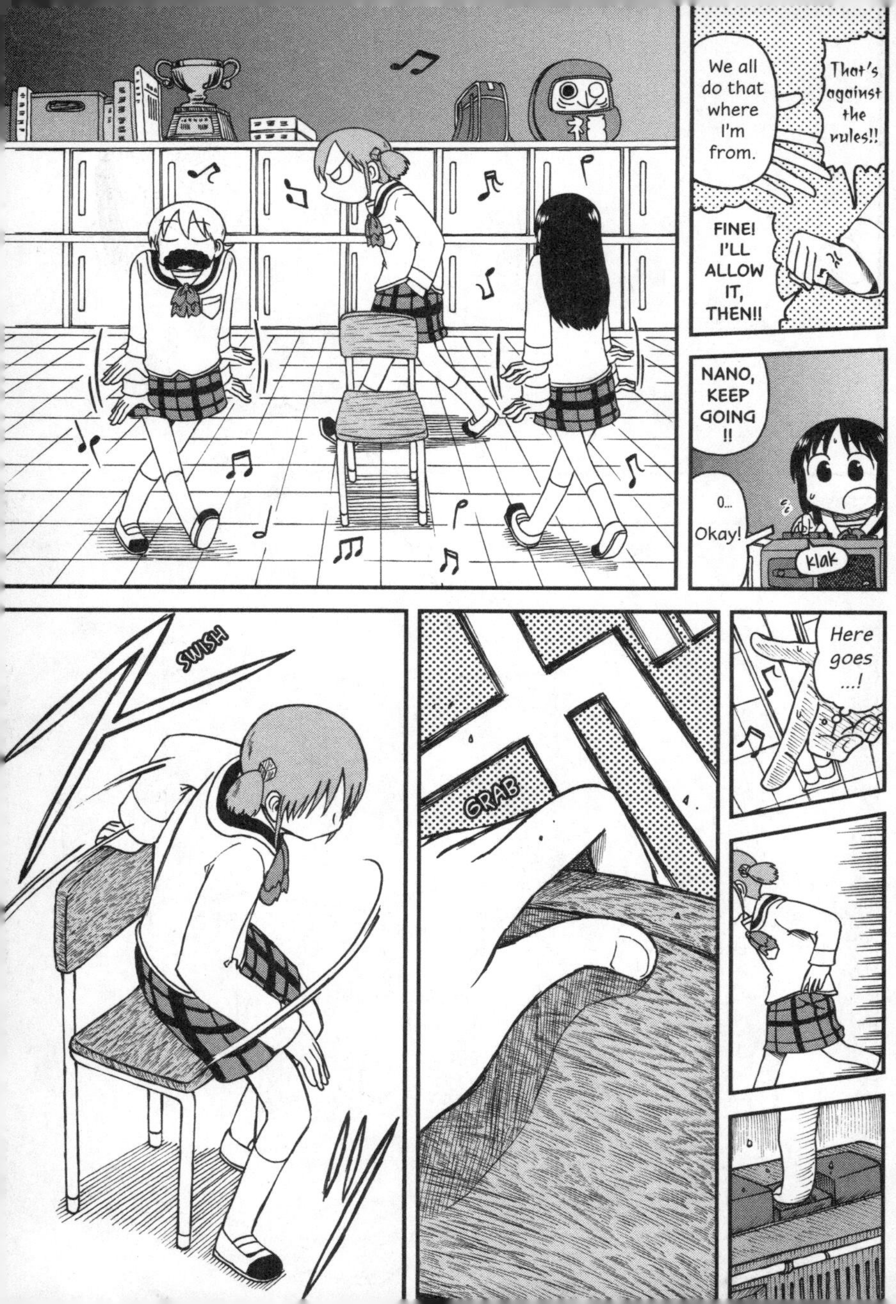
That's against the rules!!
We all do that where I'm from.
FINE! I'LL ALLOW IT, THEN!!
NANO, KEEP GOING!!
O... Okay!
KLAK
Here goes ...!
GRAB
SWISH

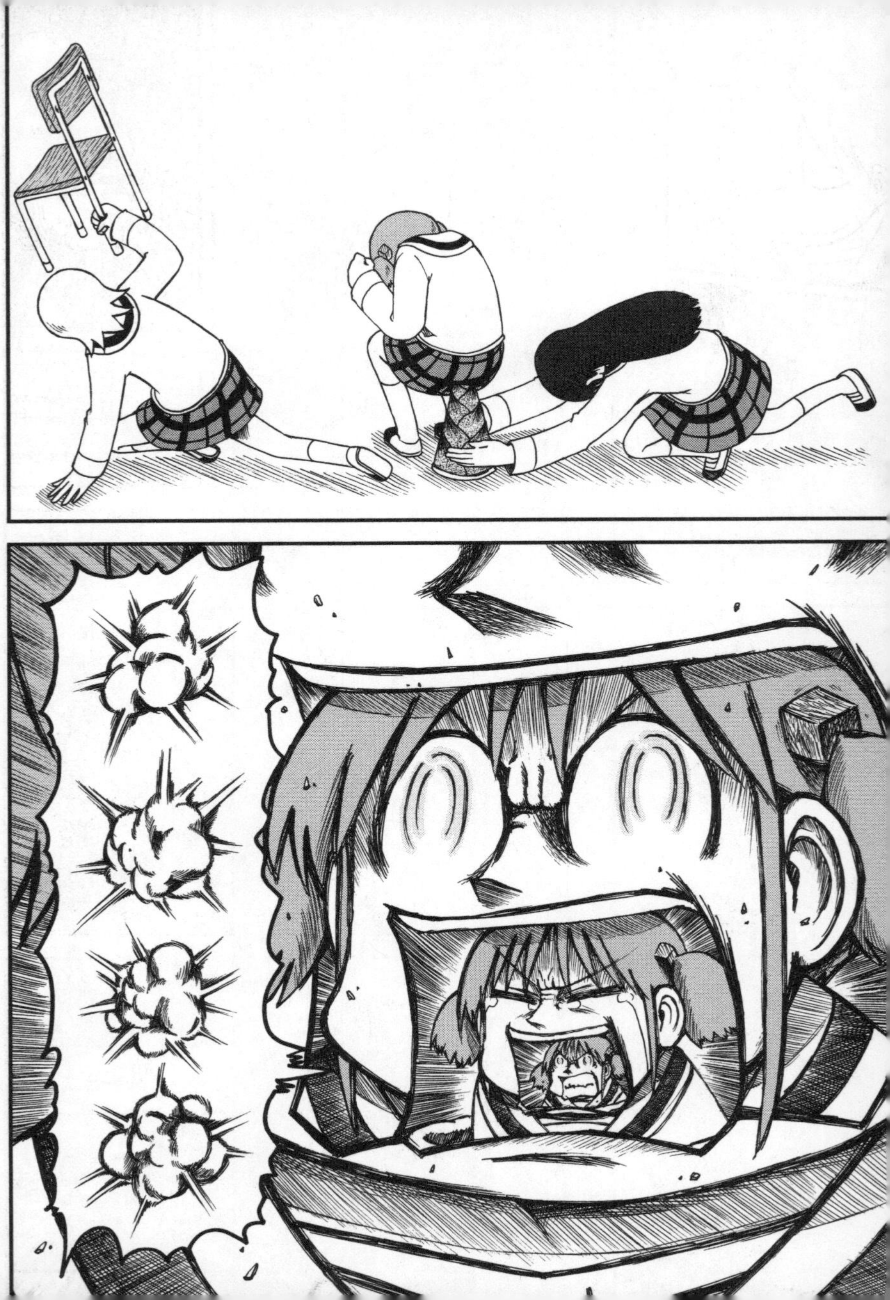

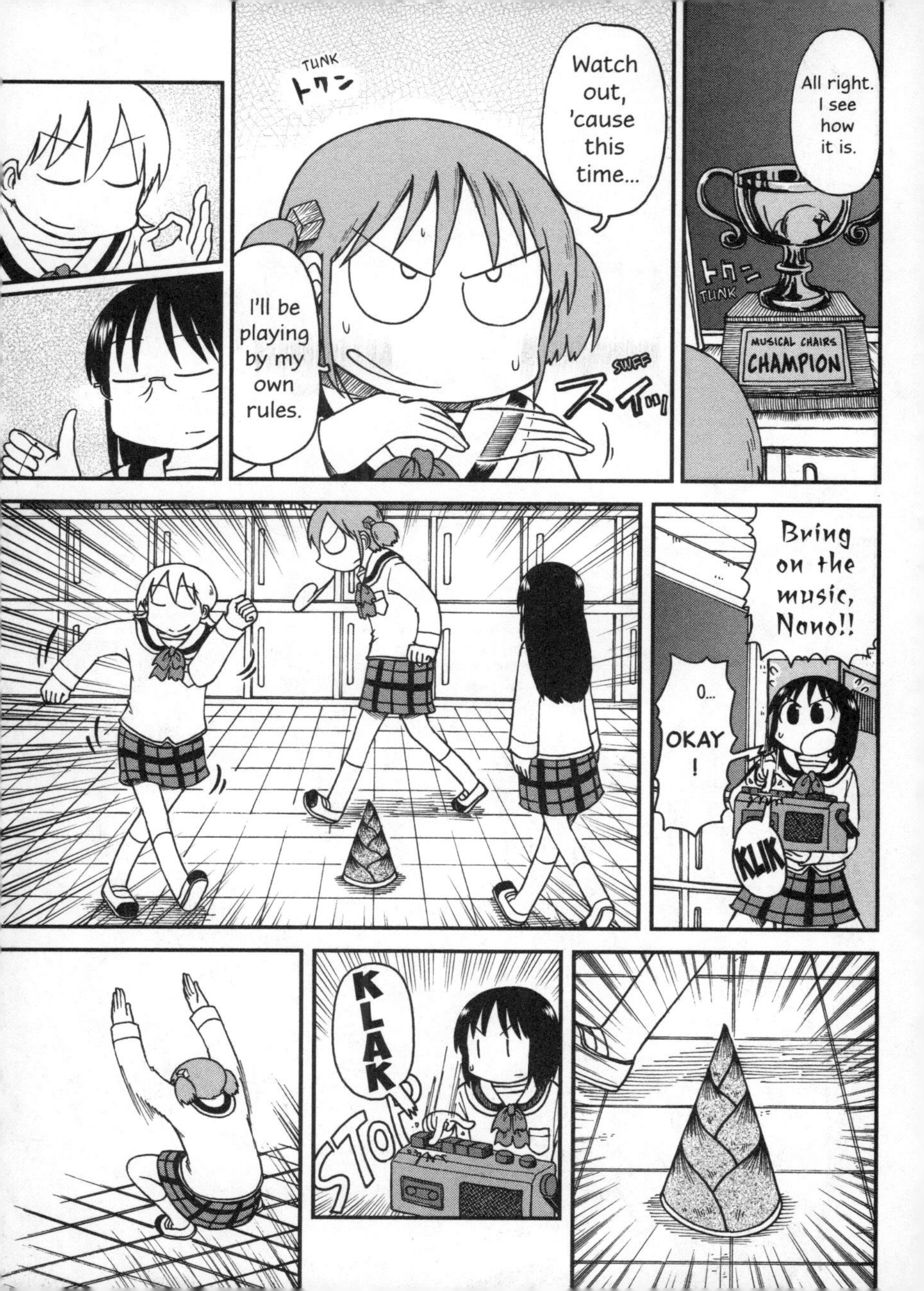
All right. I see how it is.
トクン
TUNK
MUSICAL CHAIRS
CHAMPION
TUNK
トクン
Watch out, 'cause this time...
I'll be playing by my own rules.
SWFF
スイッ
Bring on the music, Nano!!
O... OKAY!
KLIK
KLAK
STOP

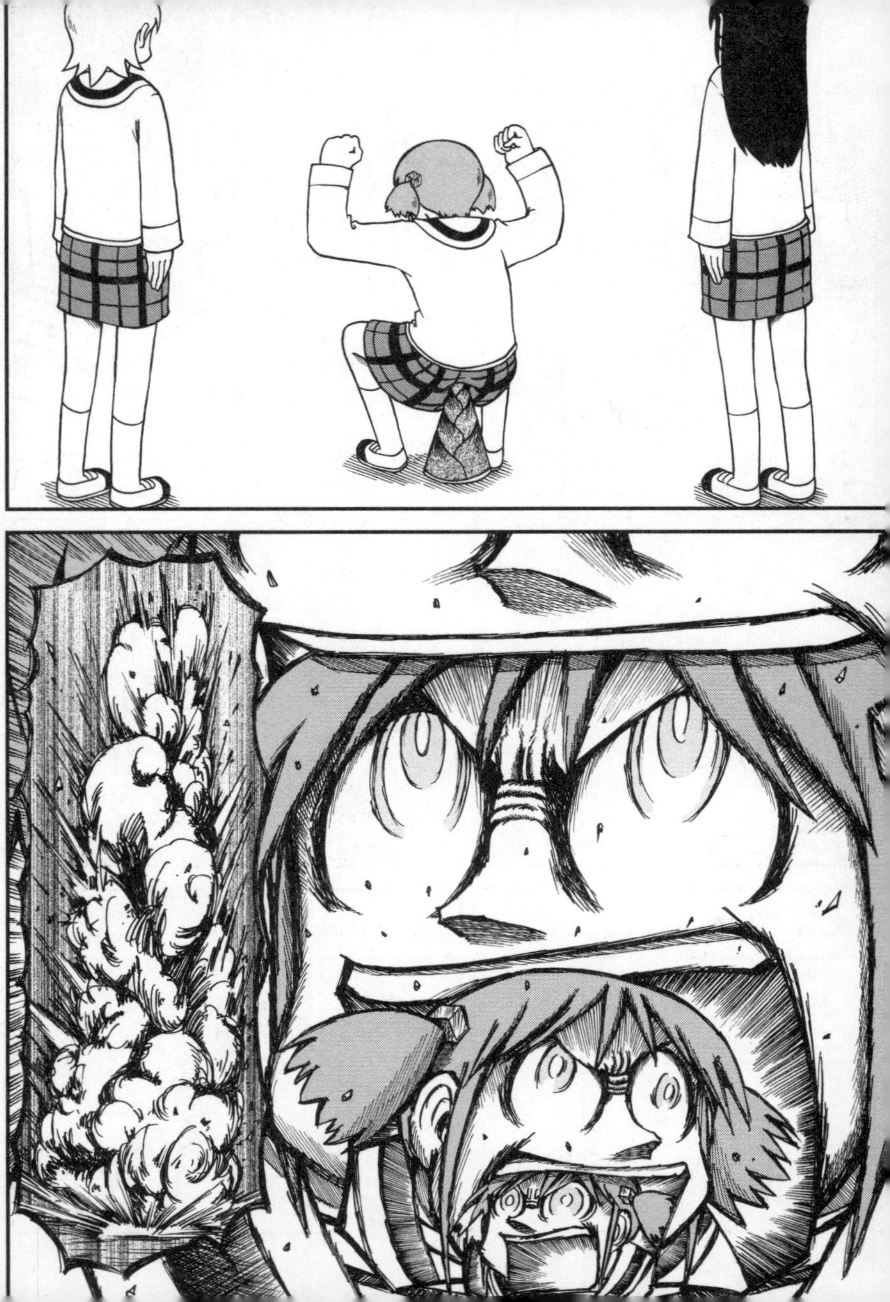

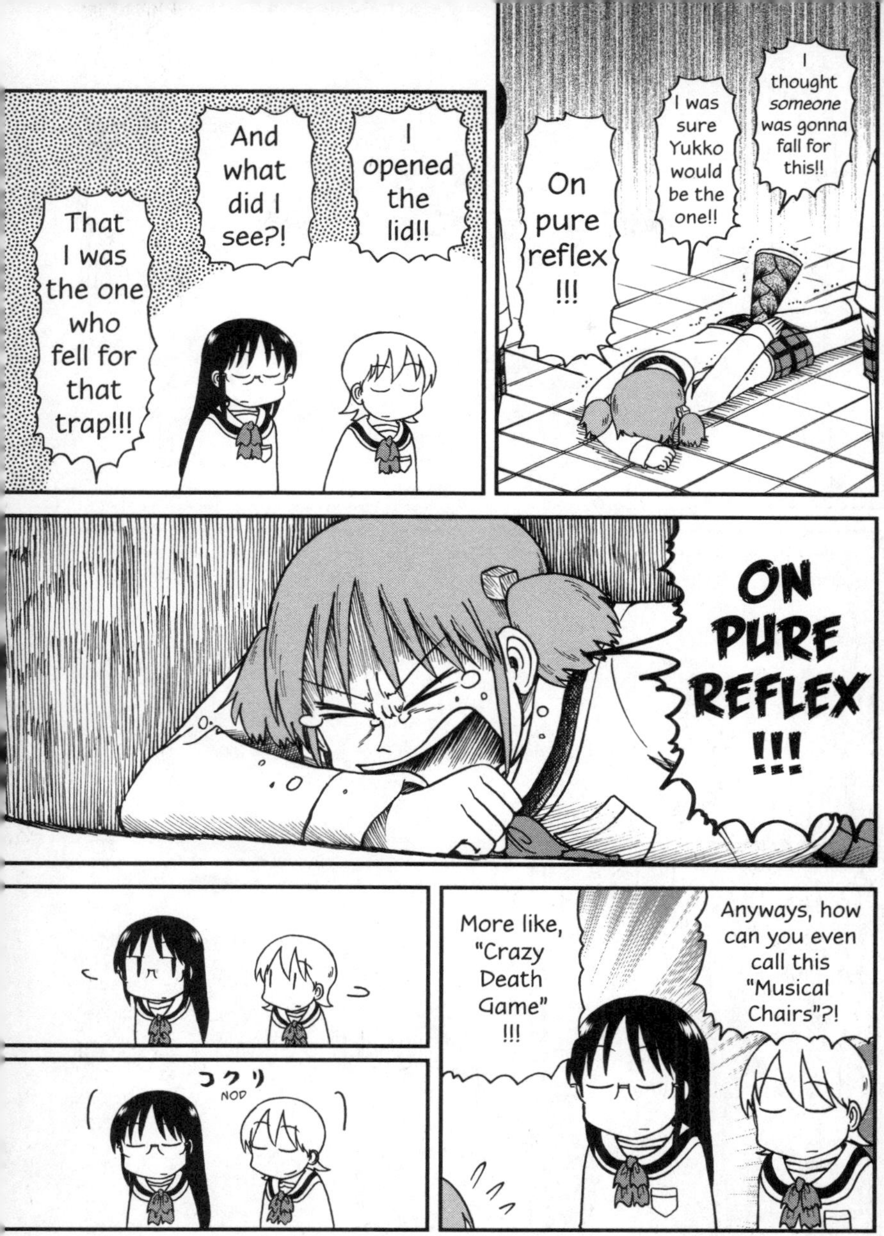
I thought someone was gonna fall for this!!
I was sure Yukko would be the one!!
On pure reflex!!!
I opened the lid!!
And what did I see?!
That I was the one who fell for that trap!!!
ON PURE REFLEX!!!
Anyways, how can you even call this "Musical Chairs"?!
More like, "Crazy Death Game"!!!
コクリ
NOD

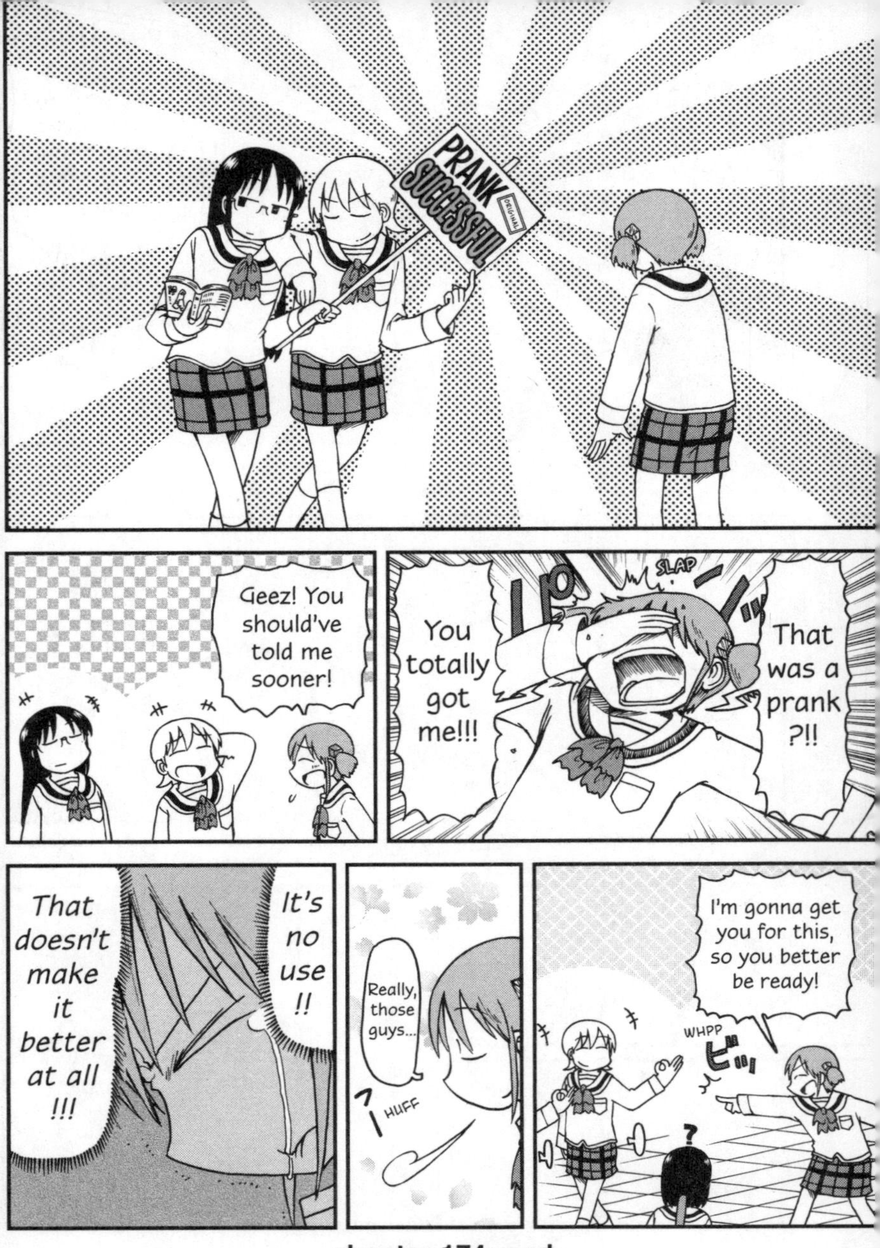
PRANK
SUCCESSFUL
ORIGINAL
That was a prank?!!
SLAP
You totally got me!!!
Geez! You should've told me sooner!
I'm gonna get you for this, so you better be ready!
WHPP
Really, those guys...
HUFF
It's no use!!
That doesn't make it better at all!!!

chapter 174: end

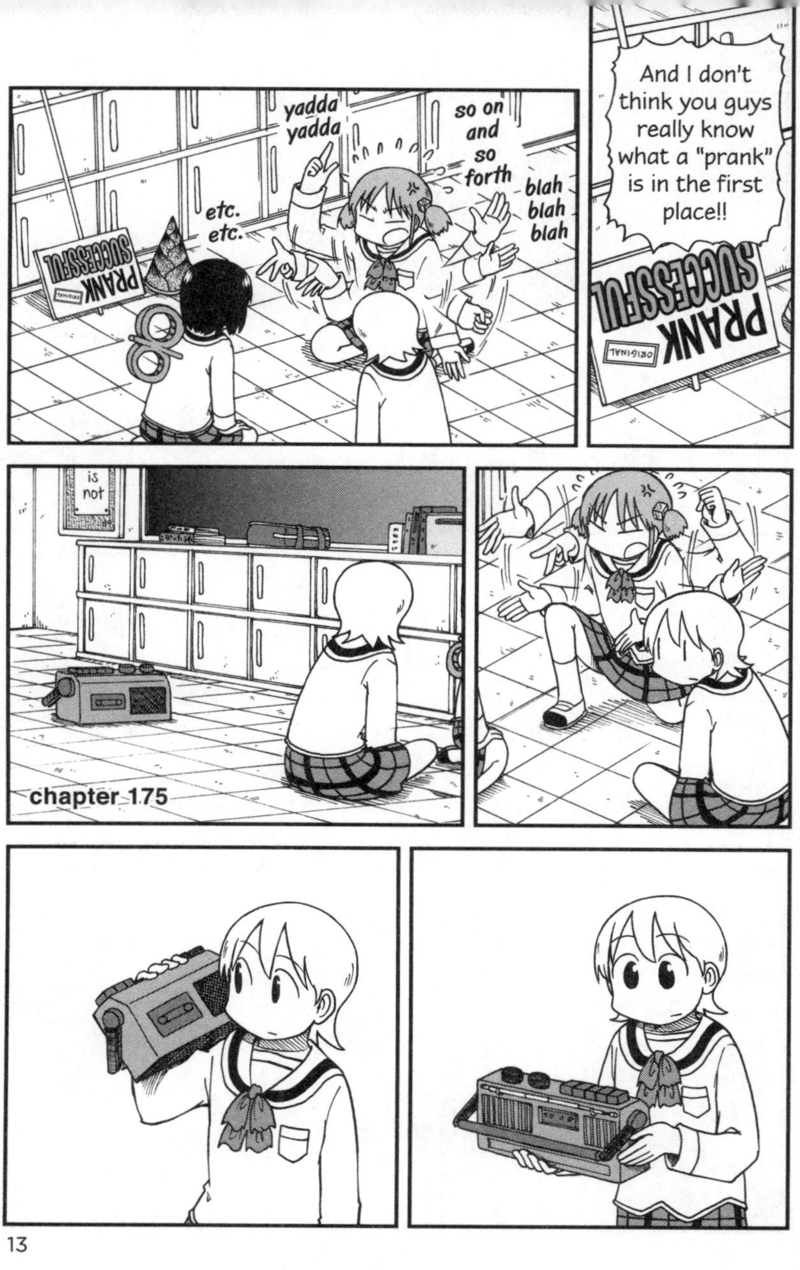
And I don't think you guys really know what a "prank" is in the first place!!
PRANK SUCCESSFUL
ORIGINAL
so on and so forth
yadda yadda
blah blah blah
etc. etc.
PRANK SUCCESSFUL
ORIGINAL
is not
chapter 175

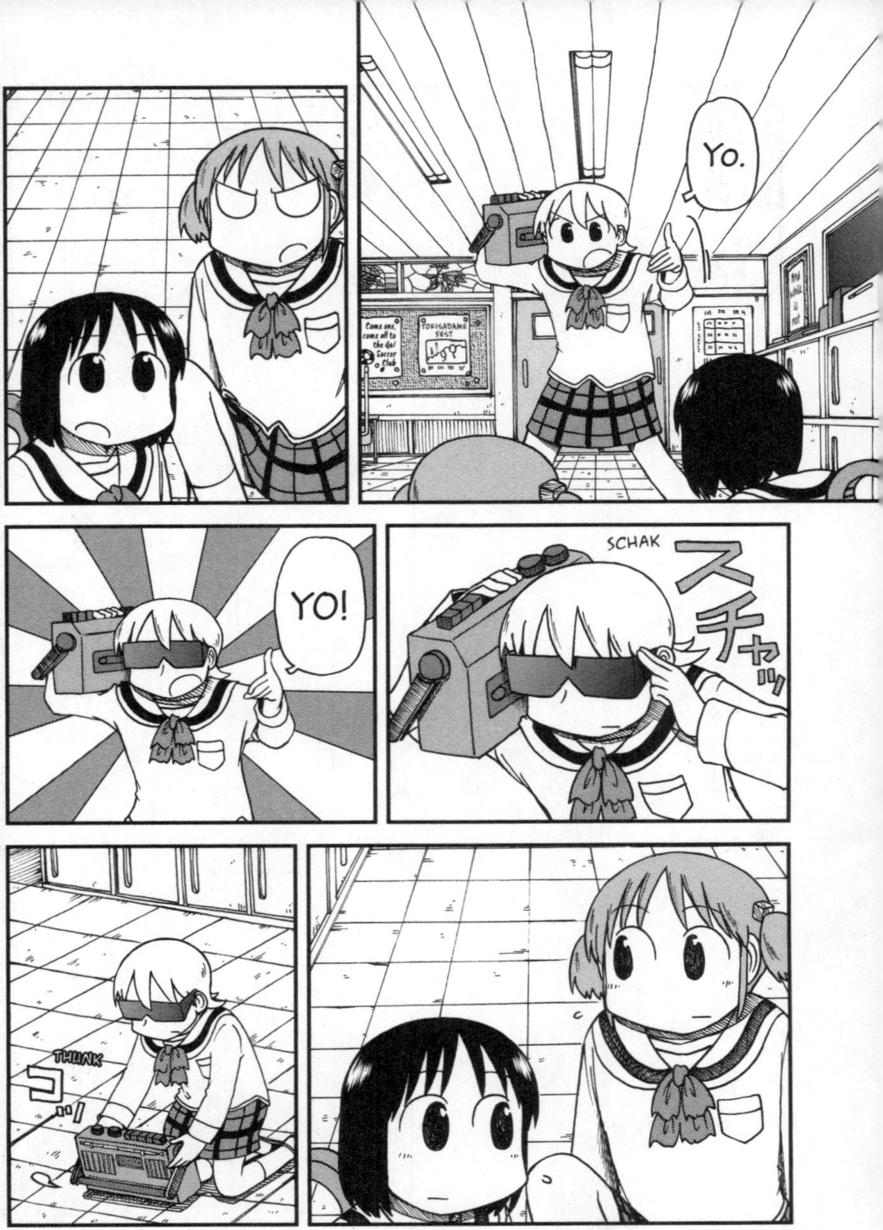

YO.
Come one, come all to the Go! Soccer Club
TOKISADAME FEST
And while is not
SCHAK
スチャッ
YO!
THUNK
コッ

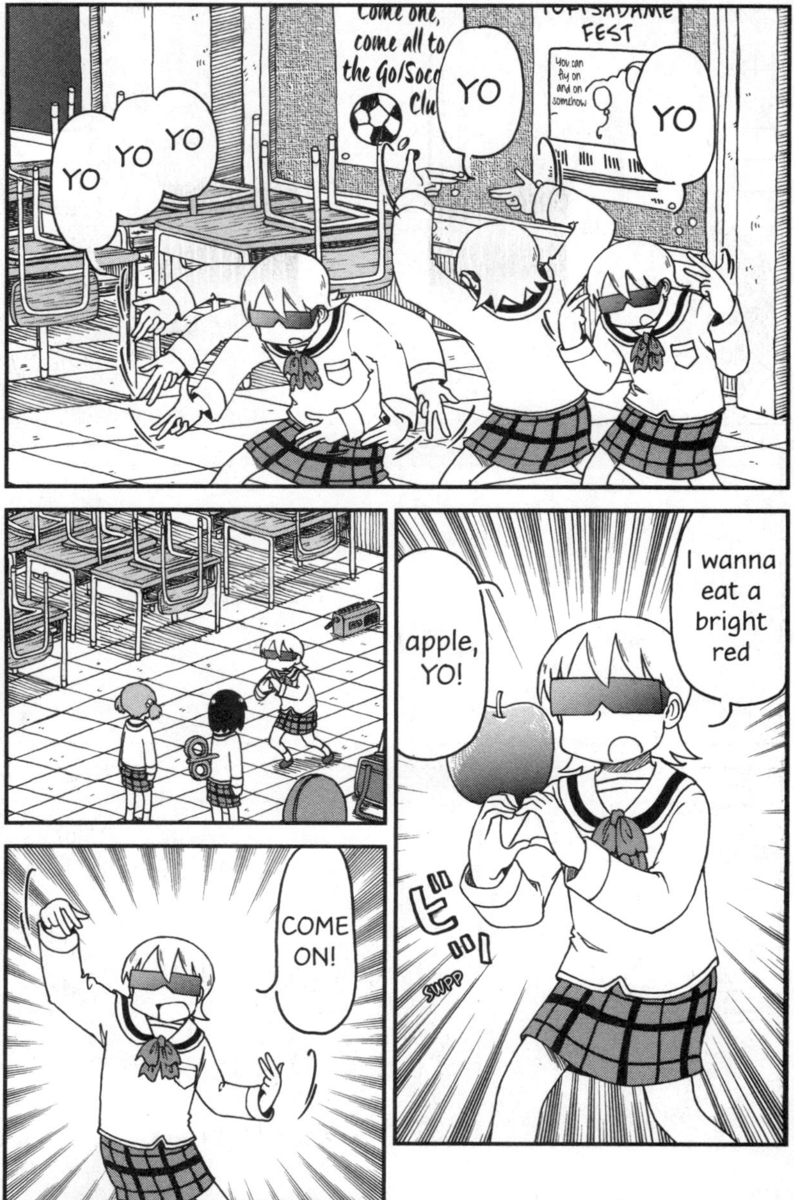
FEST
You can fly on and on somehow
come all to
YO
YO
YO YO YO
I wanna eat a bright red
apple, YO!
SWPP
COME ON!

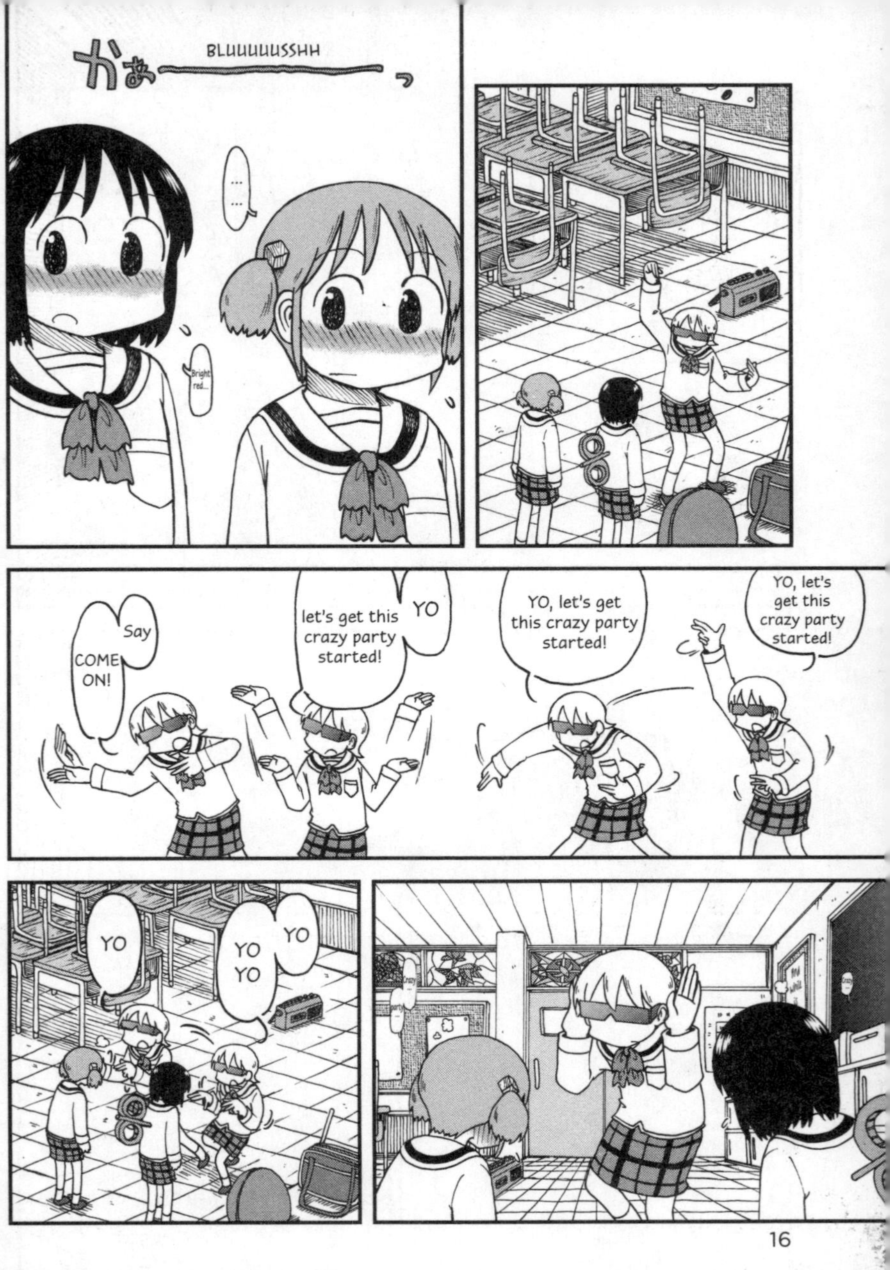
かぁーっ
BLUUUUUUSSHH
......
Bright red...
YO, let's get this crazy party started!
YO, let's get this crazy party started!
YO let's get this crazy party started!
Say COME ON!
Crazy...
Crazy...
party...
YO
YO YO
YO
YO

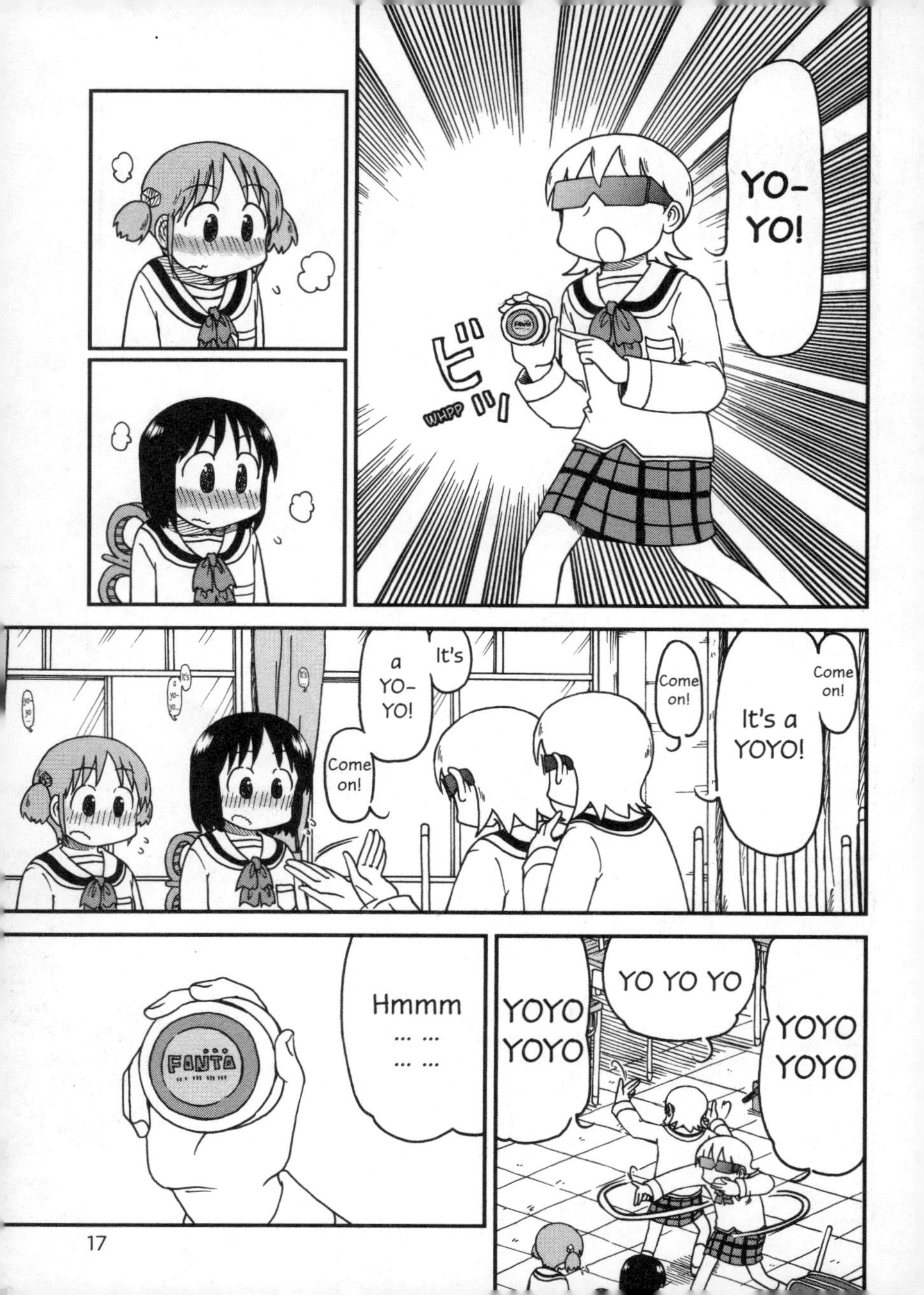
YO-YO!
ビッ
WHPP
Come on!
It's a YOYO!
Come on!
It's a YO-YO!
Come on!
YOYO YOYO
YO YO YO
YOYO YOYO
Hmmm ... ...
FANTA

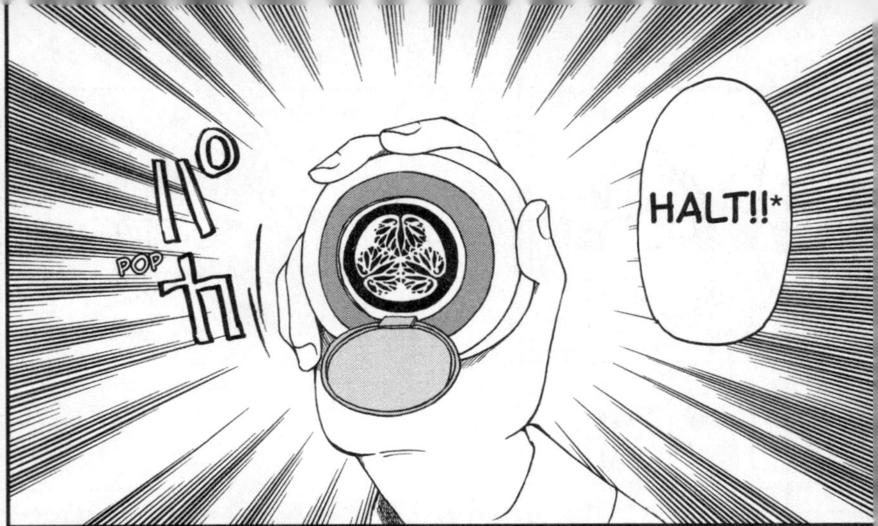
HALT!!*
パカ
POP

*reference to the period drama Mito Koumon, in which the main character goes undercover to solve crimes. at the climax of each episode, he reveals his identity by flashing a lacquered badge and shouting, "Halt!"

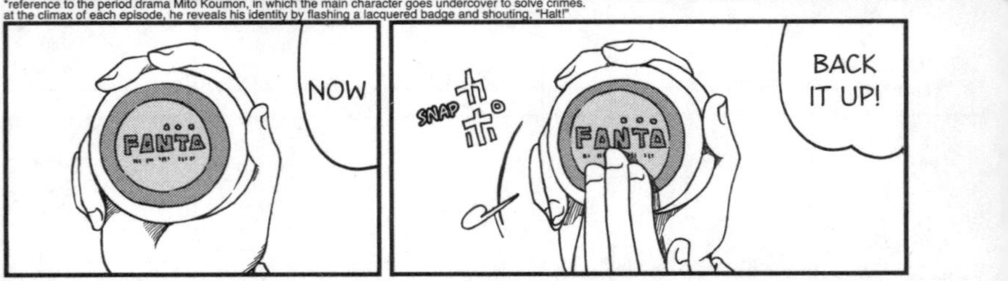
BACK IT UP!
SNAP
カポ
FANTA
NOW
FANTA

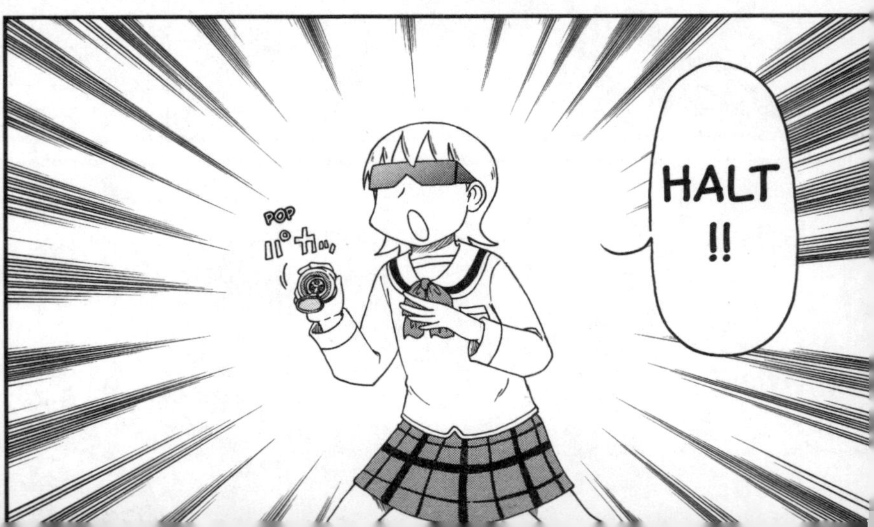
HALT !!
POP
パカッ

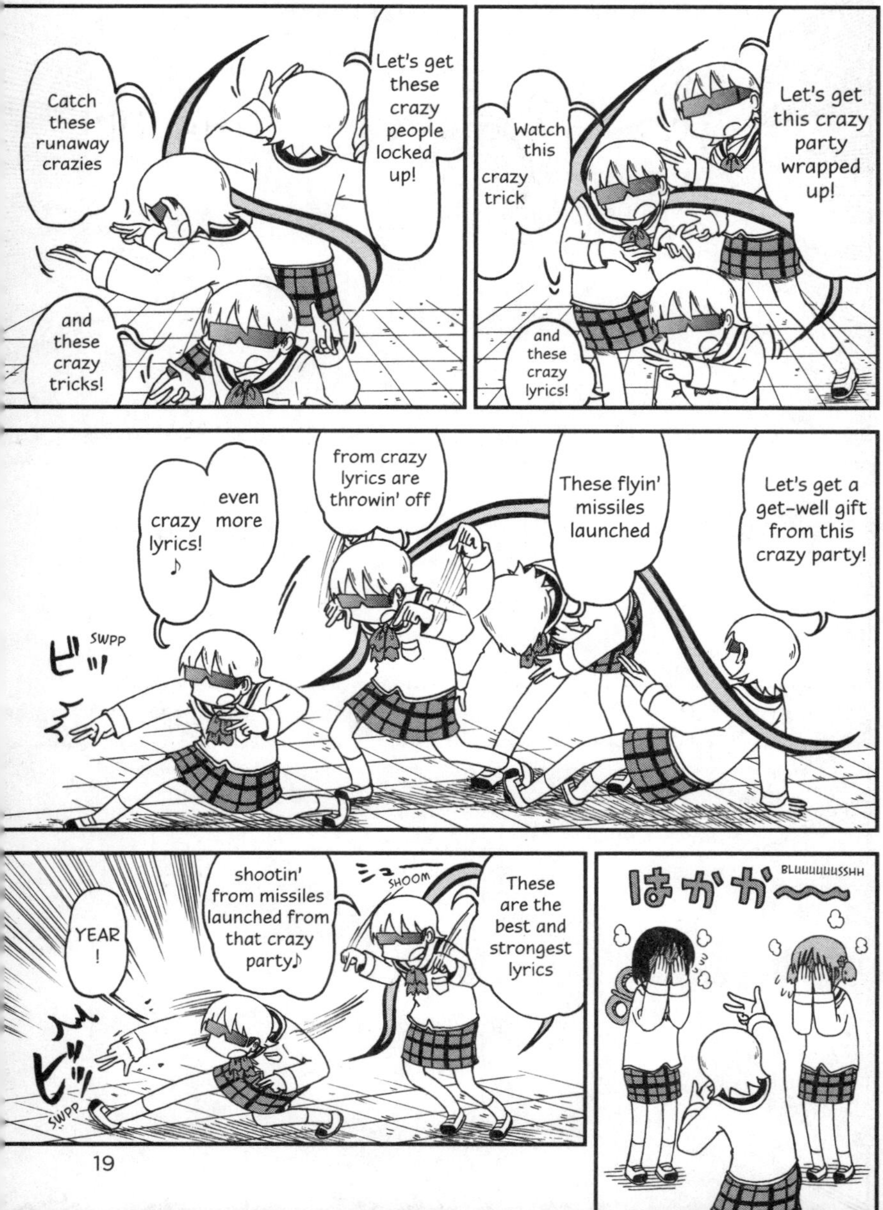
Let's get this crazy party wrapped up!
Watch this crazy trick
and these crazy lyrics!
Let's get these crazy people locked up!
Catch these runaway crazies
and these crazy tricks!
Let's get a get-well gift from this crazy party!
These flyin' missiles launched
from crazy lyrics are throwin' off
even more crazy lyrics! ♪
SWPP
ビッ
はかが～～
BLUUUUUUSSHH
These are the best and strongest lyrics
シュー
SHOOM
shootin' from missiles launched from that crazy party♪
YEAR!
ビッ
SWPP

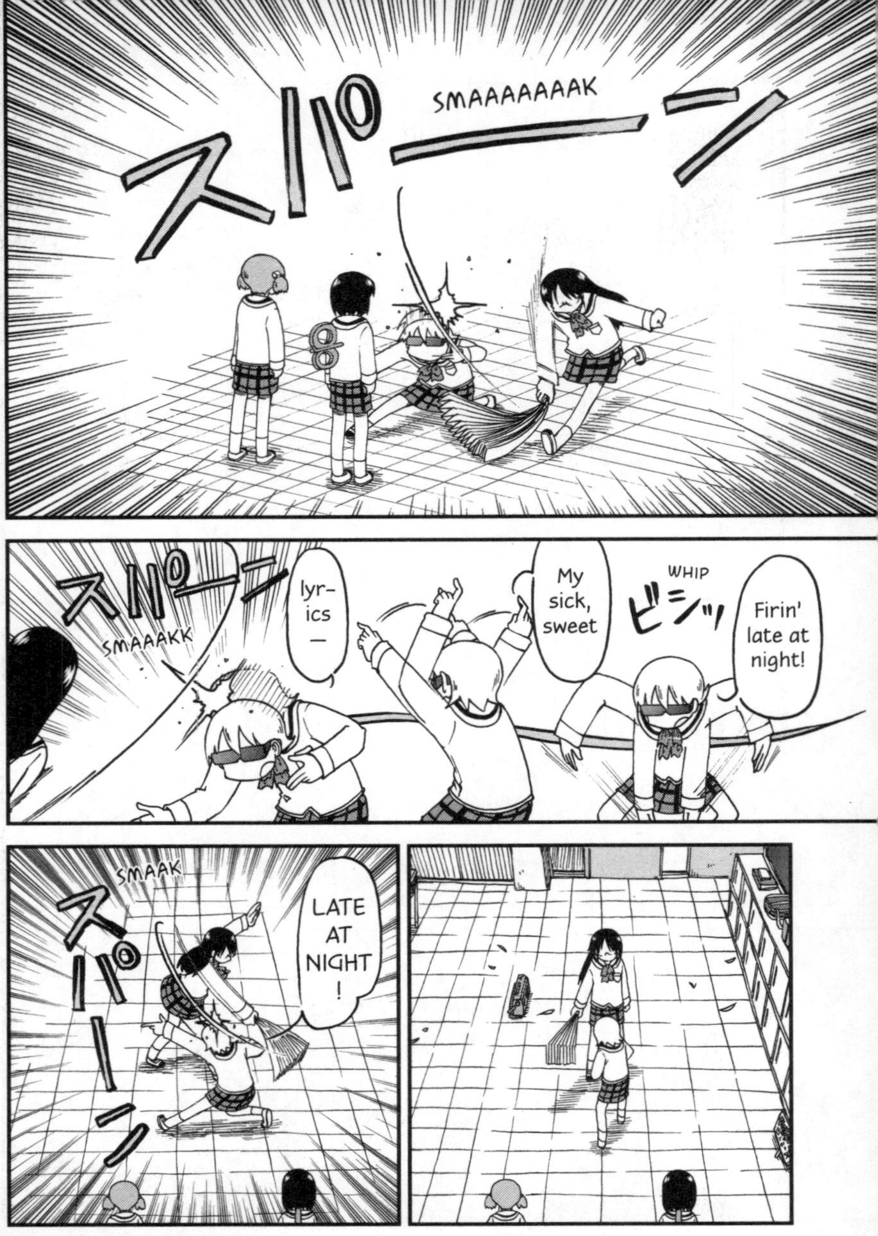
スパーーン
SMAAAAAAAK
Firin' late at night!
WHIP
ビシッ
My sick, sweet
lyr-ics —
スパーン
SMAAAKK
LATE AT NIGHT !
スパーン
SMAAK

chapter 175: end

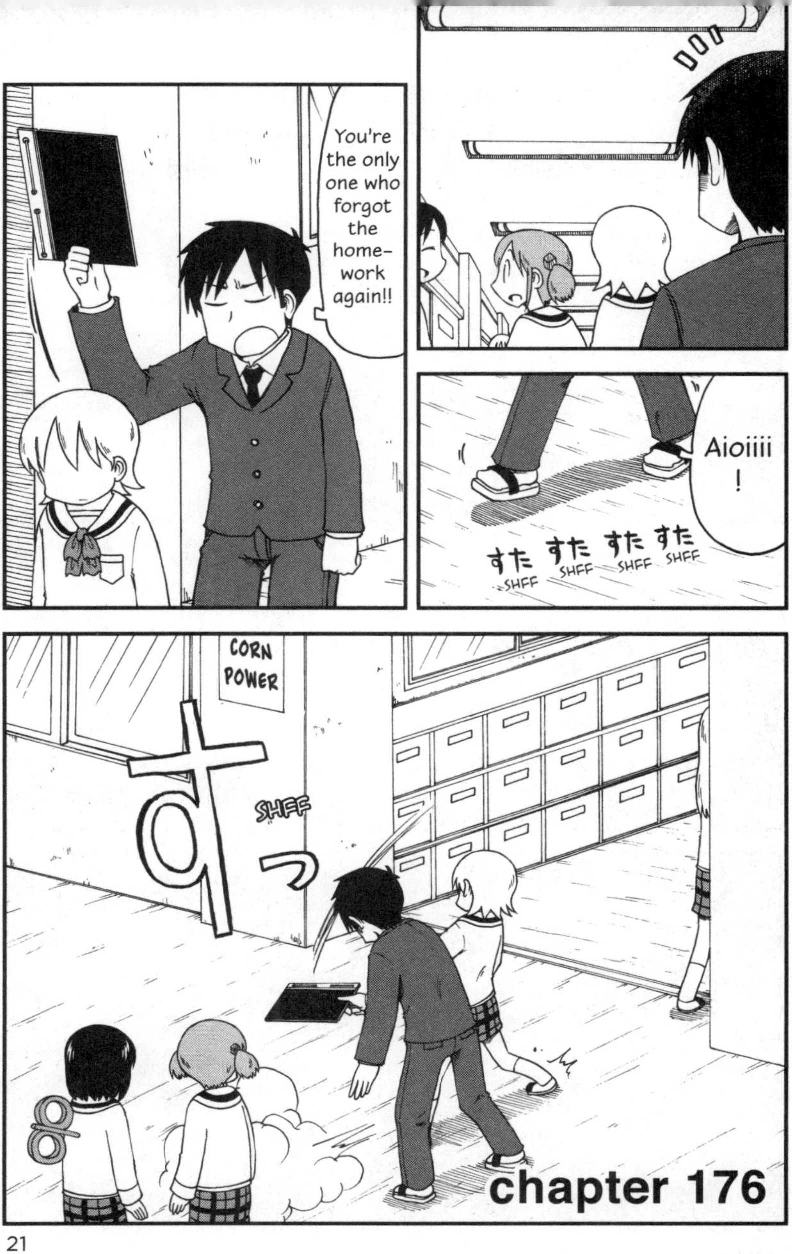
Aioiiii!
すた すた すた すた
SHFF SHFF SHFF SHFF
You're the only one who forgot the home-work again!!
CORN POWER
すっ
SHFF
chapter 176

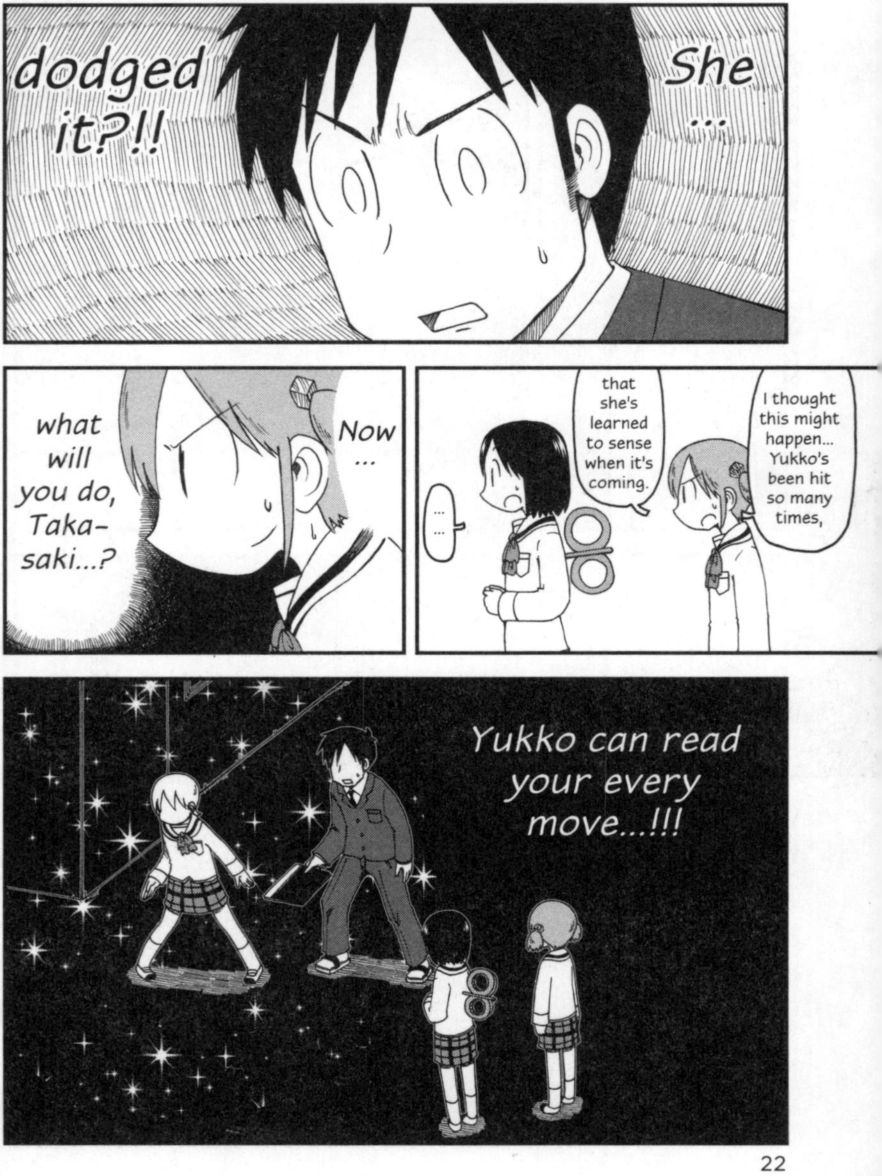
She ...
dodged it?!!
I thought this might happen... Yukko's been hit so many times,
that she's learned to sense when it's coming.
... ...
Now ...
what will you do, Taka-saki...?
Yukko can read your every move...!!!

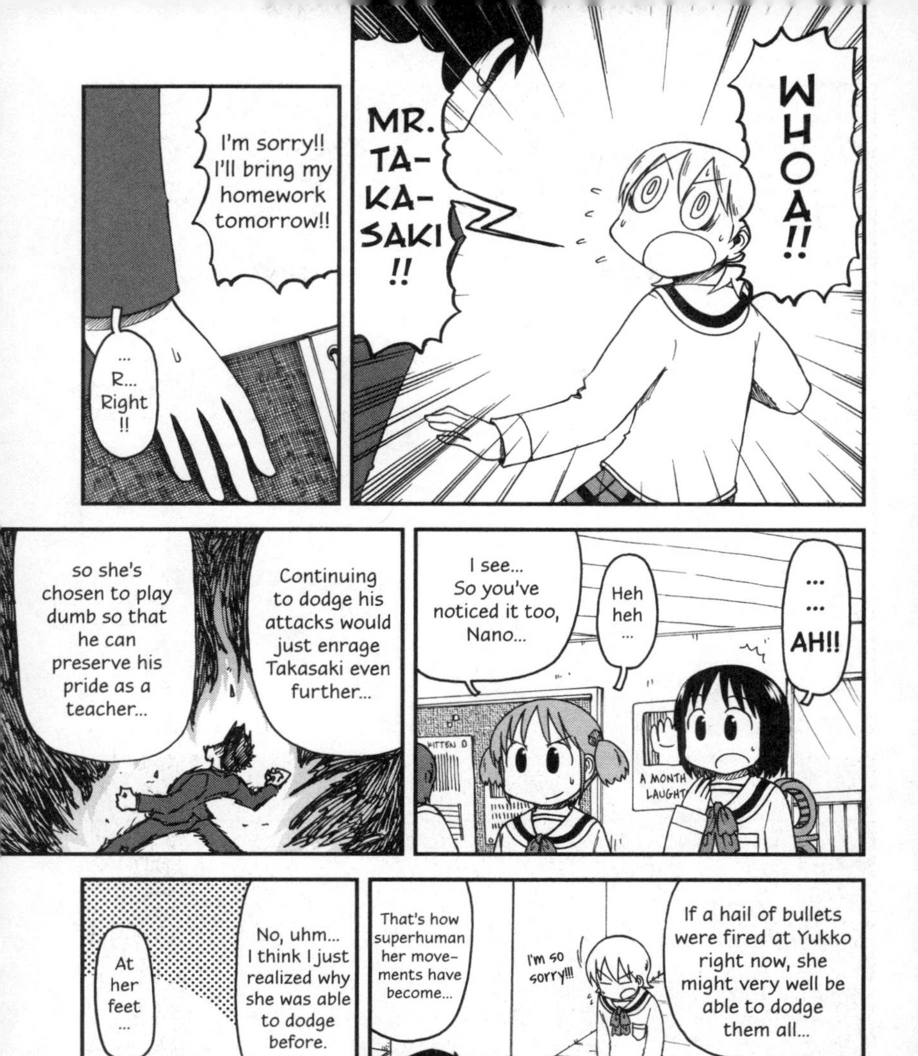
WHOA!!
MR. TA-KA-SAKI!!
I'm sorry!! I'll bring my homework tomorrow!!
... R... Right!!
... ... AH!!
Heh heh ...
I see... So you've noticed it too, Nano...
Continuing to dodge his attacks would just enrage Takasaki even further...
so she's chosen to play dumb so that he can preserve his pride as a teacher...
If a hail of bullets were fired at Yukko right now, she might very well be able to dodge them all...
I'm so sorry!!!
That's how superhuman her move-ments have become...
No, uhm... I think I just realized why she was able to dodge before.
At her feet ...

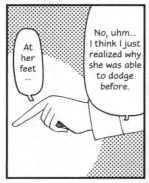

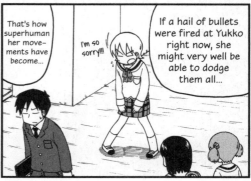

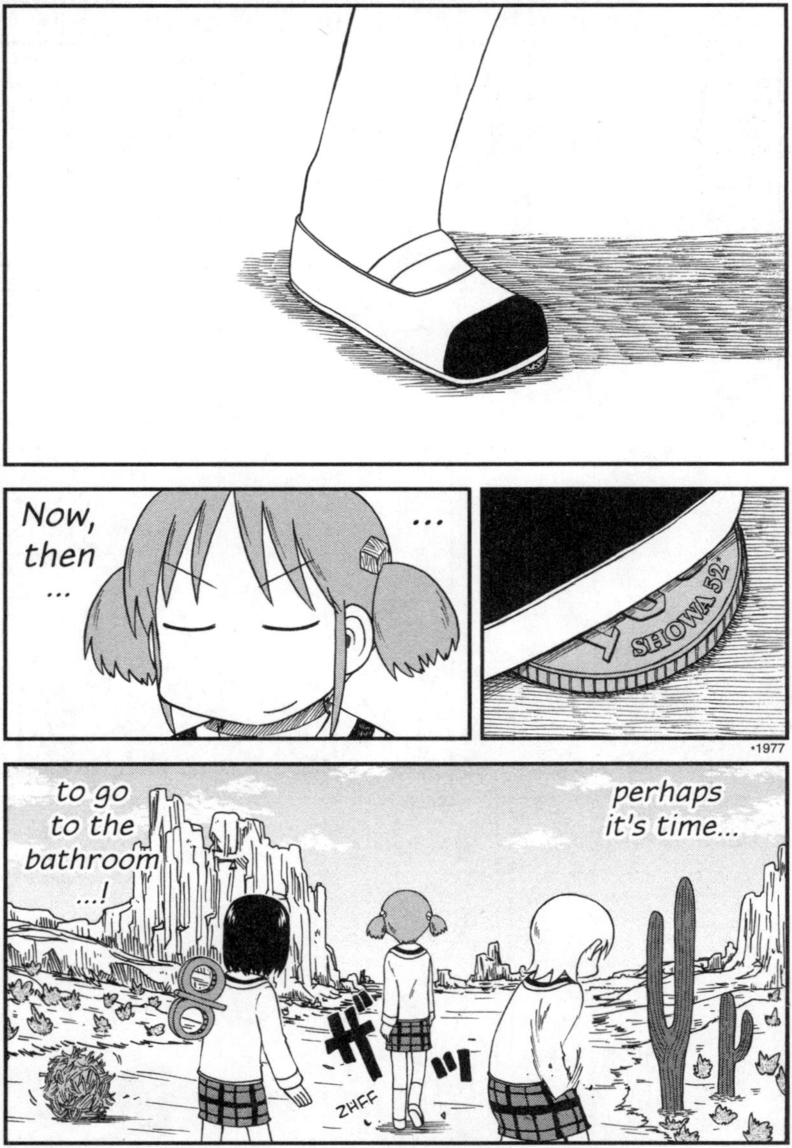
SHOWA 52*
Now, then ...
...
*1977
perhaps it's time...
to go to the bathroom ...!
ZHFF

chapter 176: end

first time at a fancy café

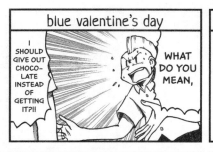

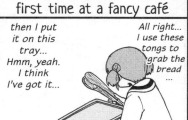

All right... I use these tongs to grab the bread ...
then I put it on this tray... Hmm, yeah. I think I've got it...

I think
I can do this, maybe!

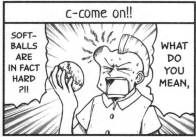

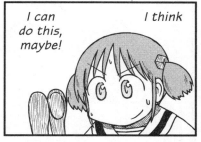

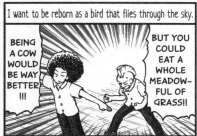

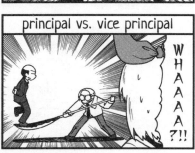

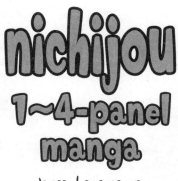

nichijou 1~4-panel manga

keiichi arawi

blue valentine's day

WHAT DO YOU MEAN,
I SHOULD GIVE OUT CHOCO-LATE INSTEAD OF GETTING IT?!!

c-come on!!

WHAT DO YOU MEAN,
SOFT-BALLS ARE IN FACT HARD ?!!

I want to be reborn as a bird that flies through the sky.

BUT YOU COULD EAT A WHOLE MEADOW-FUL OF GRASS!!
BEING A COW WOULD BE WAY BETTER !!!

principal vs. vice principal

WHAAAAAA ?!!

chapter 177

a page of smiles and charades!

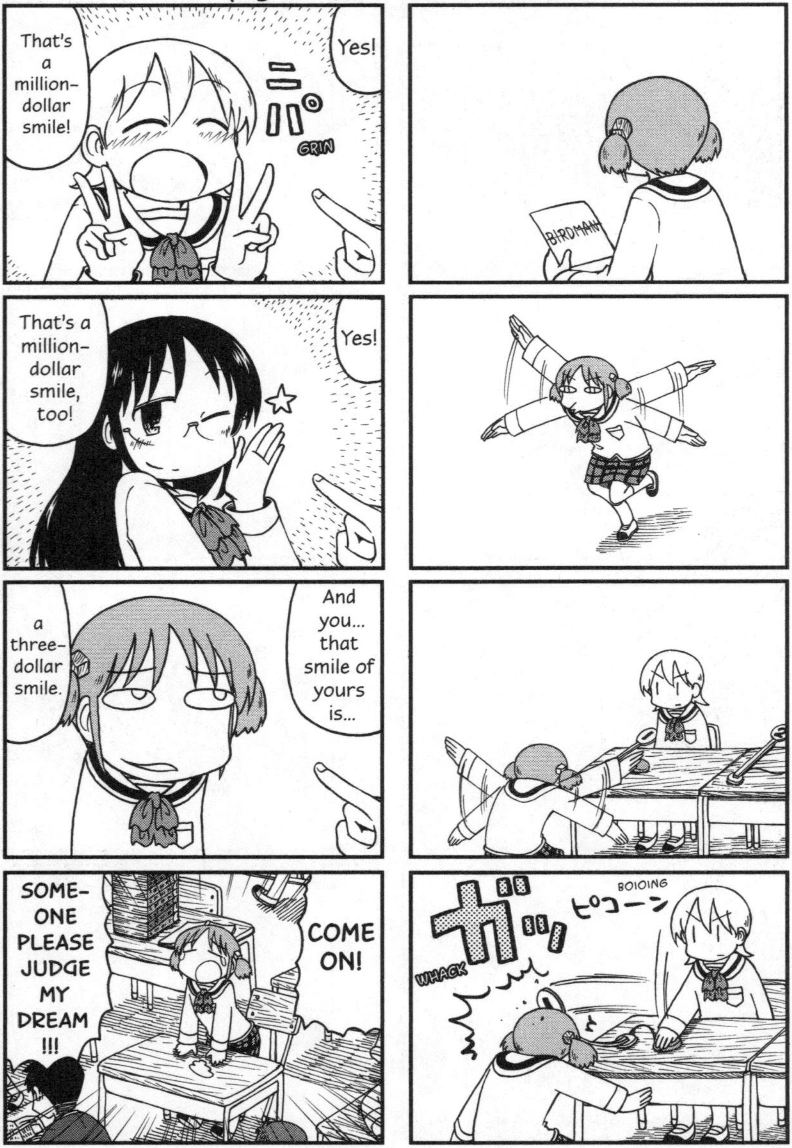
BIRDMAN
BOIOING
ピコーン
ガッ
WHACK
Yes!
That's a million-dollar smile!
ニパ
GRIN
Yes!
That's a million-dollar smile, too!
And you... that smile of yours is...
a three-dollar smile.
COME ON!
SOME-ONE PLEASE JUDGE MY DREAM!!!

phantom thief potato

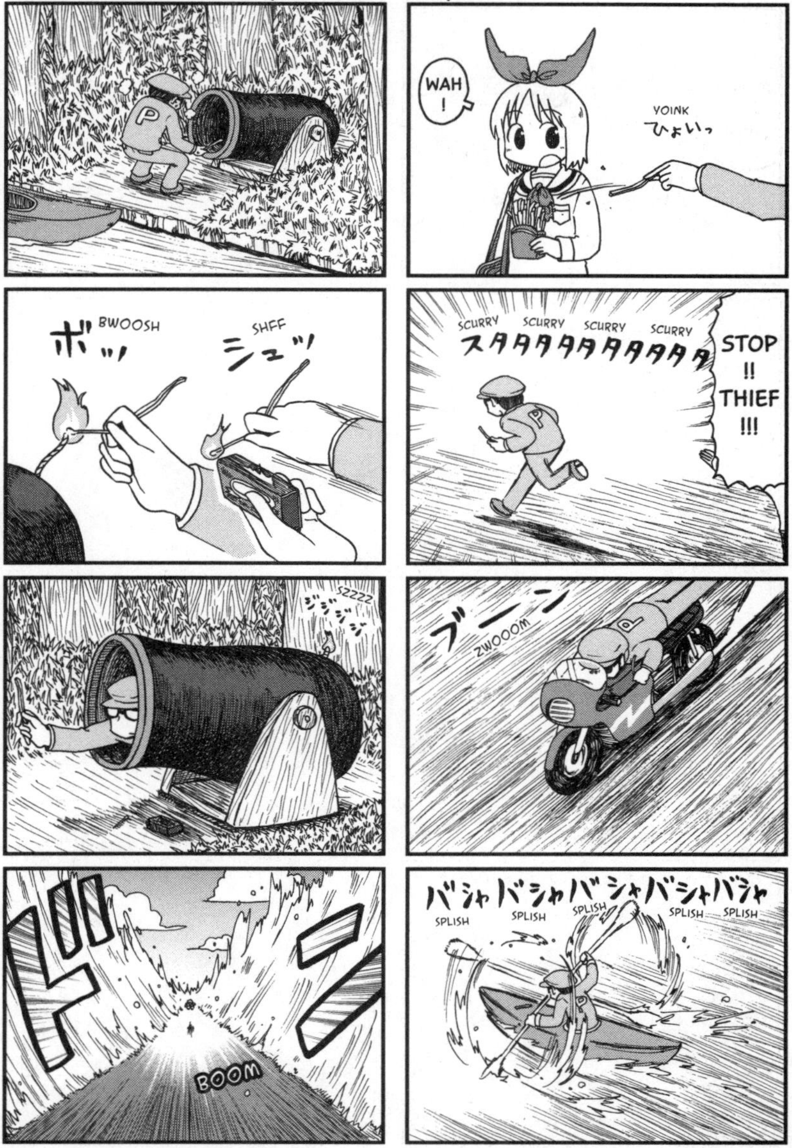
WAH !
YOINK
ひょいっ
SCURRY SCURRY SCURRY SCURRY
スタタタタタタタタタタ
STOP !! THIEF !!!
ブーン
ZWOOOM
バシャバシャバシャバシャバシャ
SPLISH SPLISH SPLISH SPLISH SPLISH
SHFF
シュッ
BWOOSH
ボッ
SZZZZ
ジジジジジ
ドーン
BOOM

bridge of promises

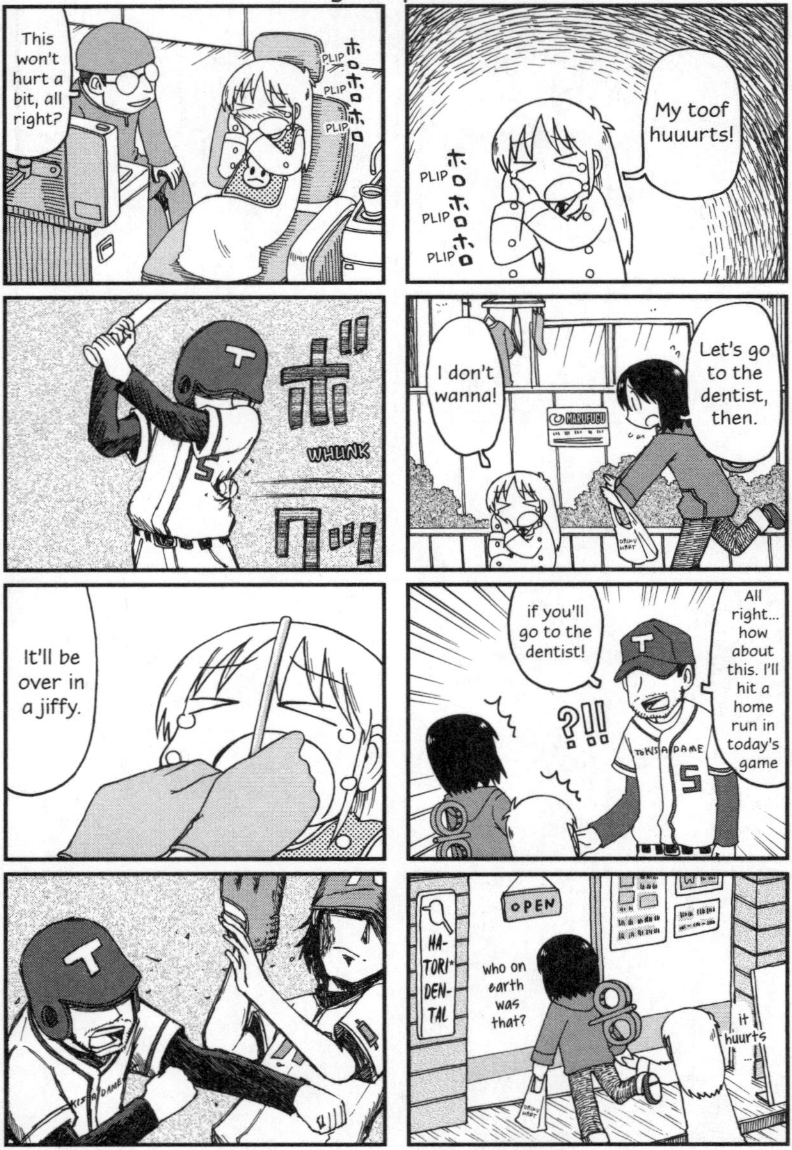
My toof huuurts!
PLIP ホロ PLIP ホロ PLIP ホロ
Let's go to the dentist, then.
I don't wanna!
MARUFUGU
All right... how about this. I'll hit a home run in today's game
if you'll go to the dentist!
?!!
OPEN
HA-TORI* DEN-TAL
who on earth was that?
it huurts ...
This won't hurt a bit, all right?
PLIP ホロ PLIP ホロ PLIP ホロ
ボワッ
WHUNK
It'll be over in a jiffy.

*literally, "tooth removal"

forgery

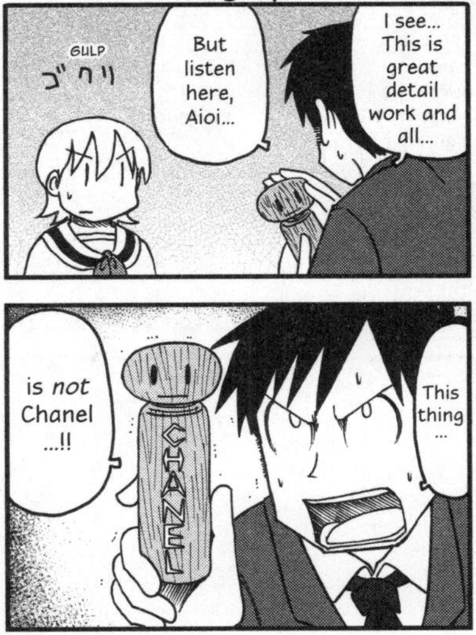
I see... This is great detail work and all...
But listen here, Aioi...
GULP
ゴクリ
This thing...
is *not* Chanel ...!!
CHANEL

grief

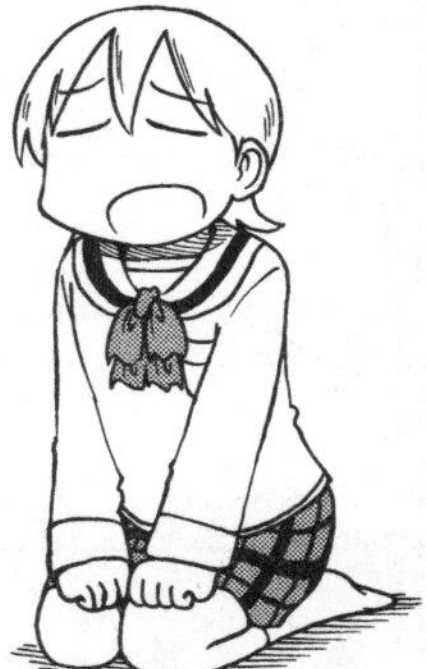

dejection

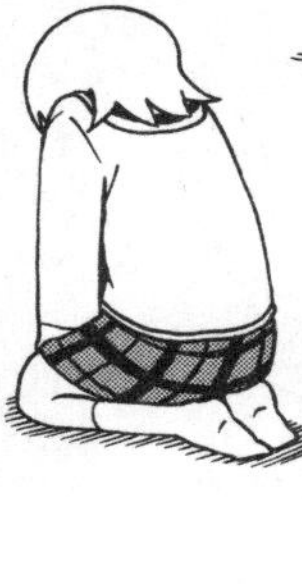

matryoshka of tears

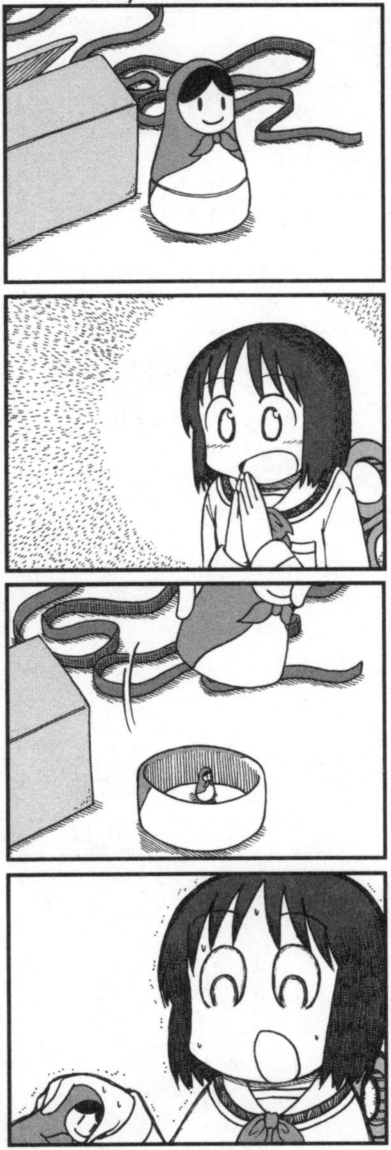

the night before a band is born

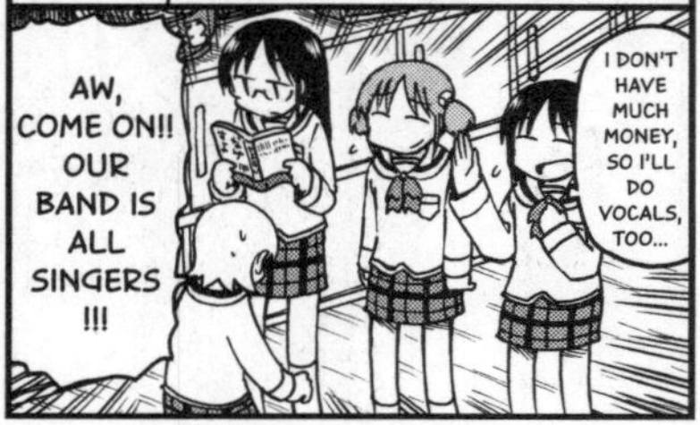
I DON'T HAVE MUCH MONEY, SO I'LL DO VOCALS, TOO...
AW, COME ON!! OUR BAND IS ALL SINGERS !!!

lingering snow

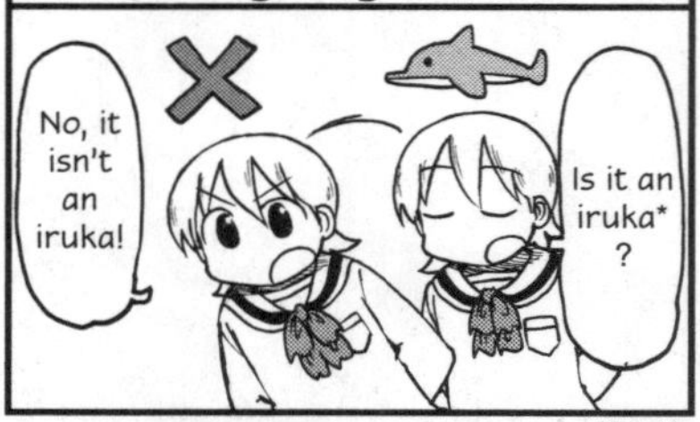
Is it an iruka* ?
No, it isn't an iruka!

*dolphin

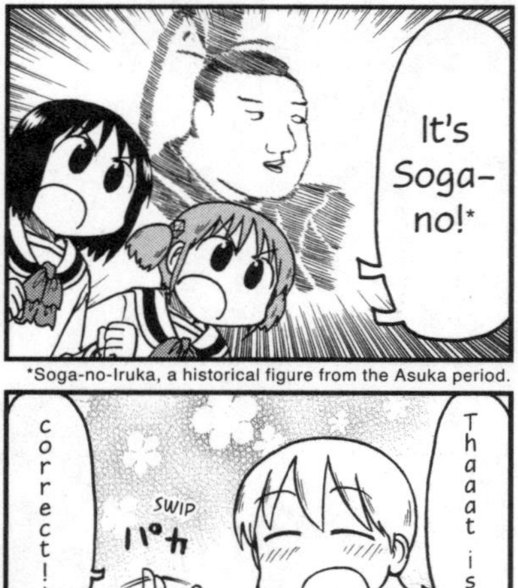
It's Soga-no!*

*Soga-no-Iruka, a historical figure from the Asuka period.

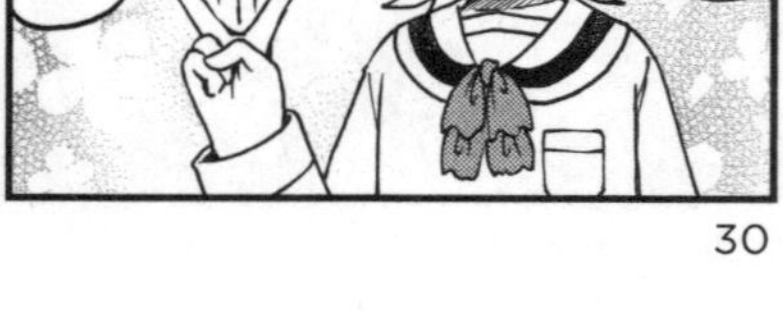
Thaaat is
correct!♪
SWIP

limiter removed

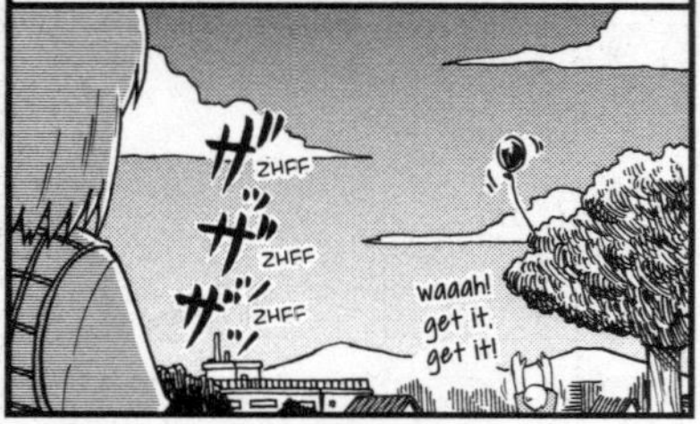
waaah! get it, get it!
ZHFF
ZHFF
ZHFF

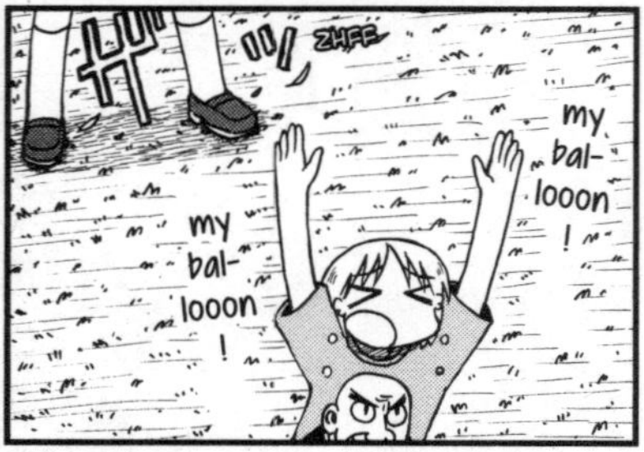
ZHFF
my bal-looon !
my bal-looon !

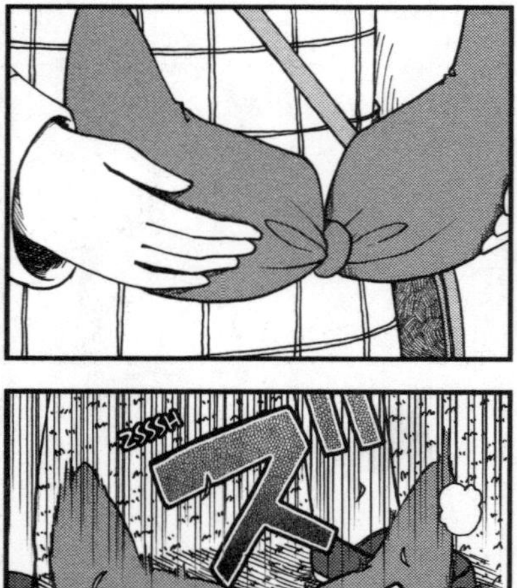

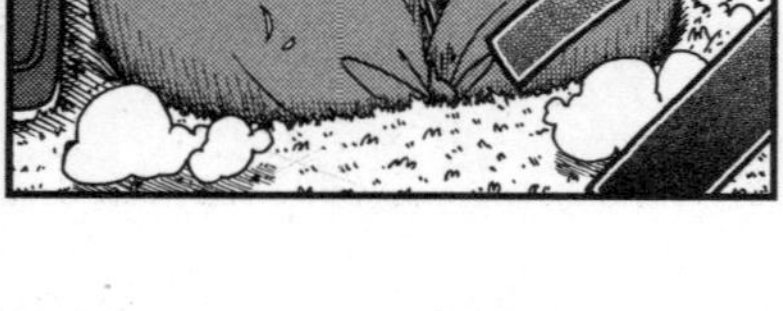
ZSSSH

growth spurt

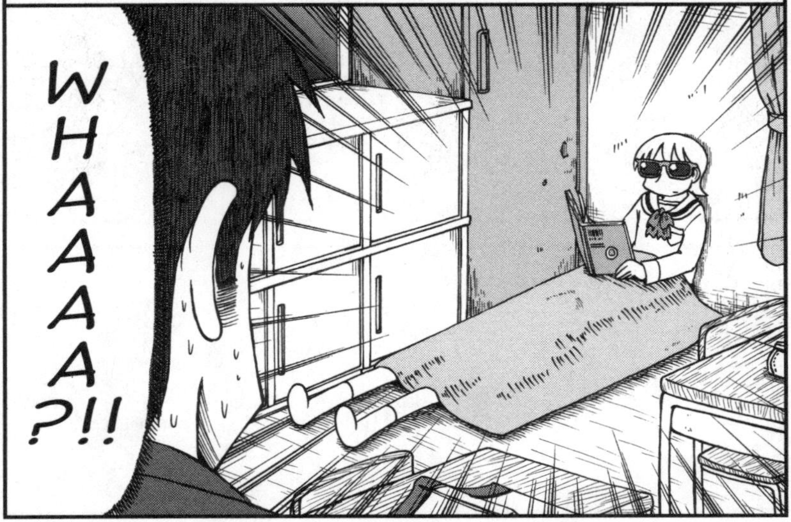
WHAAAAA?!!

subliminal

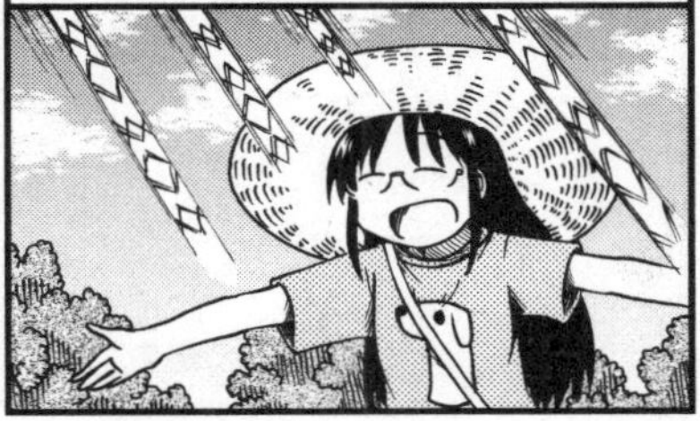

my principal, the substitute pitcher

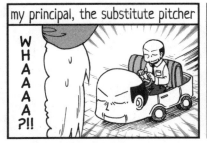

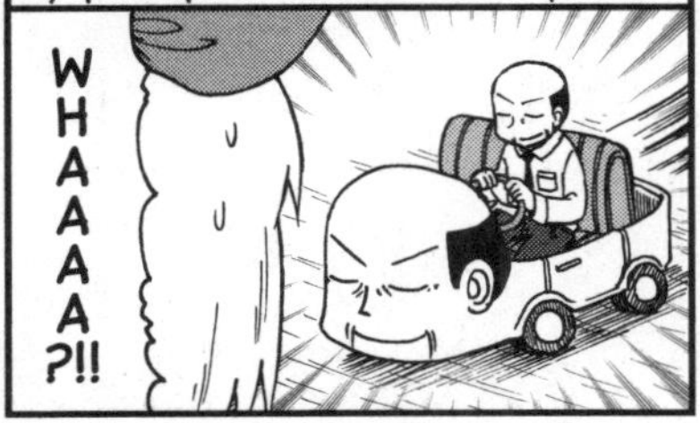
WHAAAAA?!!

oh, no!!

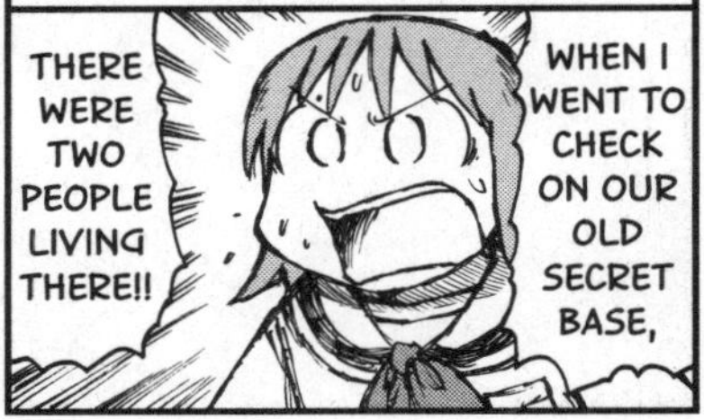
WHEN I WENT TO CHECK ON OUR OLD SECRET BASE,
THERE WERE TWO PEOPLE LIVING THERE!!

subliminal

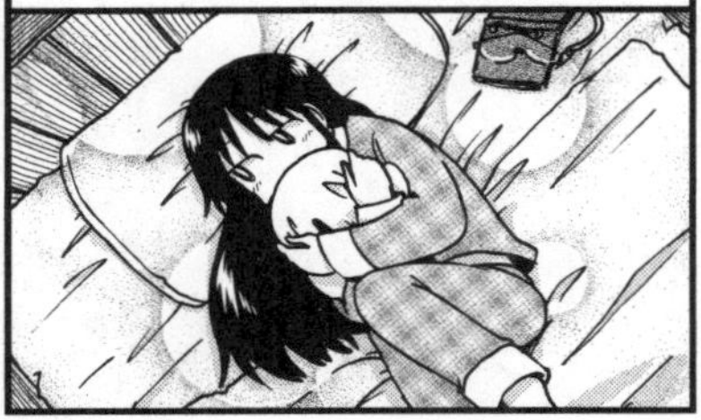

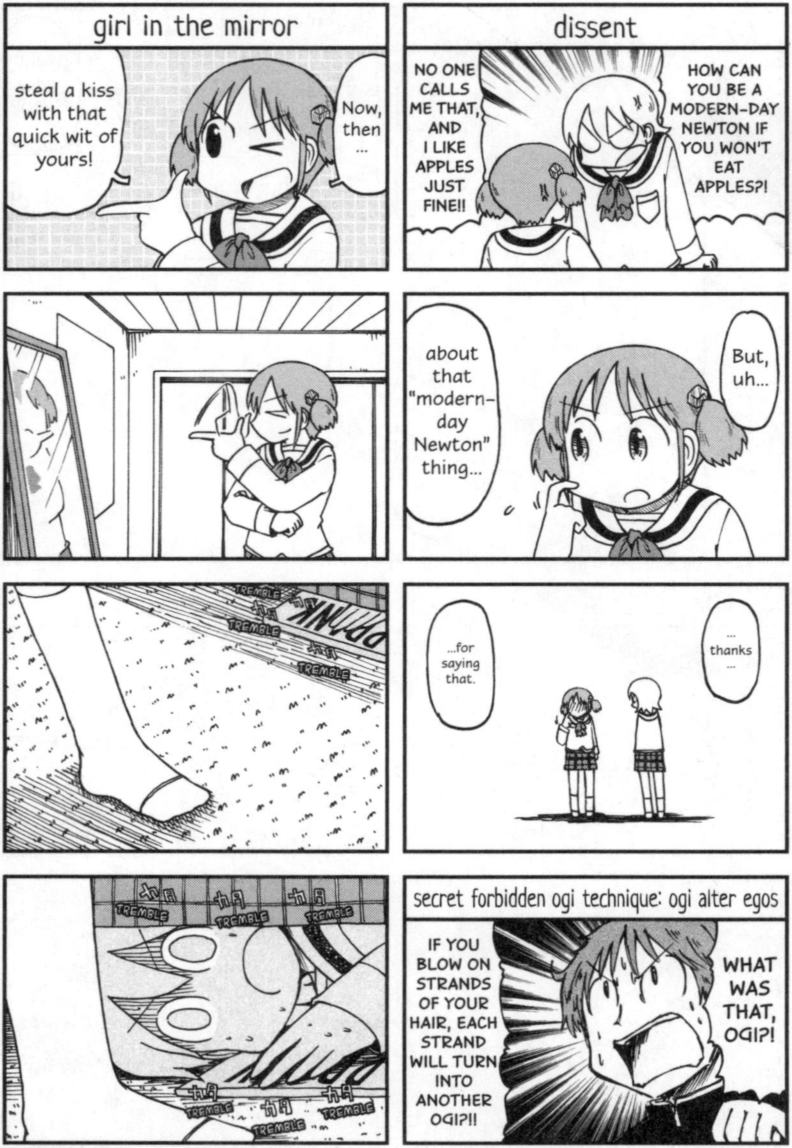
dissent
HOW CAN YOU BE A MODERN-DAY NEWTON IF YOU WON'T EAT APPLES?!
NO ONE CALLS ME THAT, AND I LIKE APPLES JUST FINE!!
But, uh...
about that "modern-day Newton" thing...
... thanks ...
...for saying that.
secret forbidden ogi technique: ogi alter egos
WHAT WAS THAT, OGI?!
IF YOU BLOW ON STRANDS OF YOUR HAIR, EACH STRAND WILL TURN INTO ANOTHER OGI?!!
girl in the mirror
Now, then ...
steal a kiss with that quick wit of yours!
TREMBLE
TREMBLE
TREMBLE
TREMBLE
TREMBLE
TREMBLE
TREMBLE
TREMBLE
TREMBLE
TREMBLE

chapter 177: end

chapter 178

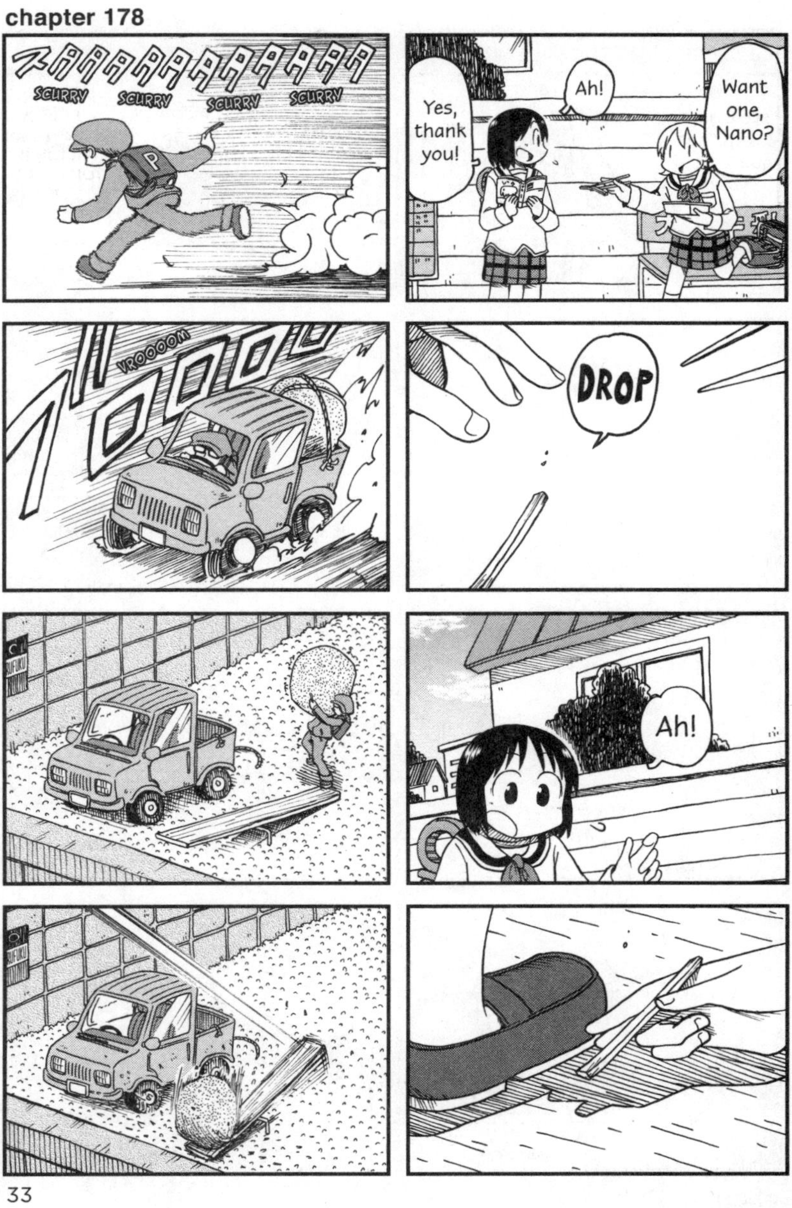
Want one, Nano?
Ah!
Yes, thank you!
SCURRY
SCURRY
SCURRY
SCURRY
DROP
VROOOOM
Ah!

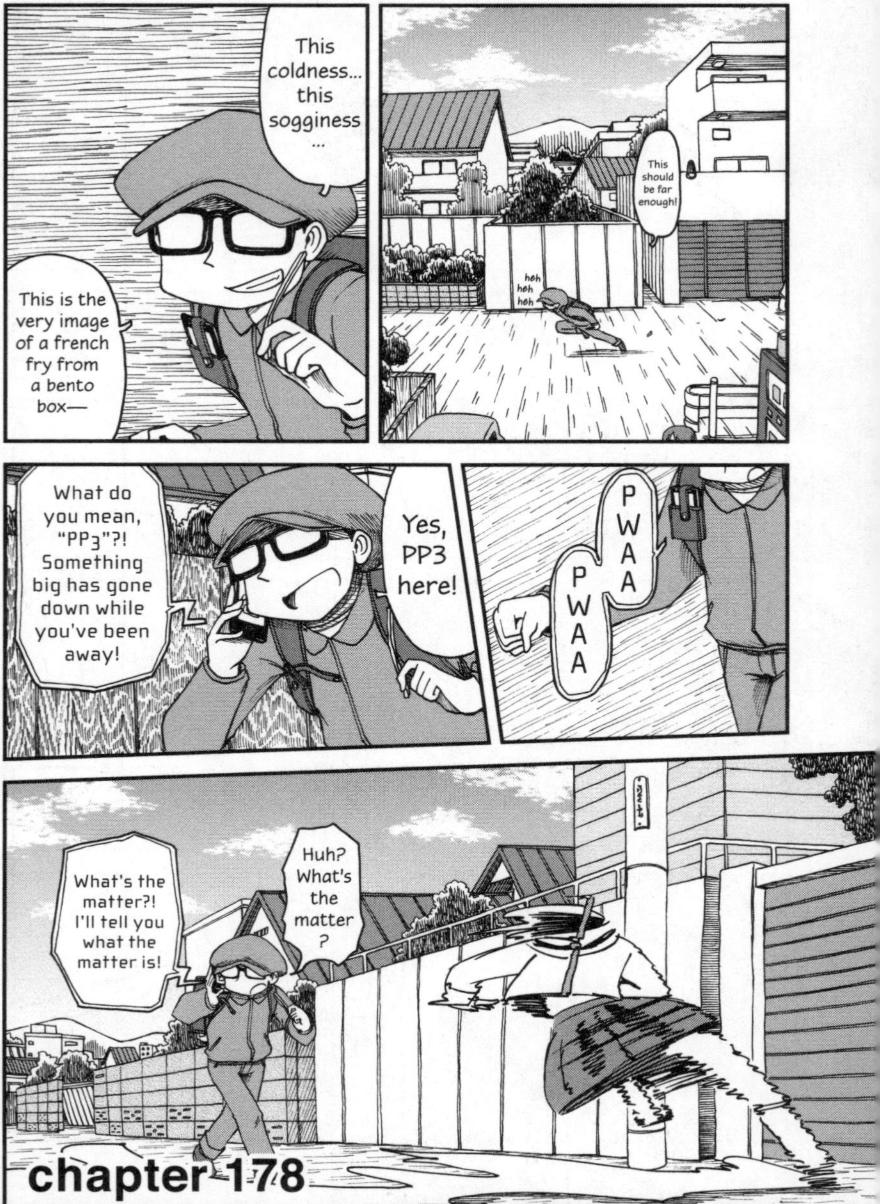
This should be far enough!
heh heh heh
This coldness... this sogginess ...
This is the very image of a french fry from a bento box—
PWAA
PWAA
Yes, PP3 here!
What do you mean, "PP3"?! Something big has gone down while you've been away!
Huh? What's the matter ?
What's the matter?! I'll tell you what the matter is!

chapter 178

ZWIPP

Master's hemorrhoids have gotten worse—!

VWOOSH

IP1

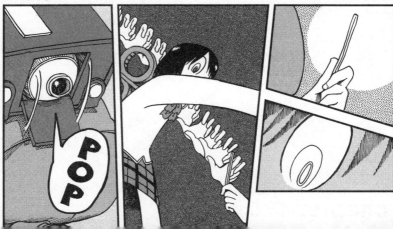

POP

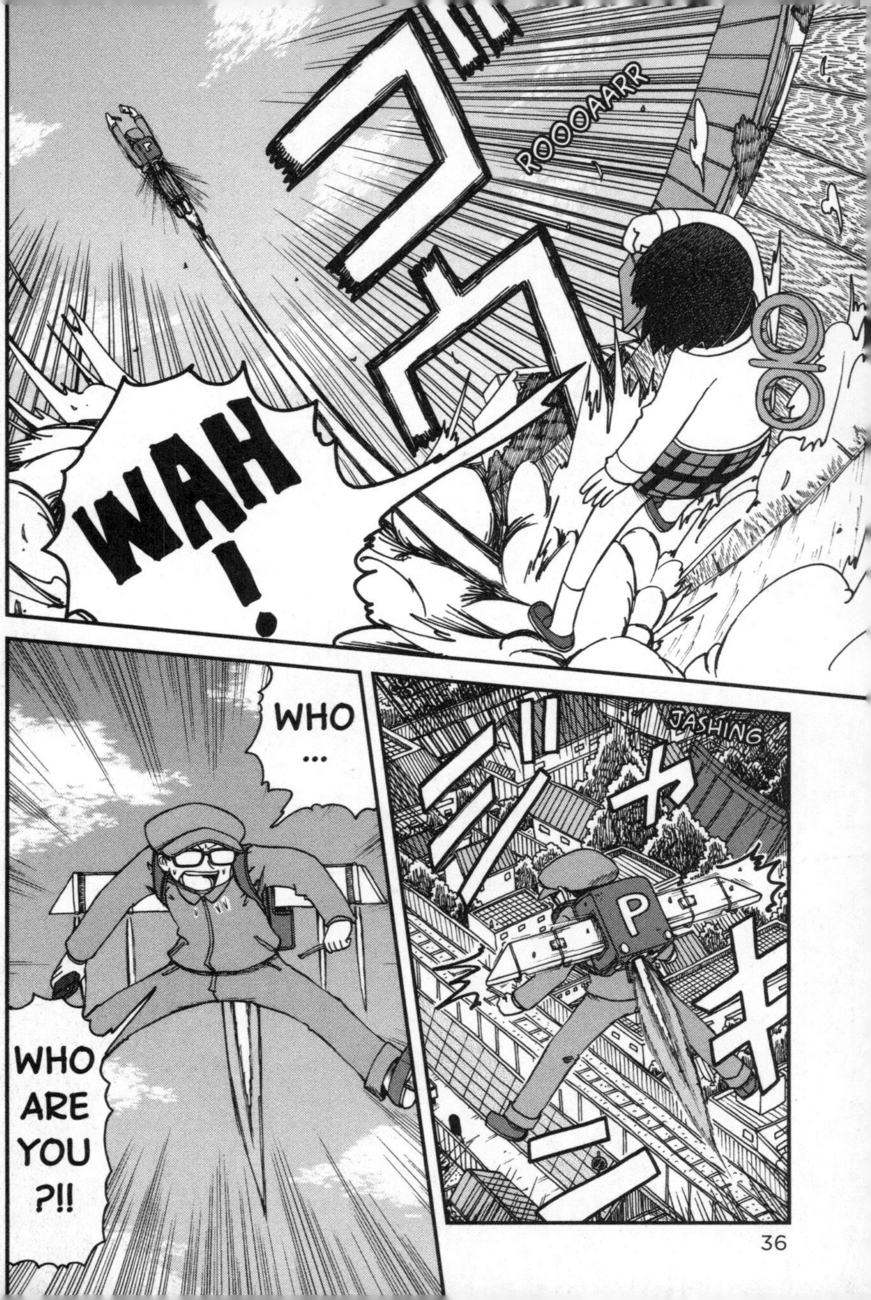
ROOOAARR
WAH!
JASHING
WHO ...
WHO ARE YOU ?!!

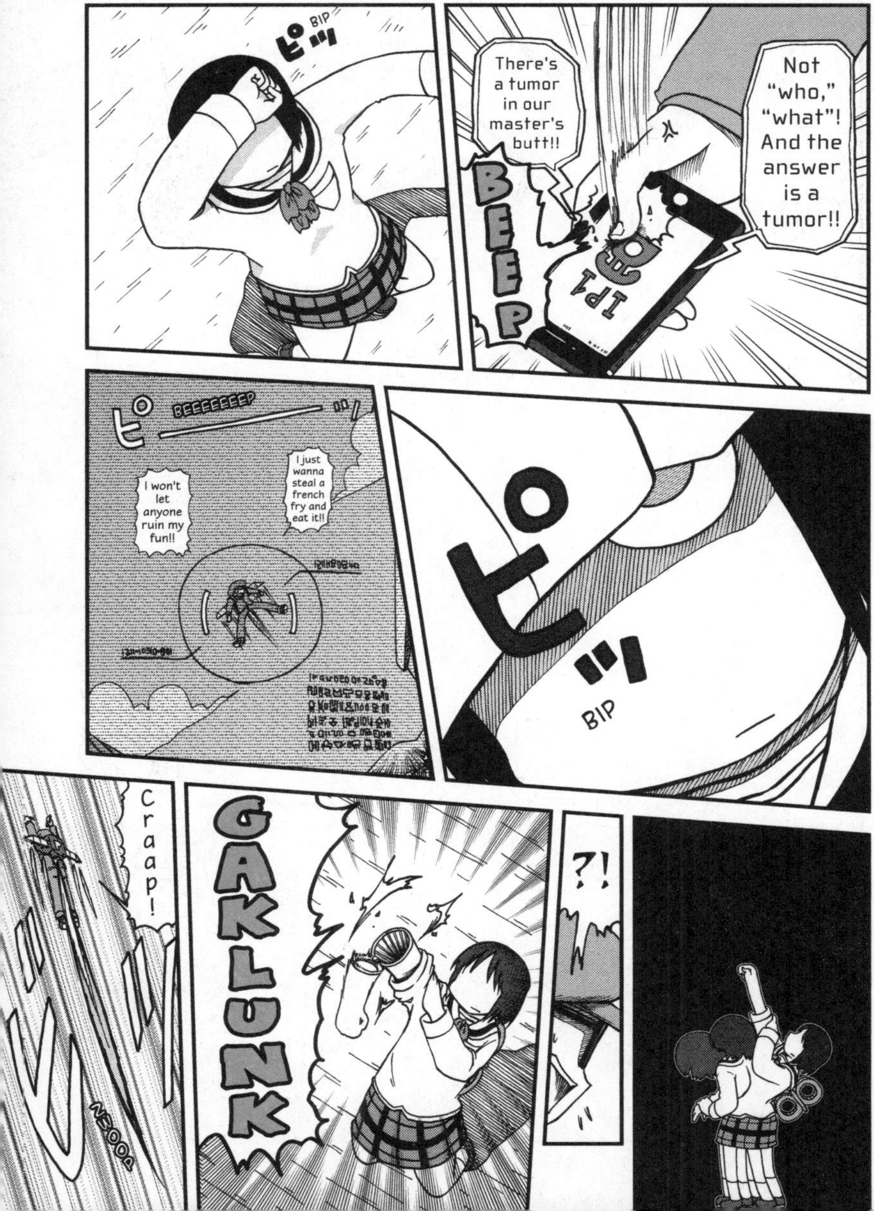
Not "who," "what"! And the answer is a tumor!!
There's a tumor in our master's butt!!
BEEEP
BIP
BIP
BEEEEEEEP
I just wanna steal a french fry and eat it!!
I won't let anyone ruin my fun!!
?!
GAKLUNK
Craap!

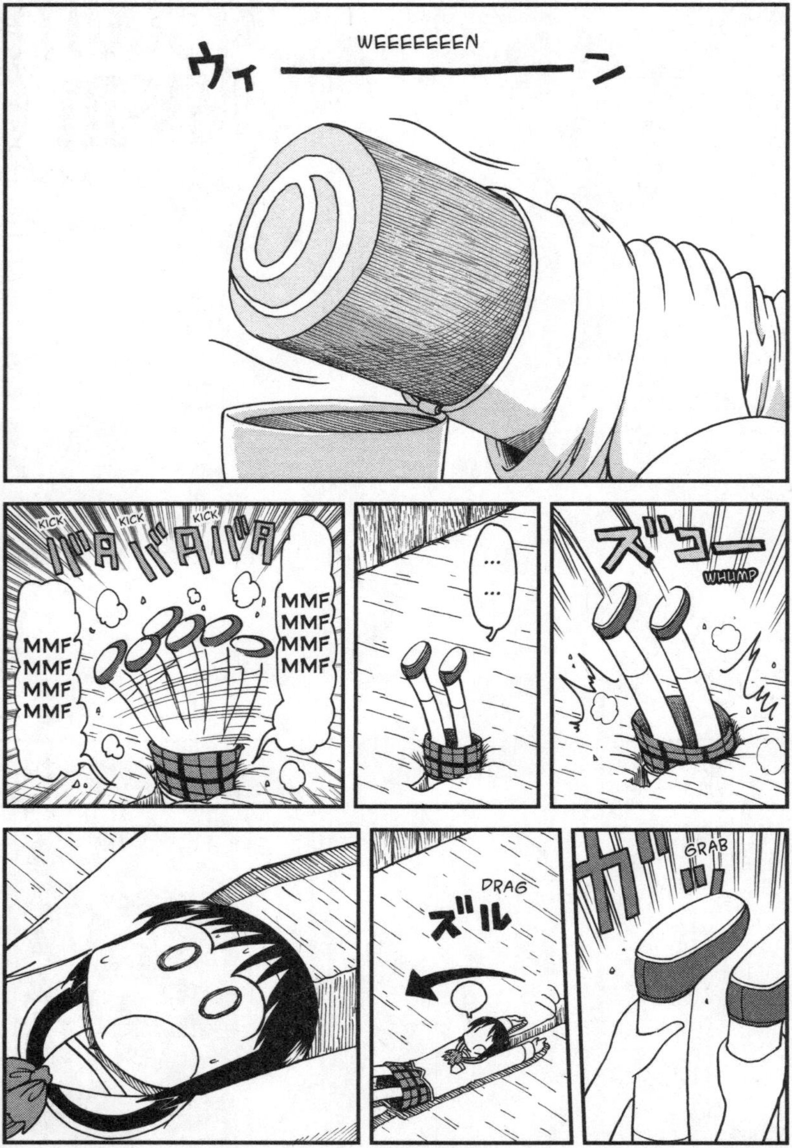

WEEEEEEEEN
ウィーーーーン
ズコー
WHUMP
…
…
KICK KICK KICK
バタバタバタ
MMF MMF MMF MMF
MMF MMF MMF MMF
GRAB
ガッ
DRAG
ズル

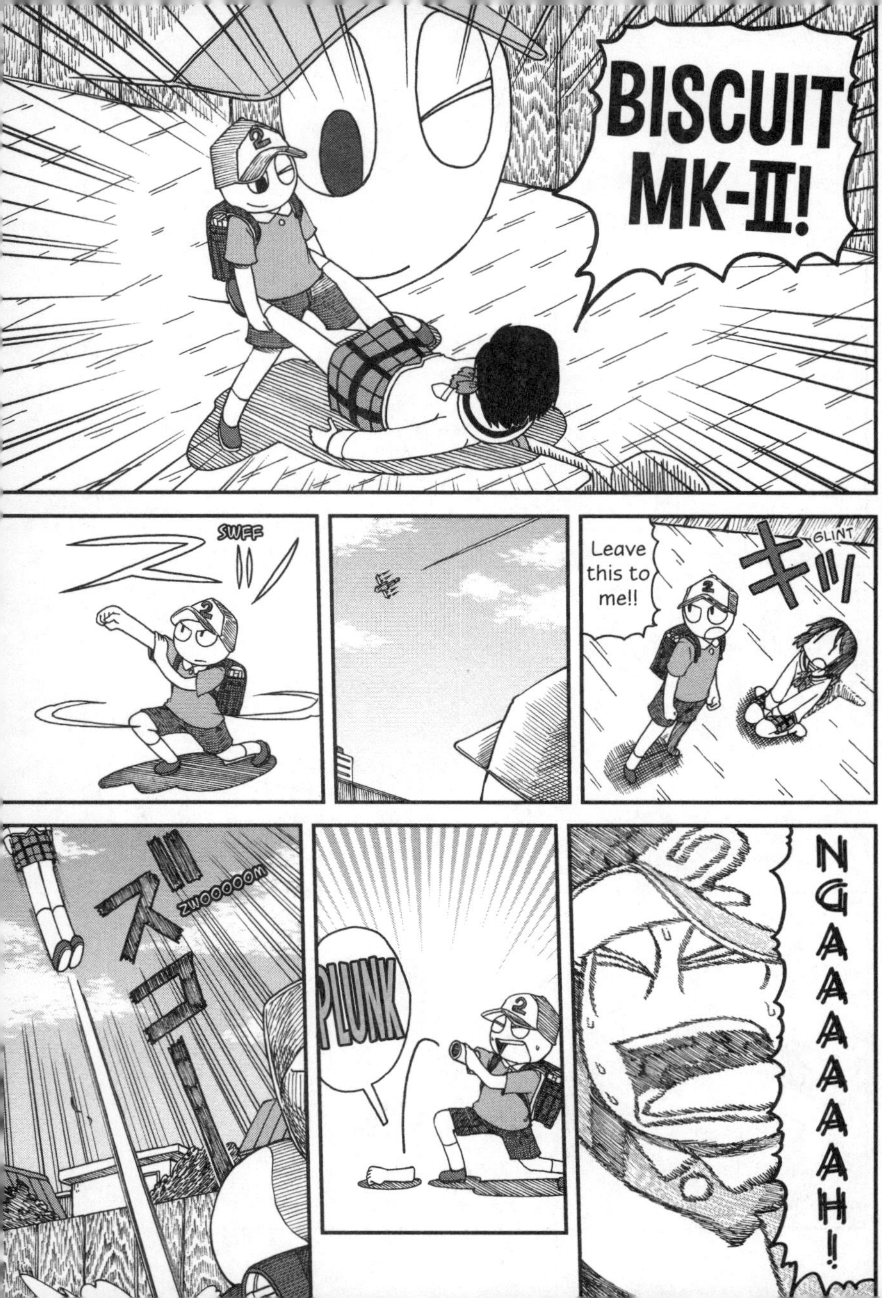
BISCUIT MK-II!
GLINT
キッ
Leave this to me!!
SWFF
NGAAAAAAH!!
PLUNK
ZWOOOOOM

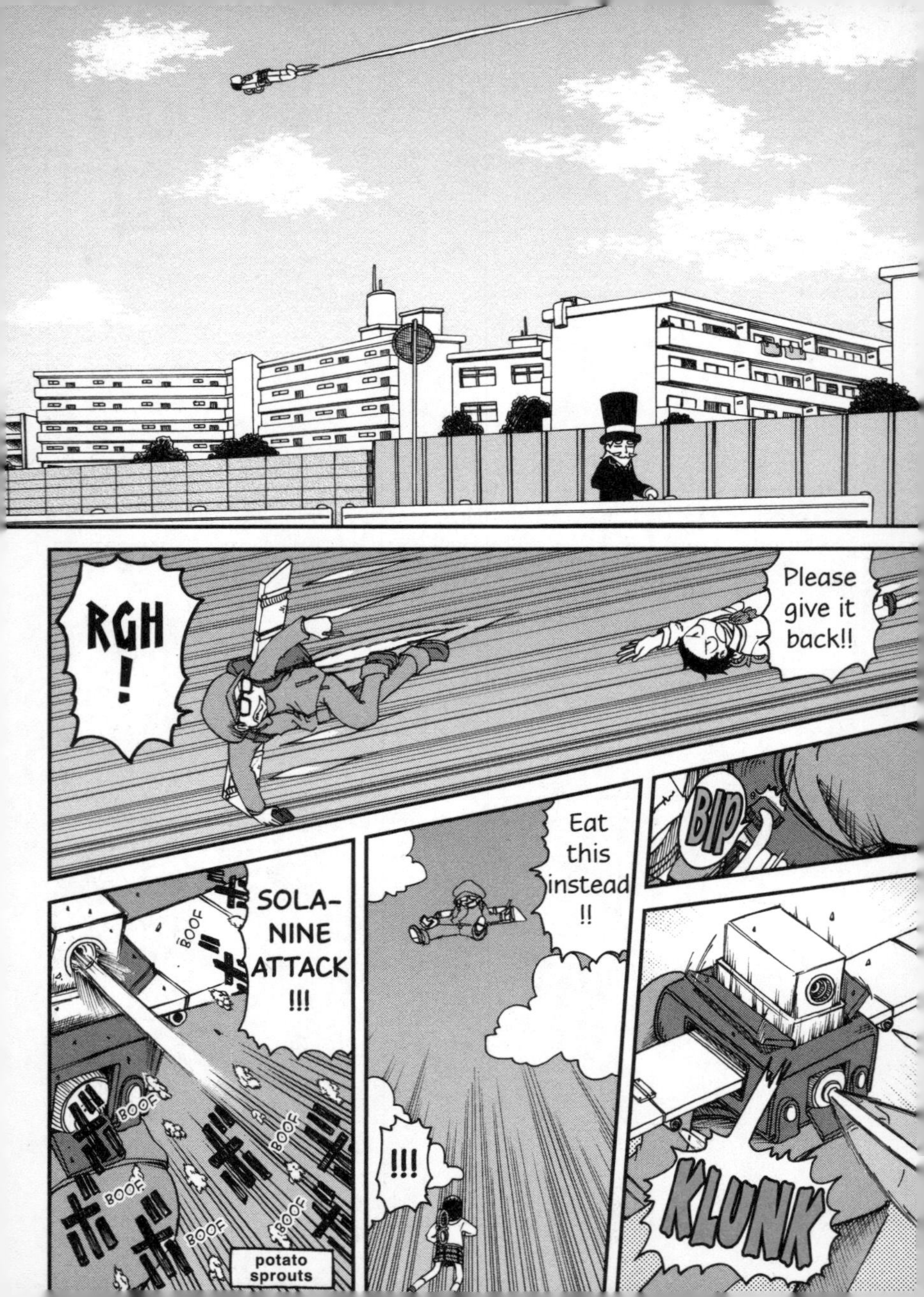
Please give it back!!
RGH!
BIP
KLUNK
Eat this instead!!
!!!
SOLA-NINE ATTACK!!!
BOOF
BOOF
BOOF
BOOF
BOOF
BOOF
potato sprouts

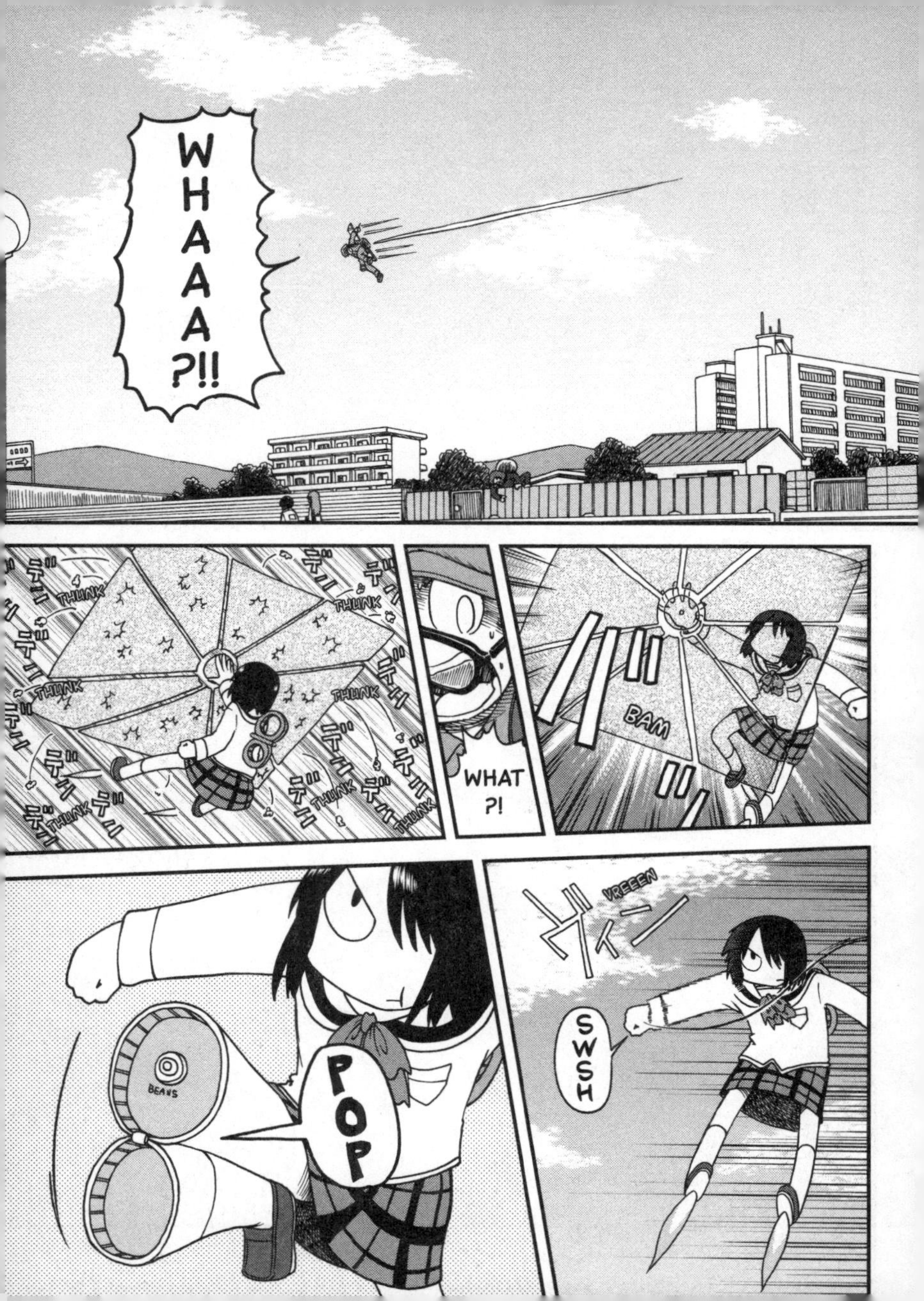
WHAAAA?!!
BAM
WHAT?!
THUNK
THUNK
THUNK
THUNK
THUNK
THUNK
THUNK
VREEEN
SWSH
POP
BEANS

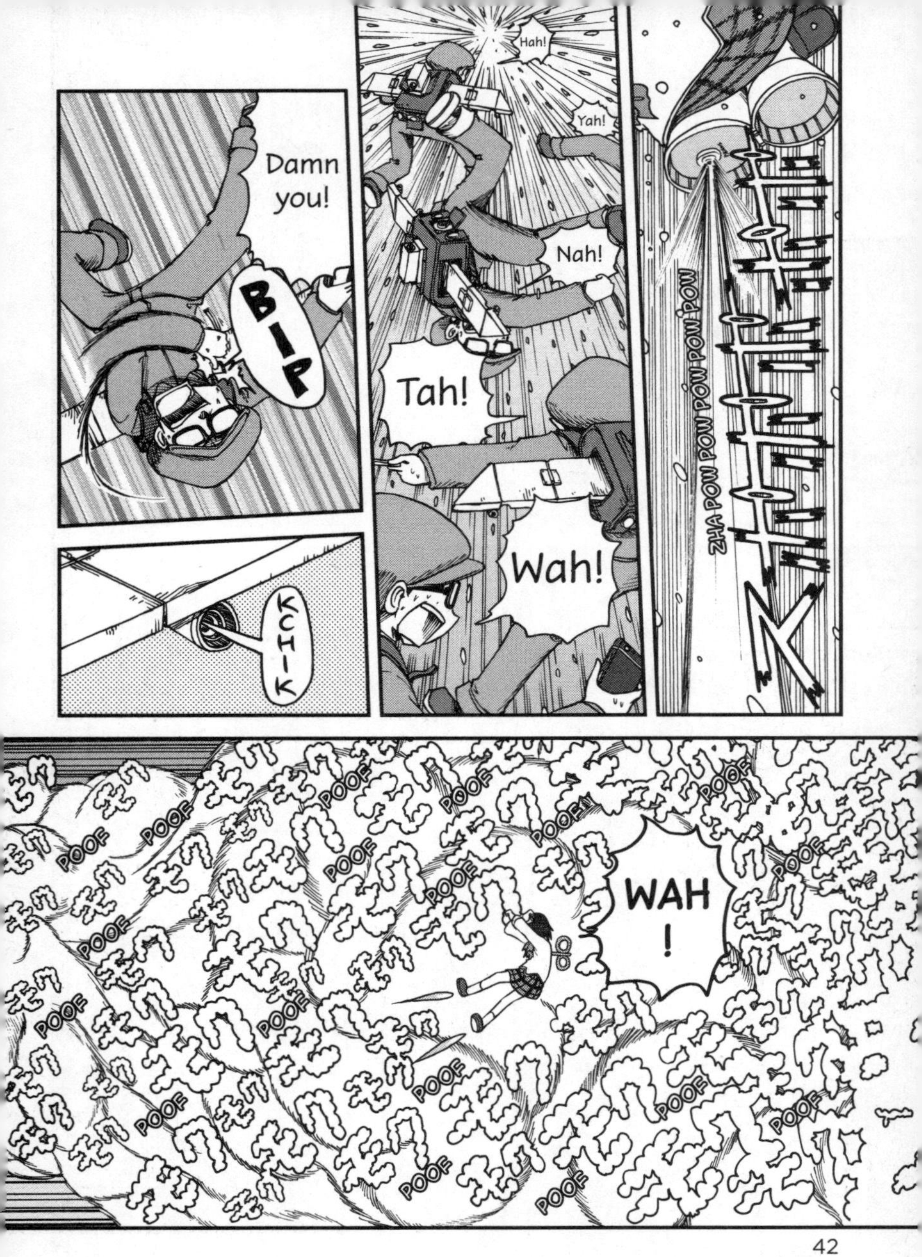
ZHA POW POW POW POW POW
Hah!
Yah!
Nah!
Tah!
Wah!
Damn you!
BIP
KCHIK
POOF
POOF
POOF
POOF
POOF!
POOF
POOF
POOF
POOF
WAH!
POOF
POOF
POOF
POOF
POOF
POOF
POOF
POOF
POOF

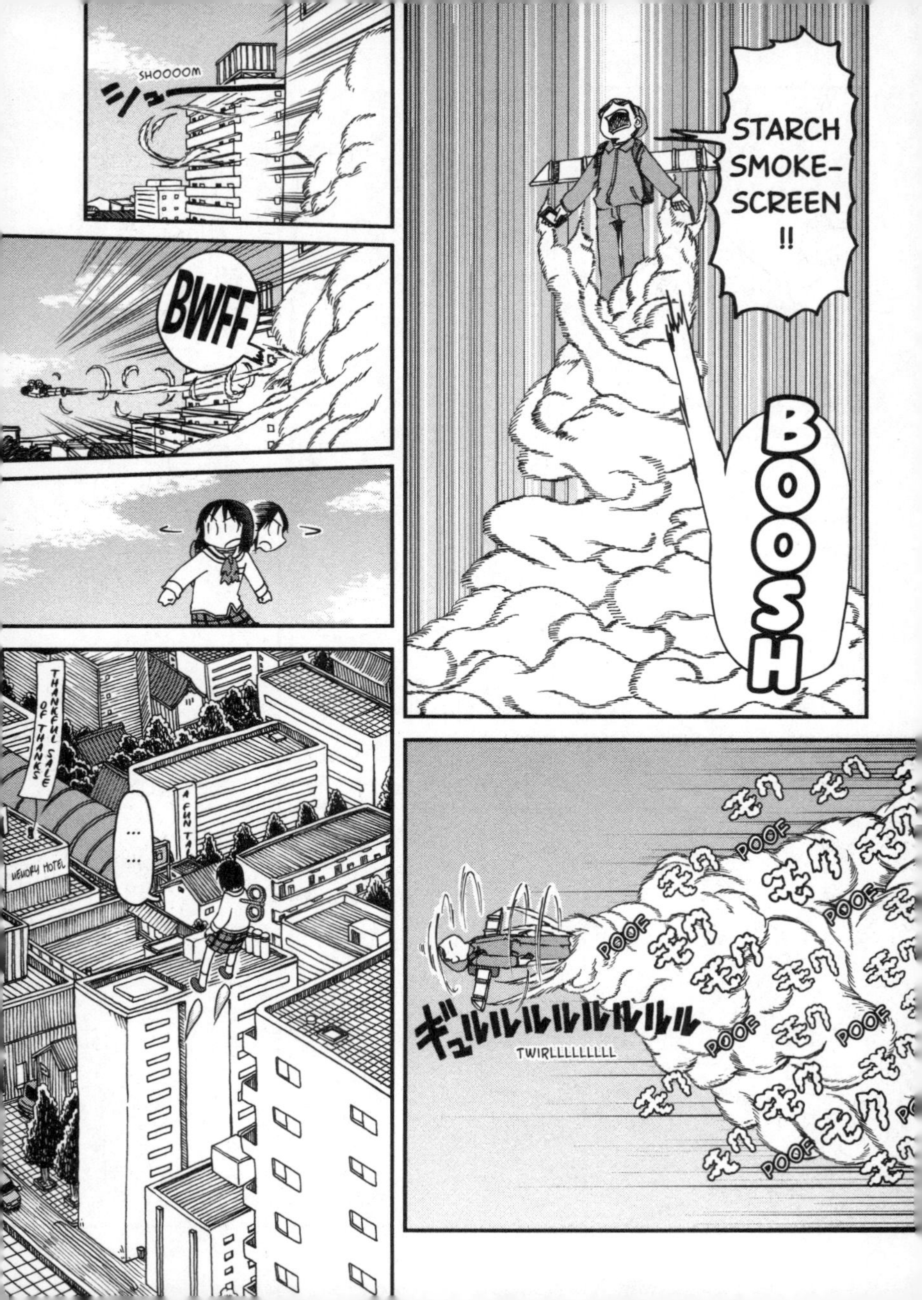

STARCH SMOKE-SCREEN !!
BOOSH
シュー
SHOOOM
BWFF
POOF
TWIRLLLLLLLLLL
...
...
THANKFUL SALE OF THANKS
A FUN TA
MEMORY HOTEL

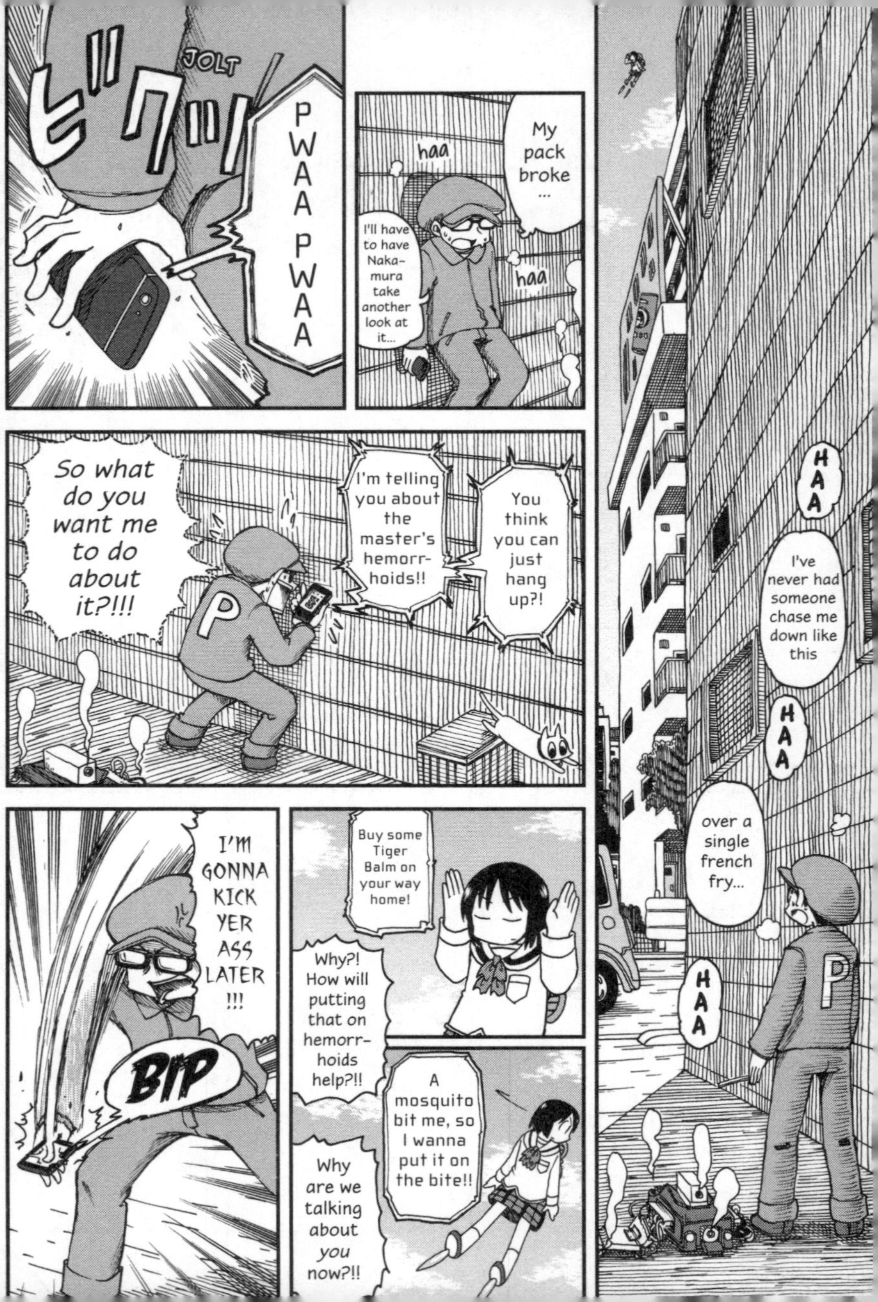
HAA
I've never had someone chase me down like this
HAA
over a single french fry...
HAA
My pack broke...
haa
haa
I'll have to have Nakamura take another look at it...
JOLT
PWAA PWAA
You think you can just hang up?!
I'm telling you about the master's hemorrhoids!!
So what do you want me to do about it?!!!
Buy some Tiger Balm on your way home!
Why?! How will putting that on hemorrhoids help?!!
A mosquito bit me, so I wanna put it on the bite!!
Why are we talking about you now?!!
I'M GONNA KICK YER ASS LATER!!!
BIP

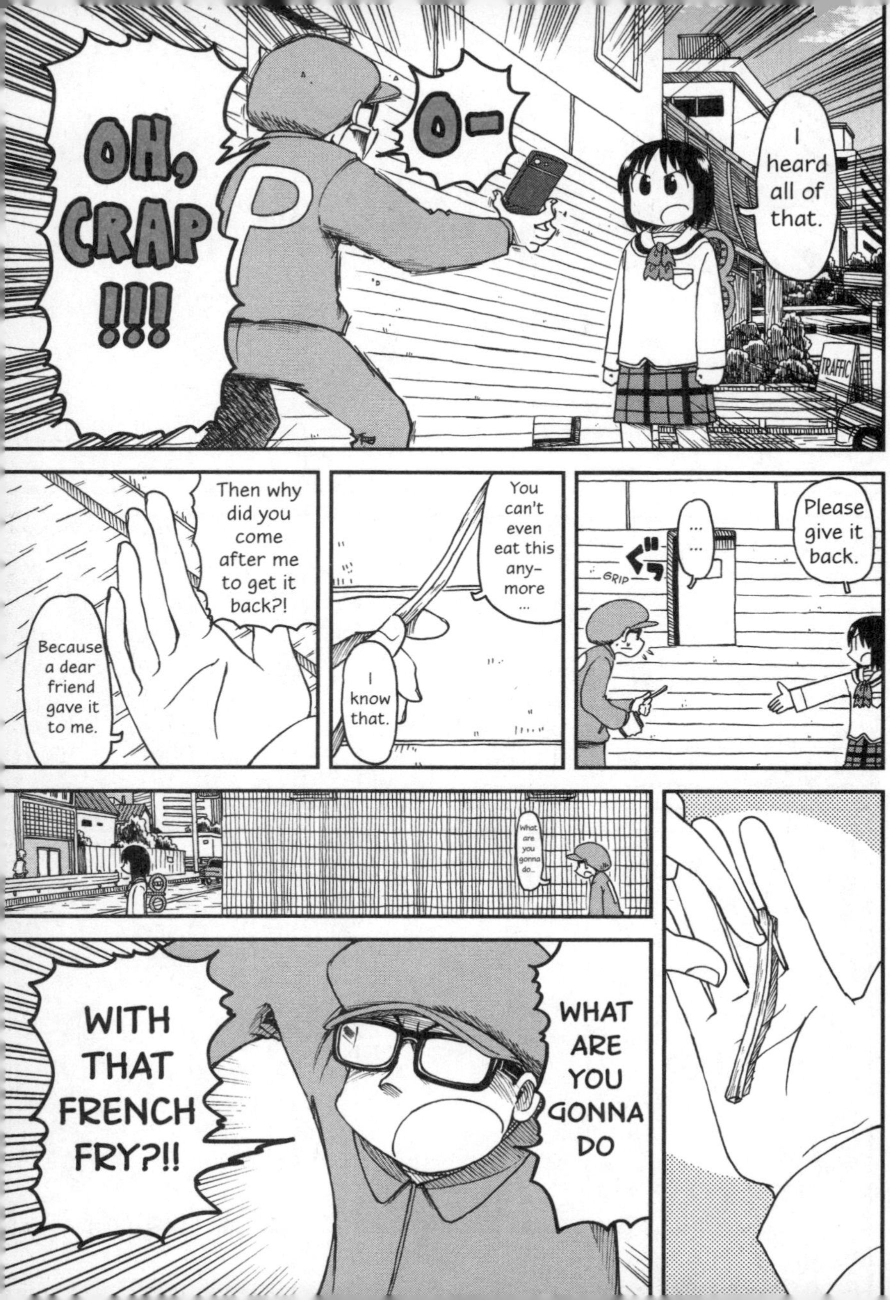
I heard all of that.
TRAFFIC
O-
OH, CRAP!!!
Please give it back.
GRIP
... ...
You can't even eat this any-more ...
I know that.
Then why did you come after me to get it back?!
Because a dear friend gave it to me.
What are you gonna do...
WHAT ARE YOU GONNA DO
WITH THAT FRENCH FRY?!!

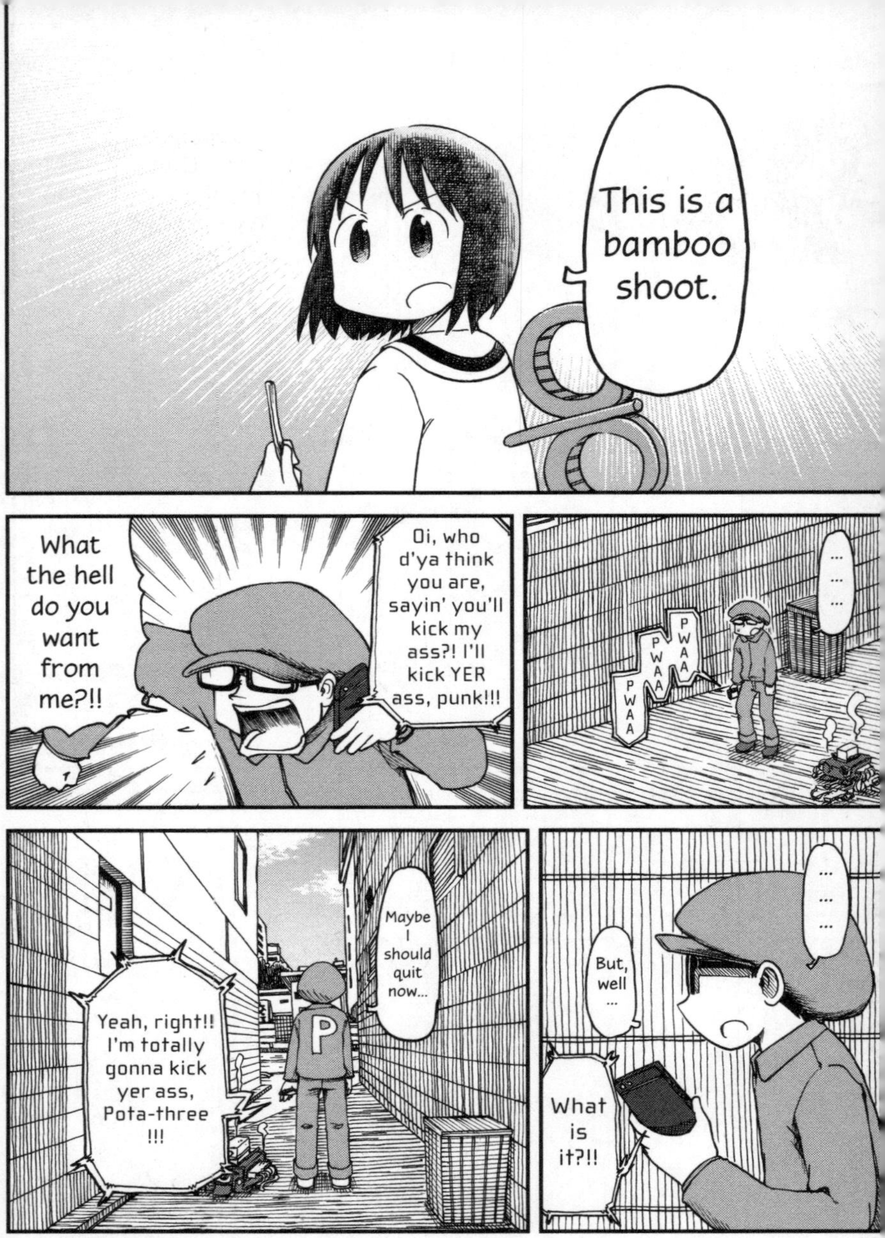
This is a bamboo shoot.
...
...
...
PWAA
PWAA
PWAA
Oi, who d'ya think you are, sayin' you'll kick my ass?! I'll kick YER ass, punk!!!
What the hell do you want from me?!!
...
...
...
But, well ...
What is it?!!
Maybe I should quit now...
Yeah, right!! I'm totally gonna kick yer ass, Pota-three !!!

chapter 178: end

chapter 179

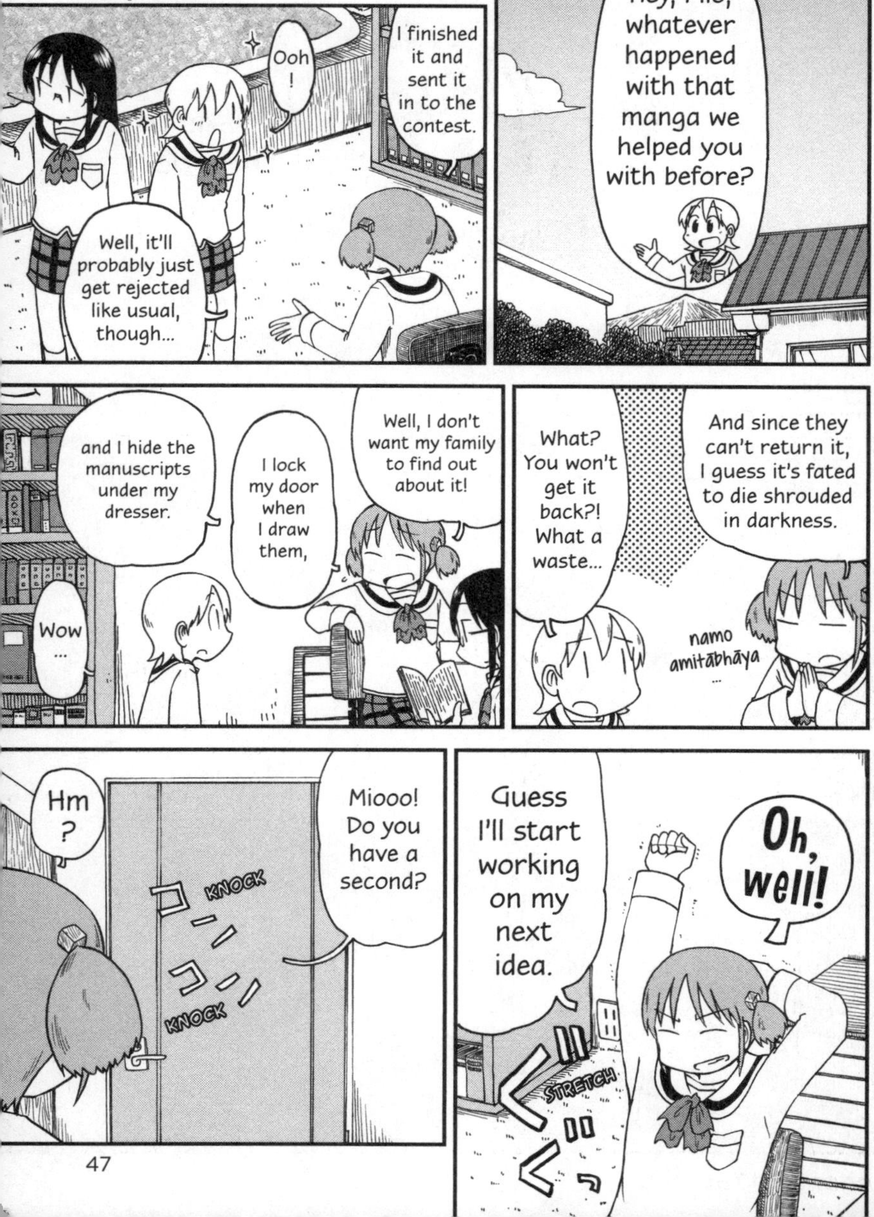
Hey, Mio, whatever happened with that manga we helped you with before?
I finished it and sent it in to the contest.
Ooh!
Well, it'll probably just get rejected like usual, though...
And since they can't return it, I guess it's fated to die shrouded in darkness.
What? You won't get it back?! What a waste...
namo amitābhāya ...
Well, I don't want my family to find out about it!
I lock my door when I draw them,
and I hide the manuscripts under my dresser.
Wow ...
Oh, well!
Guess I'll start working on my next idea.
STRETCH
Miooo! Do you have a second?
KNOCK
KNOCK
Hm?

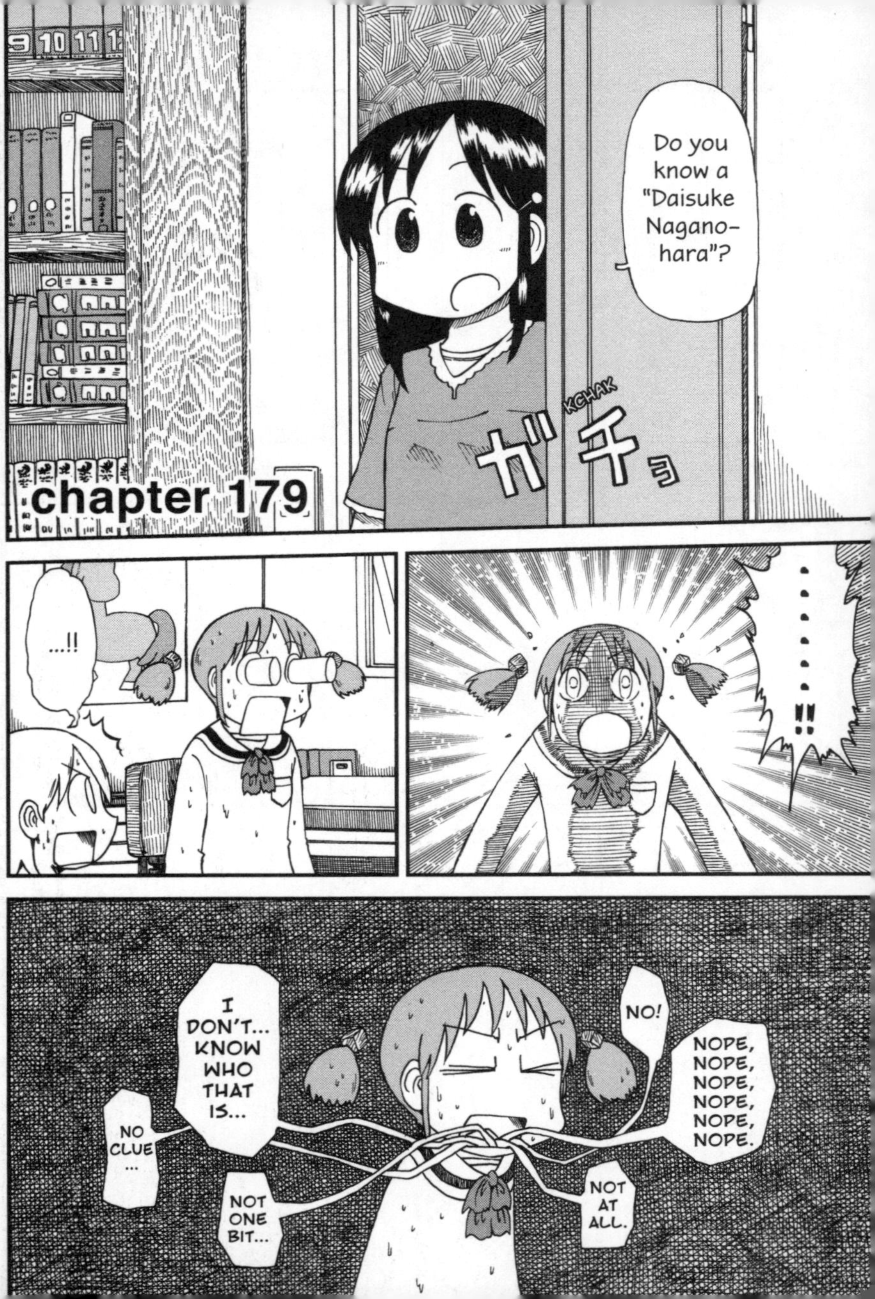
chapter 179
Do you know a "Daisuke Nagano-hara"?
ガチョ
KCHAK
......!!
...!!
NO!
NOPE, NOPE, NOPE, NOPE, NOPE, NOPE.
NOT AT ALL.
I DON'T... KNOW WHO THAT IS...
NOT ONE BIT...
NO CLUE...

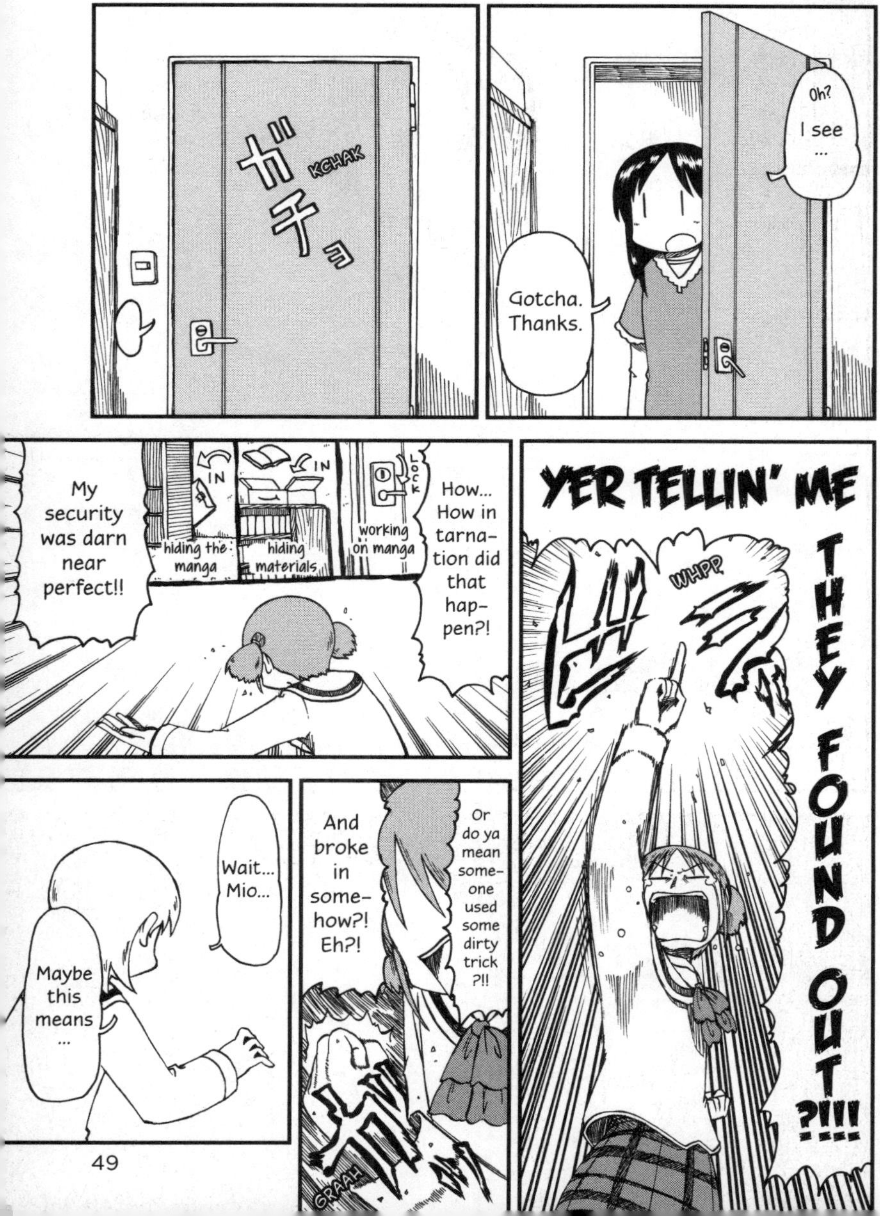
Oh?
I see ...
Gotcha. Thanks.
ガチョ
KCHAK
YER TELLIN' ME THEY FOUND OUT?!!!
WHPP
How... How in tarna-tion did that hap-pen?!
working on manga
LOCK
IN
hiding materials
IN
hiding the manga
My security was darn near perfect!!
Or do ya mean some-one used some dirty trick ?!!
And broke in some-how?! Eh?!
GRAAH
Wait... Mio...
Maybe this means ...

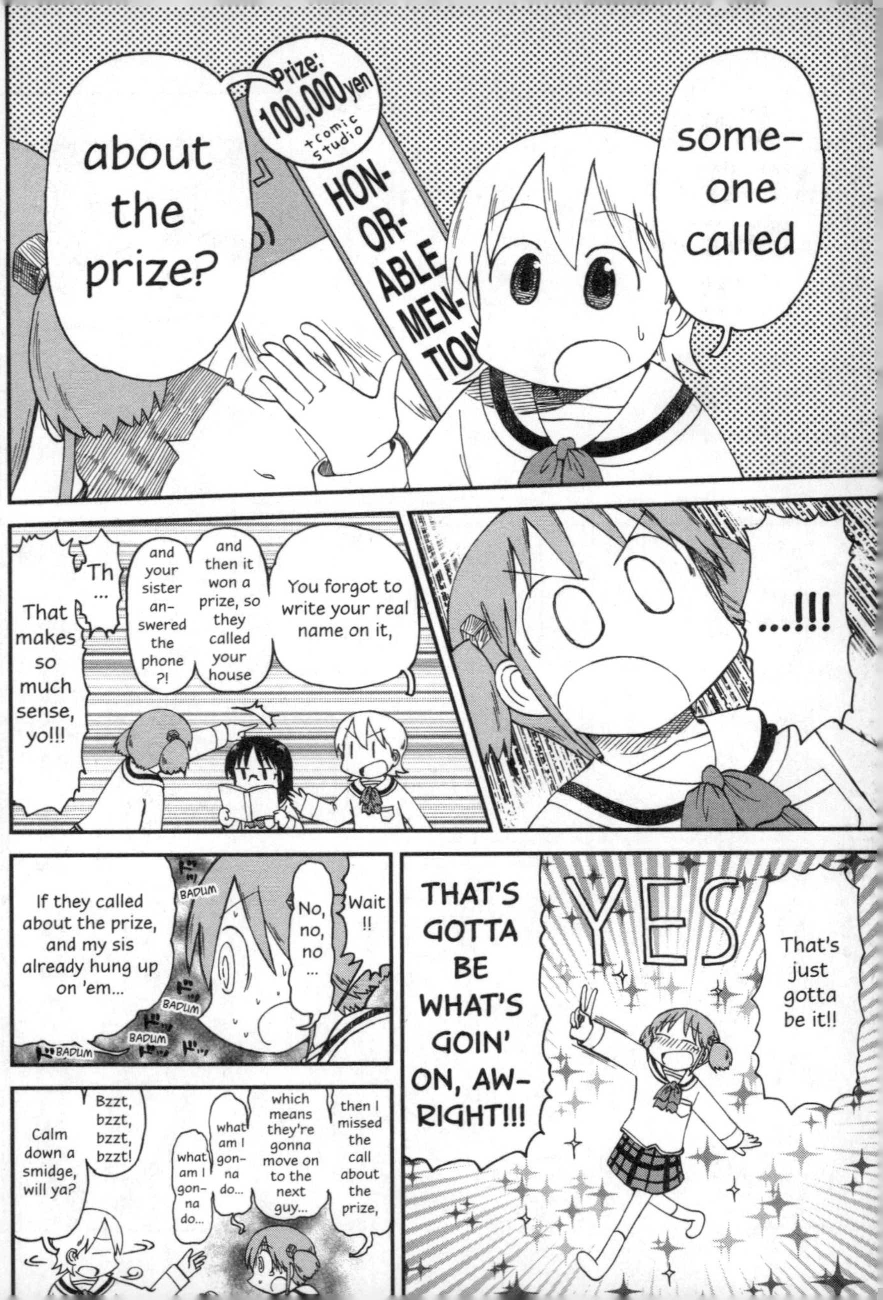
some-one called
Prize: 100,000yen +comic studio
HON-OR-ABLE MEN-TION
about the prize?
...!!!
You forgot to write your real name on it,
and then it won a prize, so they called your house
and your sister an-swered the phone ?!
Th ...
That makes so much sense, yo!!!
YES
That's just gotta be it!!
THAT'S GOTTA BE WHAT'S GOIN' ON, AW-RIGHT!!!
Wait !!
No, no, no ...
BADUM
If they called about the prize, and my sis already hung up on 'em...
BADUM
BADUM
BADUM
then I missed the call about the prize,
which means they're gonna move on to the next guy...
what am I gon-na do...
what am I gon-na do...
Bzzt, bzzt, bzzt, bzzt!
Calm down a smidge, will ya?

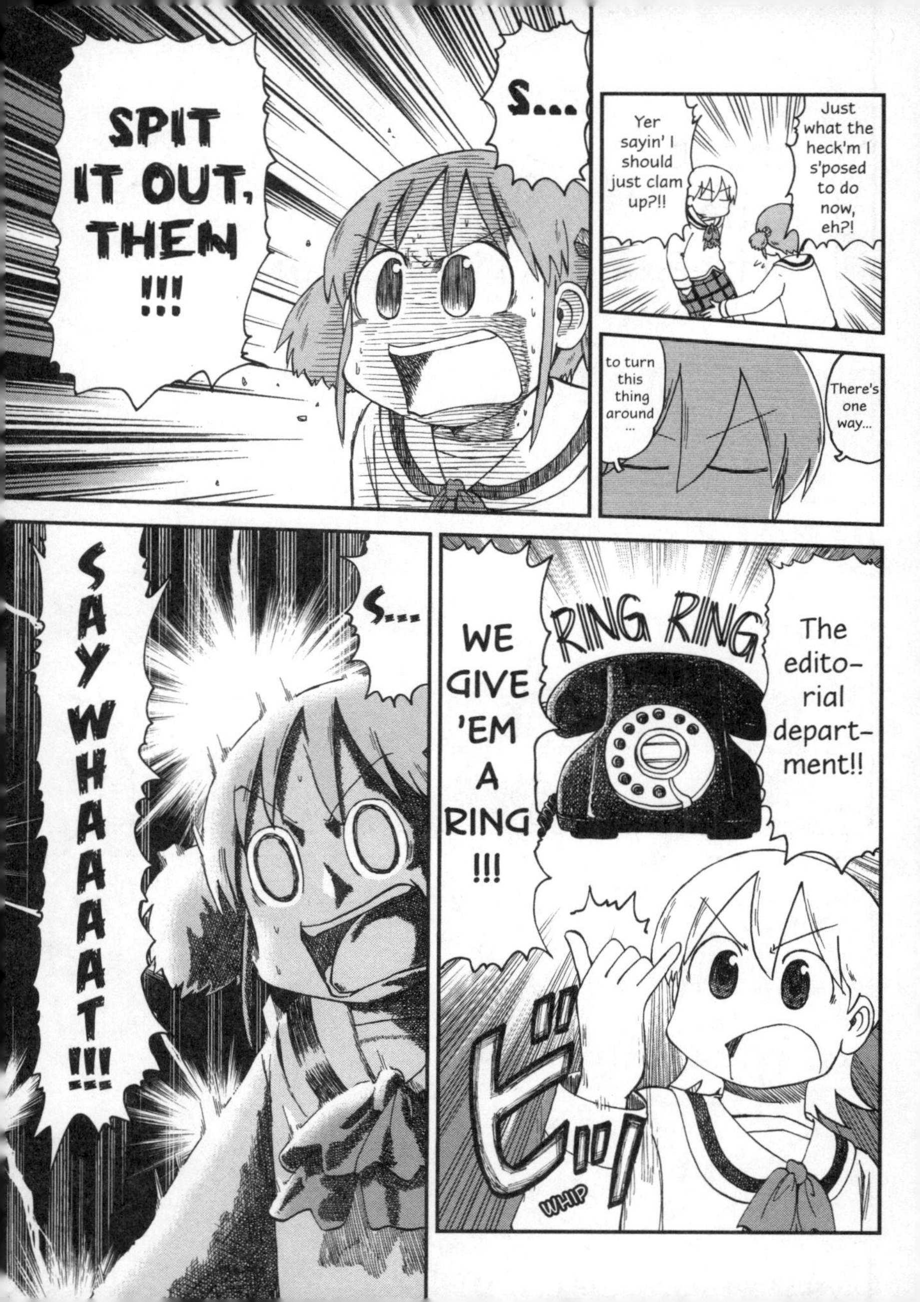
Just what the heck'm I s'posed to do now, eh?!
Yer sayin' I should just clam up?!!
There's one way...
to turn this thing around...
S...
SPIT IT OUT, THEN!!!
The editorial department!!
RING RING
WE GIVE 'EM A RING!!!
WHIP
S...
SAY WHAAAAAT!!!

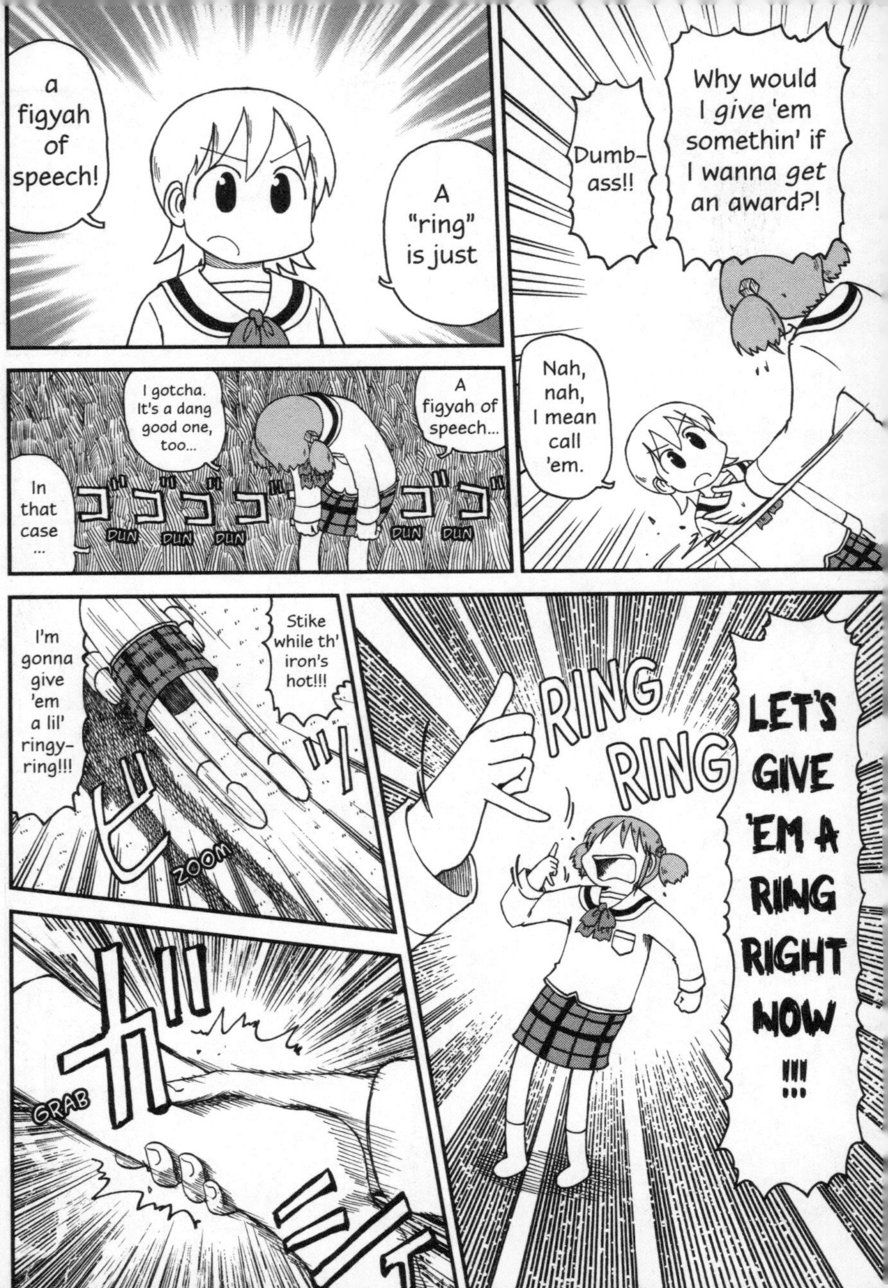
Why would I *give* 'em somethin' if I wanna *get* an award?!
Dumb-ass!!
A "ring" is just
a figyah of speech!
Nah, nah, I mean call 'em.
A figyah of speech...
I gotcha. It's a dang good one, too...
DUN DUN
DUN DUN DUN
In that case ...
LET'S GIVE 'EM A RING RIGHT NOW!!!
RING RING
Stike while th' iron's hot!!!
I'm gonna give 'em a lil' ringy-ring!!!
ZOOM
GRAB

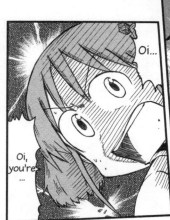

WHO DARES ?!!
GLARE
Oi...
Oi, you're ...
MAI
BAM
MINA-KAMI, AIN'T YA!!!
PINCH ME, I'M DREAMING
What's the big idea ?!!
Whatcha stoppin' me for?!!
What if it's ...
SPIT IT OUT !!!

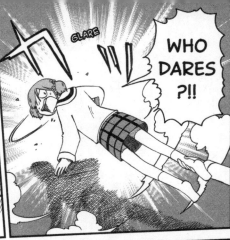

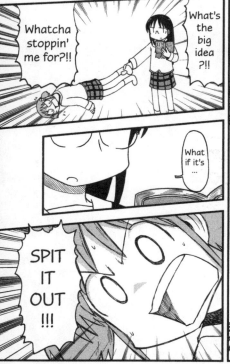

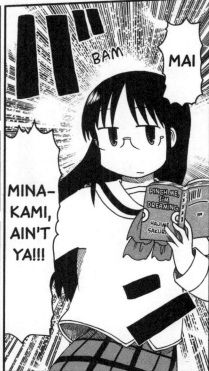

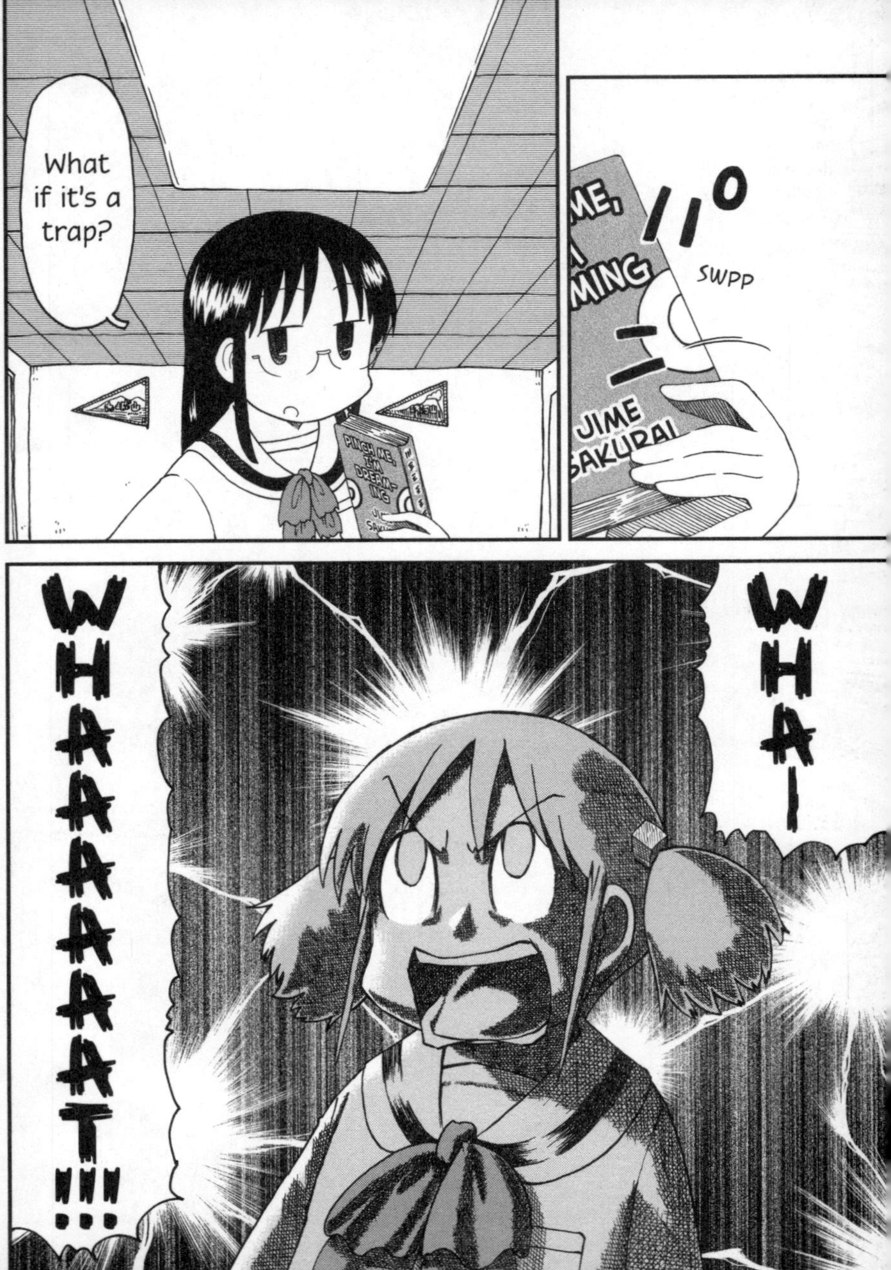
ME,
I
MING
JIME
SAKURAI
SWPP
What if it's a trap?
PINCH ME, I'M DREAMING
JIME
WHA-
WHAAAAAAT!!!

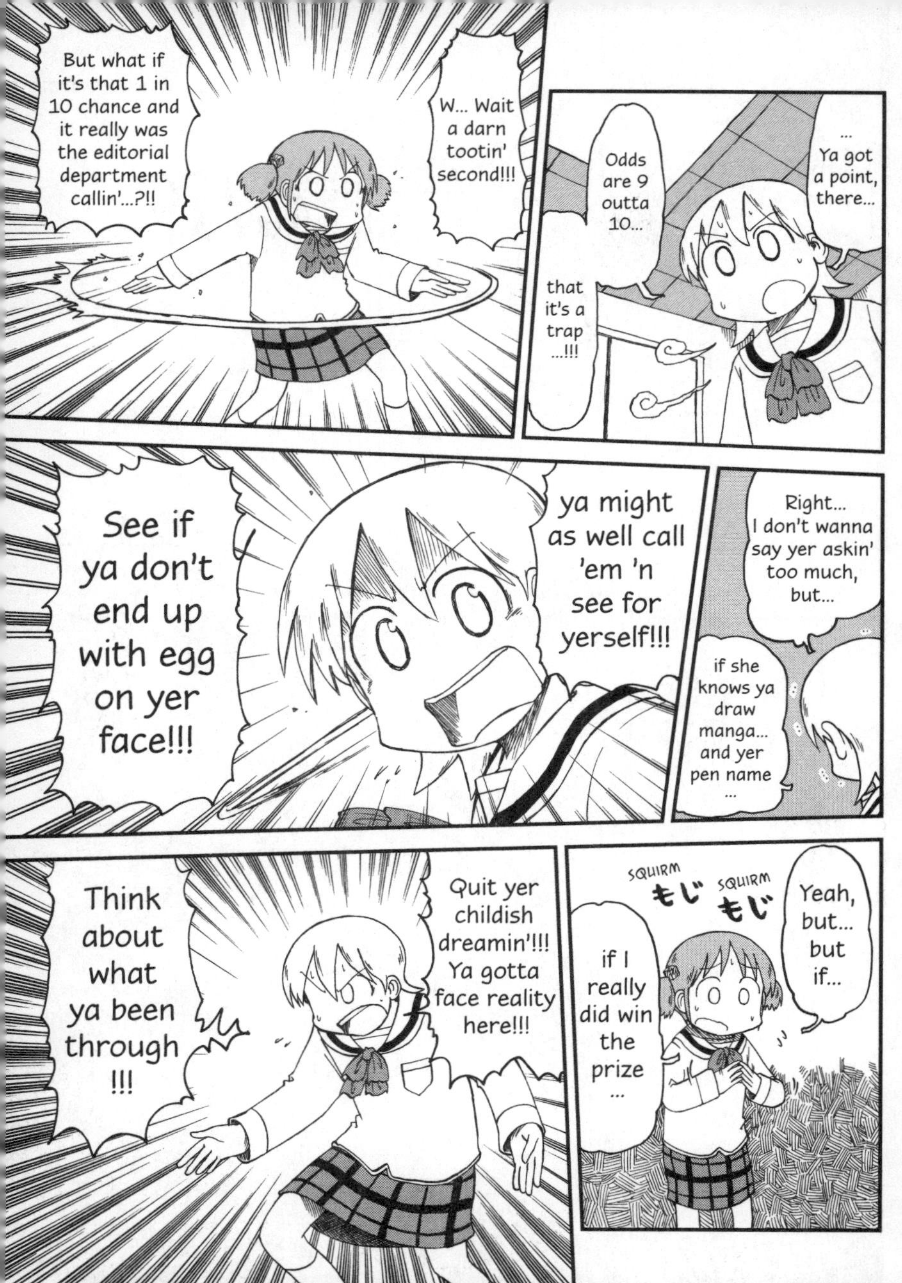
... Ya got a point, there...
Odds are 9 outta 10...
that it's a trap ...!!!
W... Wait a darn tootin' second!!!
But what if it's that 1 in 10 chance and it really was the editorial department callin'...?!!
Right... I don't wanna say yer askin' too much, but...
if she knows ya draw manga... and yer pen name ...
ya might as well call 'em 'n see for yerself!!!
See if ya don't end up with egg on yer face!!!
Yeah, but... but if...
SQUIRM
もじ
SQUIRM
もじ
if I really did win the prize ...
Quit yer childish dreamin'!!! Ya gotta face reality here!!!
Think about what ya been through !!!

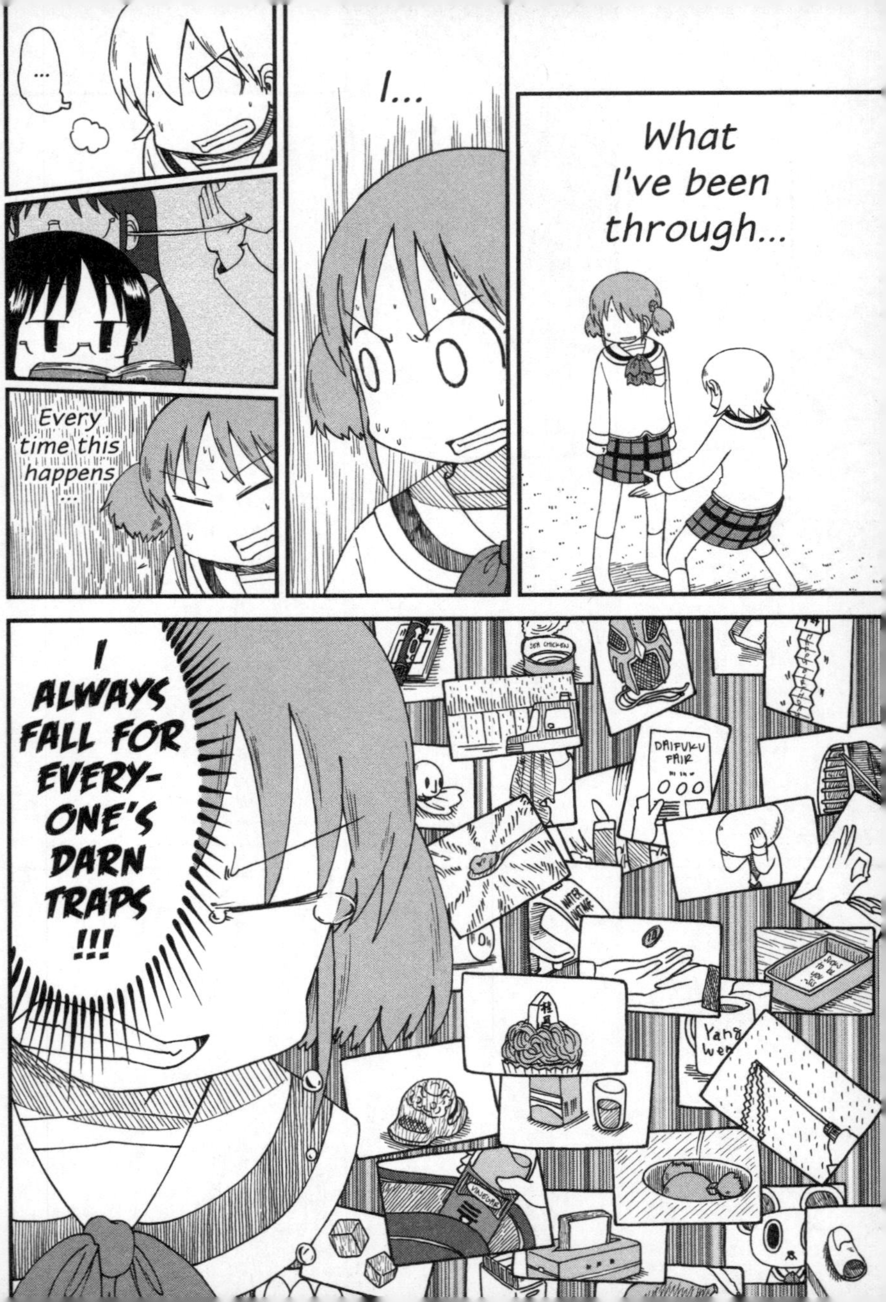

What I've been through...
I...
...
Every time this happens ...
I ALWAYS FALL FOR EVERY-ONE'S DARN TRAPS !!!
DAIFUKU FAIR

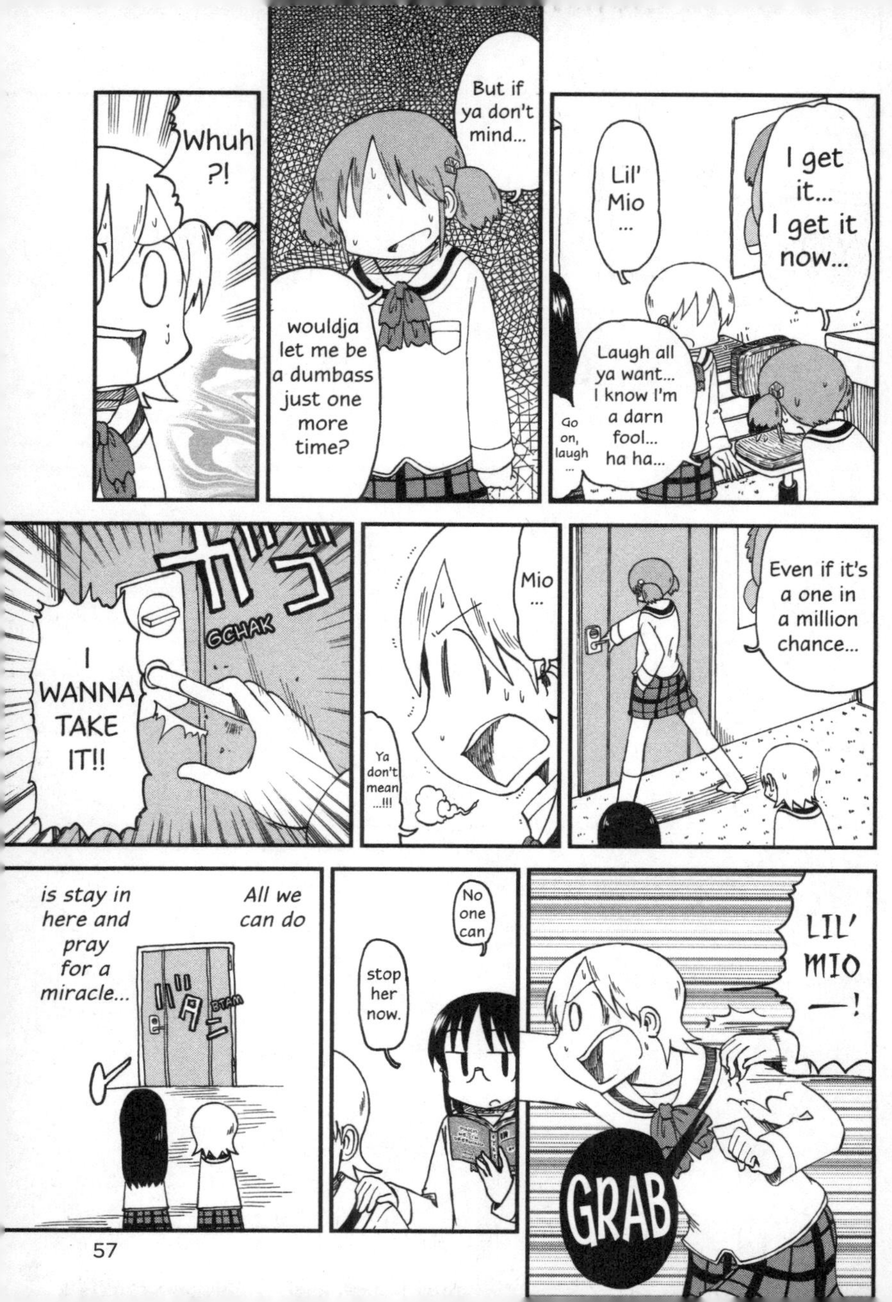
I get it... I get it now...
Lil' Mio ...
Laugh all ya want... I know I'm a darn fool... ha ha...
Go on, laugh ...
But if ya don't mind...
wouldja let me be a dumbass just one more time?
Whuh ?!
Even if it's a one in a million chance...
Mio ...
Ya don't mean ...!!!
GCHAK
I WANNA TAKE IT!!
LIL' MIO —!
GRAB
No one can
stop her now.
All we can do
is stay in here and pray for a miracle...
BTAM

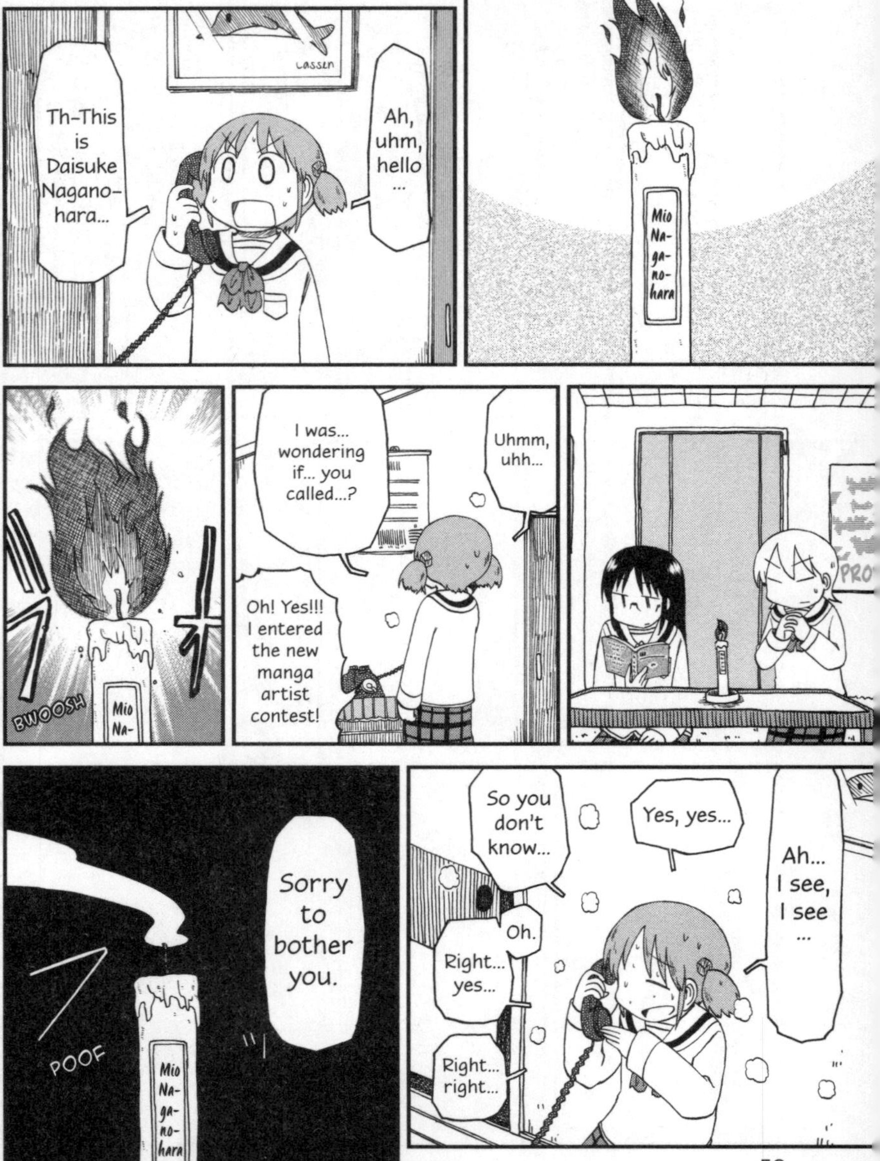
Mio Naganohara
Lassen
Ah, uhm, hello...
Th-This is Daisuke Naganohara...
PRO
Uhmm, uhh...
I was... wondering if... you called...?
Oh! Yes!!! I entered the new manga artist contest!
BWOOSH
Mio Na-
Ah... I see, I see...
Yes, yes...
So you don't know...
Oh.
Right... yes...
Right... right...
Sorry to bother you.
POOF
Mio Naganohara

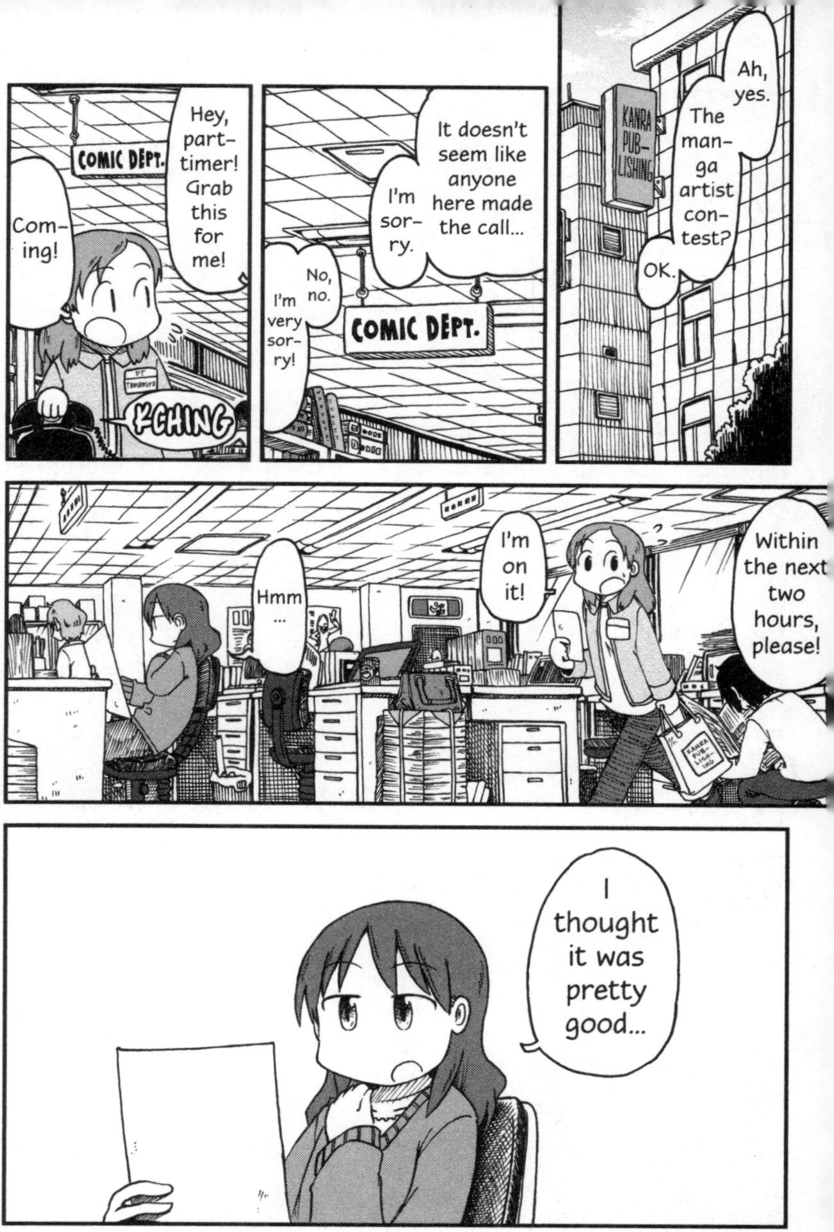
KANRA PUB-LISHING
Ah, yes. The manga artist contest?
OK.
It doesn't seem like anyone here made the call...
I'm sorry.
No, no.
I'm very sorry!
COMIC DEPT.
Hey, part-timer! Grab this for me!
COMIC DEPT.
Coming!
KCHING
Within the next two hours, please!
I'm on it!
KANRA PUB-LISHING
Hmm...
I thought it was pretty good...

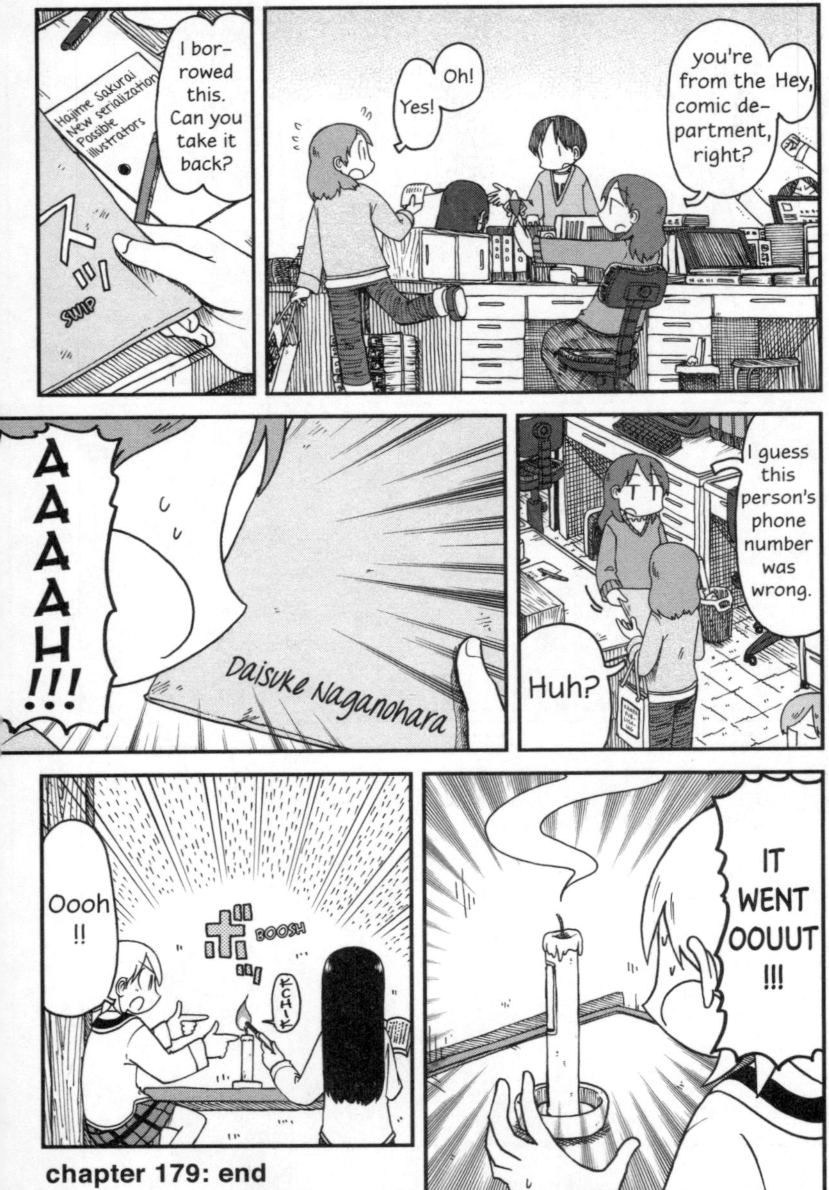
you're from the Hey, comic de-partment, right?
Oh!
Yes!
I bor-rowed this. Can you take it back?
Hajime Sakurai New serialization Possible illustrators
SWIP
I guess this person's phone number was wrong.
Huh?
Daisuke Naganohara
AAAAAH!!!
IT WENT OOUUT !!!
Oooh !!
BOOSH
KCHIK

chapter 179: end

chapter 180

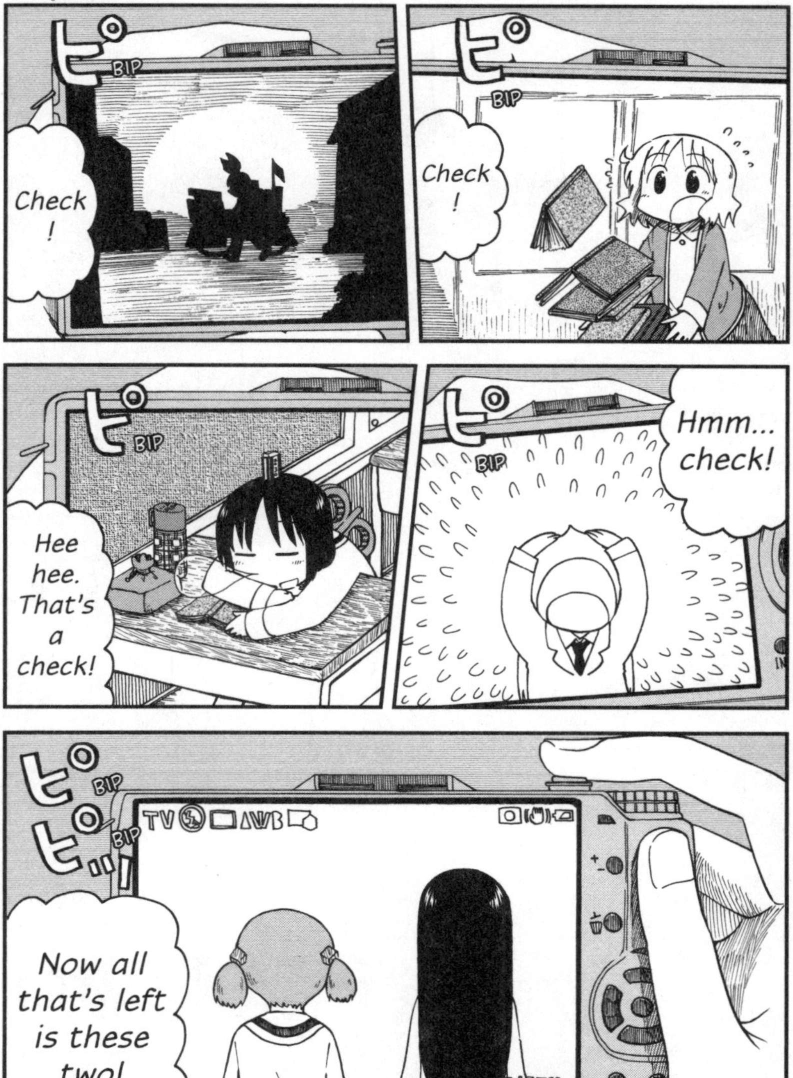
ピ
BIP
Check !
ピ
BIP
Check !
ピ
BIP
Hmm... check!
ピ
BIP
Hee hee. That's a check!
ピ
BIP
ピ
BIP
ピ...!
Now all that's left is these two!

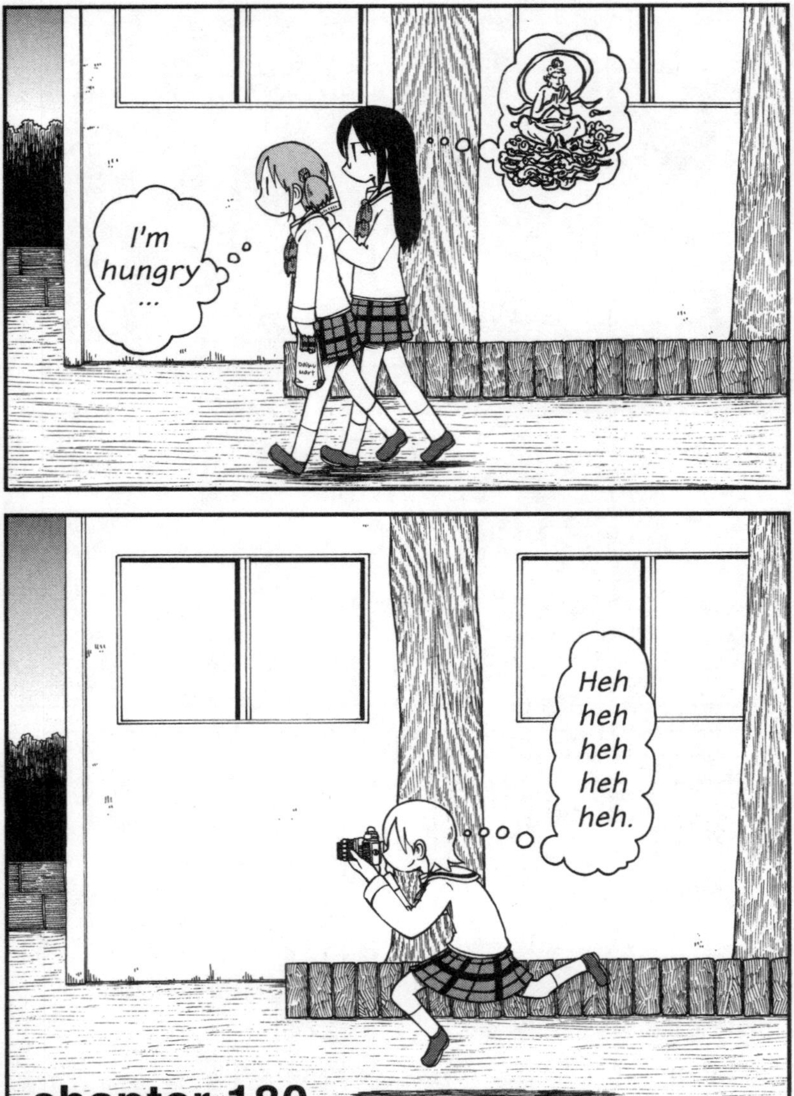
I'm hungry ...
Heh heh heh heh heh.
chapter 180

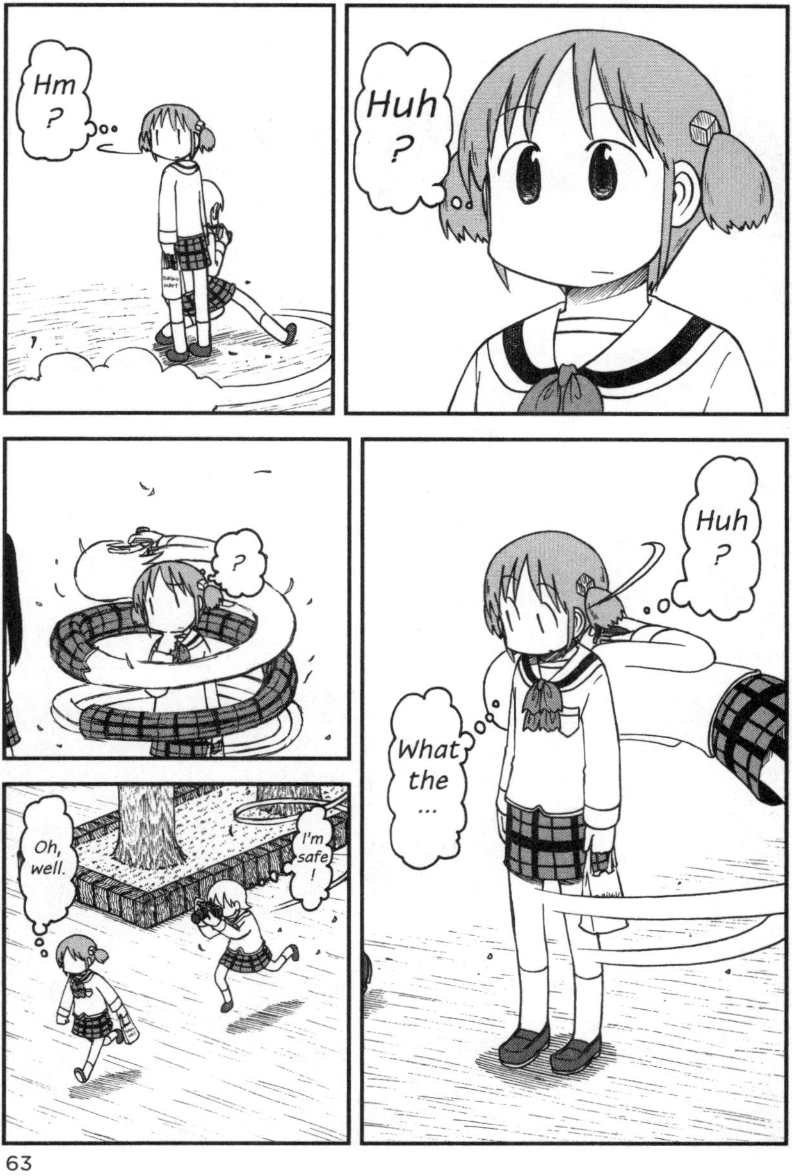
Huh ?
Hm ?
Huh ?
What the ...
?
I'm safe !
Oh, well.

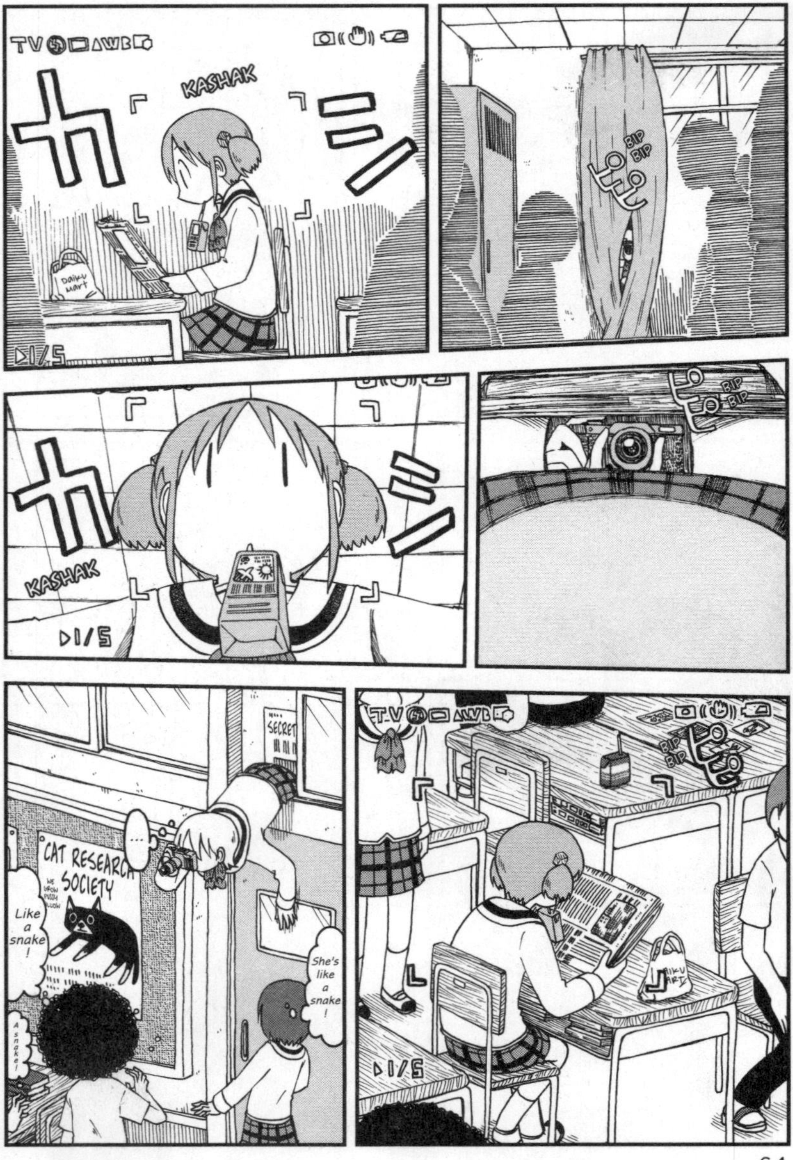
BIP BIP
KASHAK
Daiku Mart
BIP BIP
KASHAK
BIP BIP
SECRET
...
CAT RESEARCH SOCIETY
She's like a snake!
Like a snake!
A snake!

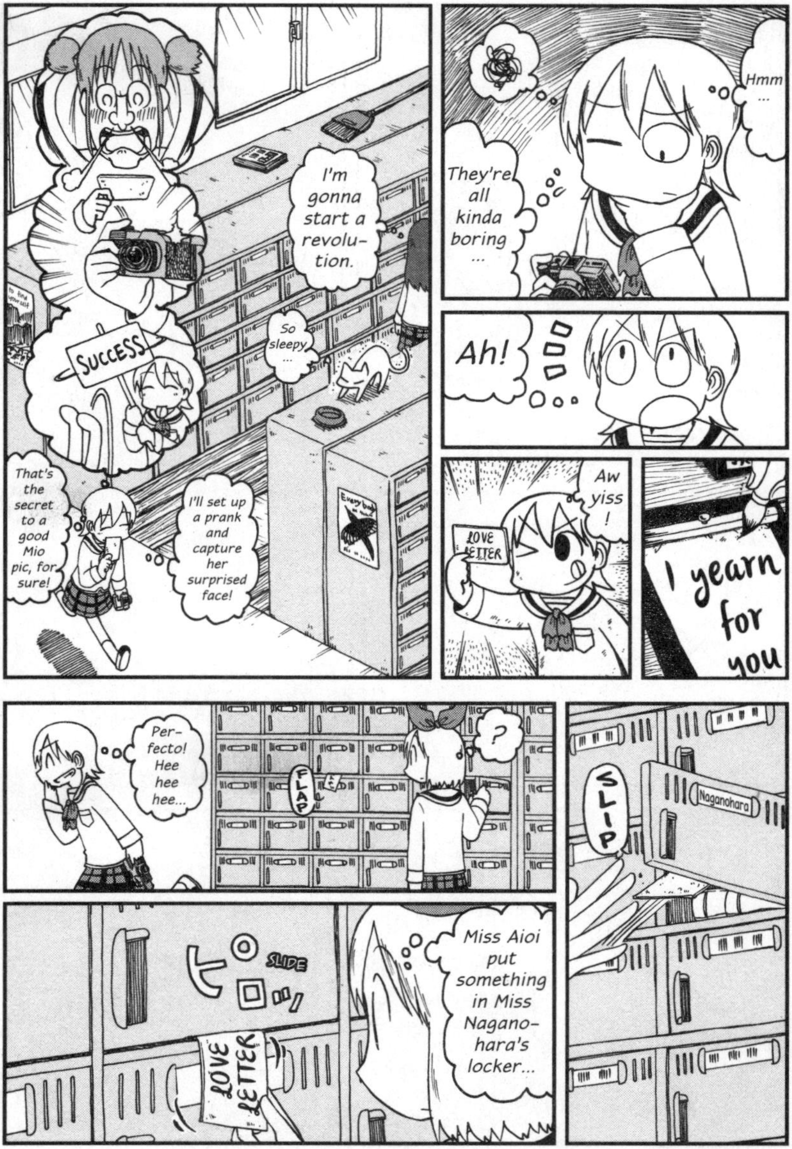
Hmm
...
They're all kinda boring
...
Ah!
I yearn for you
Aw yiss
!
LOVE LETTER
I'm gonna start a revolution.
So sleepy
...
SUCCESS
I'll set up a prank and capture her surprised face!
That's the secret to a good Mio pic, for sure!
SLIP
Naganohara
?
FLAP
Per-fecto! Hee hee hee...
Miss Aioi put something in Miss Nagano-hara's locker...
SLIDE
LOVE LETTER

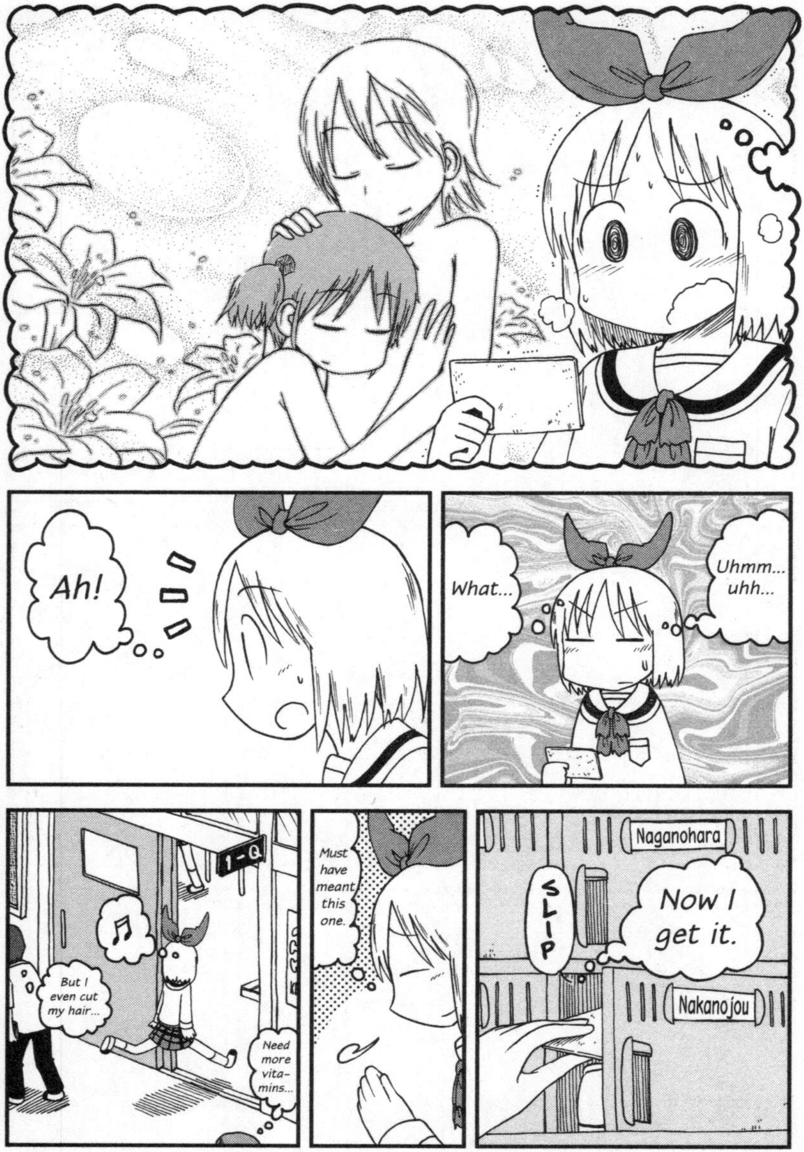
Uhmm... uhh...
What...
Ah!
Naganohara
Now I get it.
SLIP
Nakanojou
Must have meant this one.
1-Q
Need more vita-mins...
But I even cut my hair...

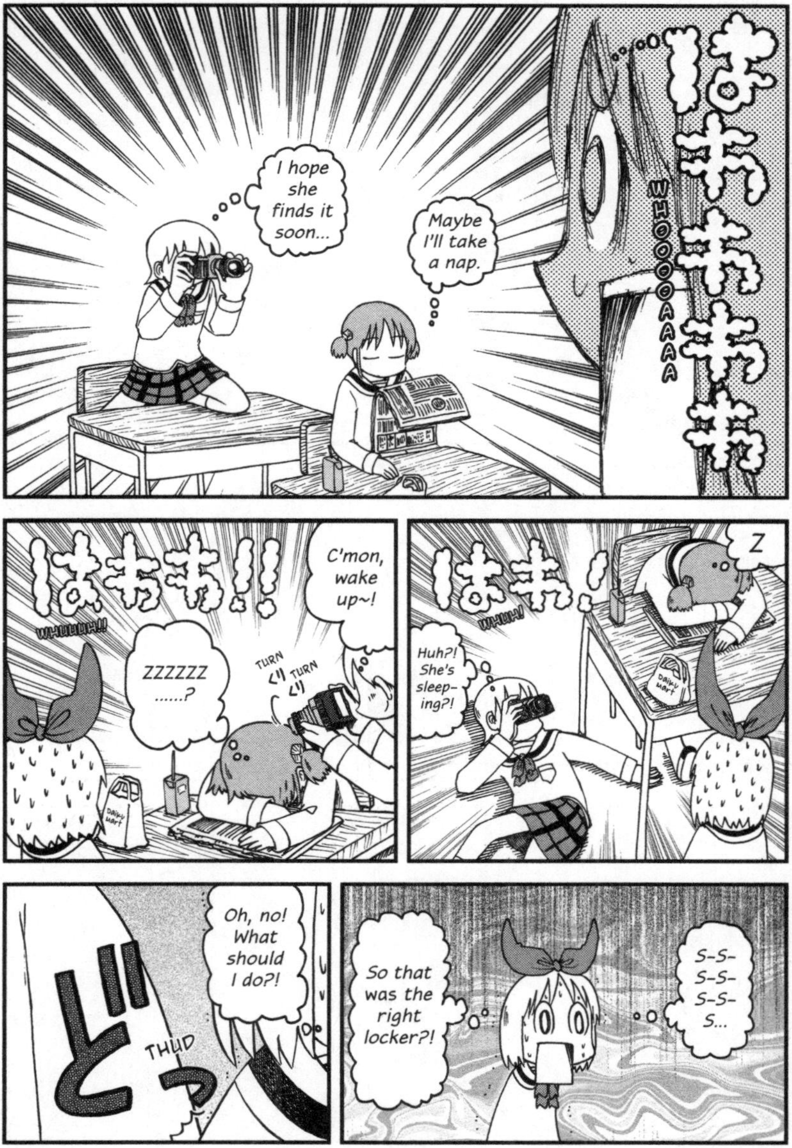
はおおおお
WHOOOOOAAAA
Maybe I'll take a nap.
I hope she finds it soon...
Z
はお!
WHUH!
Huh?! She's sleep-ing?!
Daiku Mart
C'mon, wake up~!
はおお!!
WHUUUH!!
TURN くり TURN くり
ZZZZZZ ......?
Daiku Mart
S-S-S-S-S-S-S...
So that was the right locker?!
Oh, no! What should I do?!
どっ
THUD

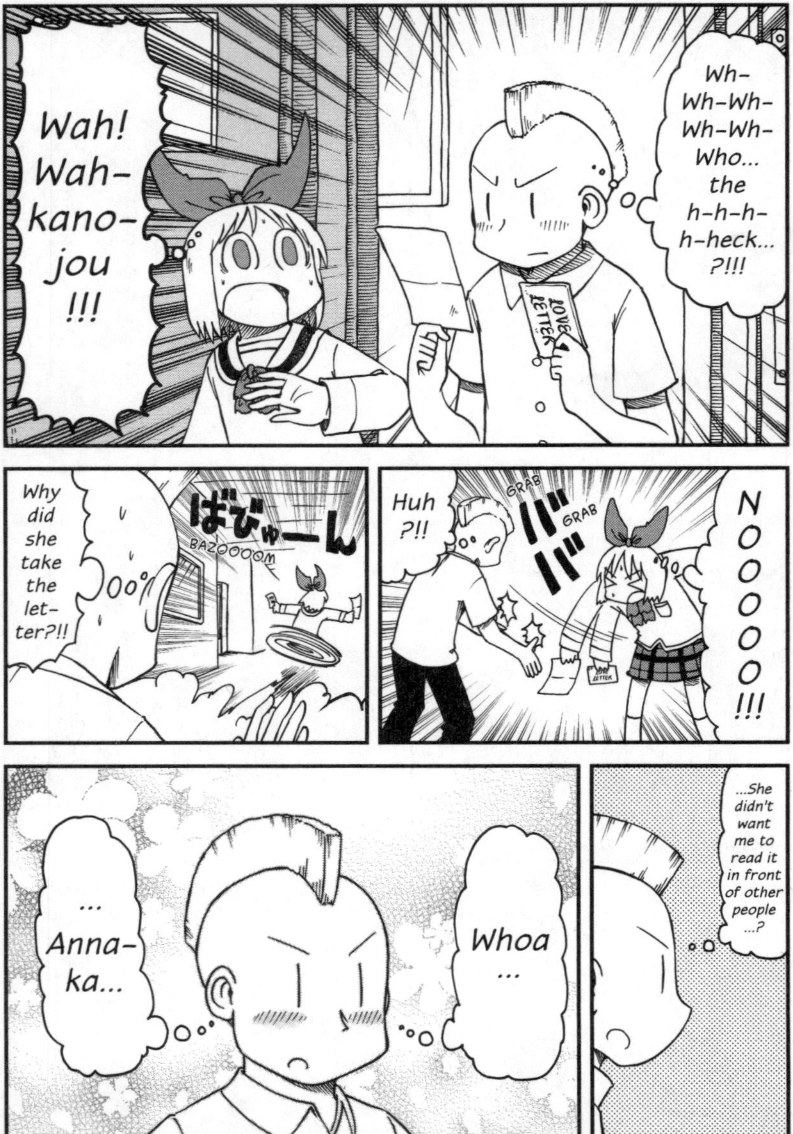
Wh-Wh-Wh-Wh-Wh-Who... the h-h-h-h-heck...?!!!
LOVE LETTER
Wah! Wah-kano-jou!!!
NOOOOOOO!!!
バ GRAB
バ GRAB
Huh?!!
LETTER
Why did she take the letter?!!
ばびゅーん
BAZOOOOOM
...She didn't want me to read it in front of other people...?
Whoa...
...Anna-ka...

chapter 180: end

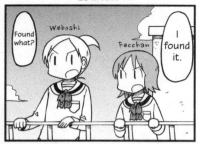

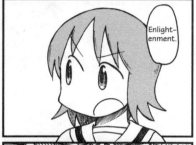

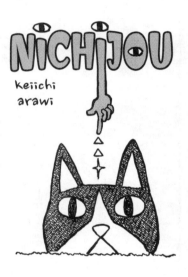

NICHIJOU
keiichi arawi

chapter 181

counter

I found it.
Fecchan
Weboshi
Found what?
Enlightenment.
What a coincidence.
What?
So did I.

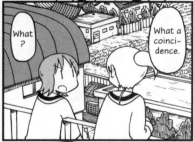

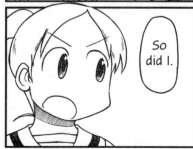

enlightenment is...

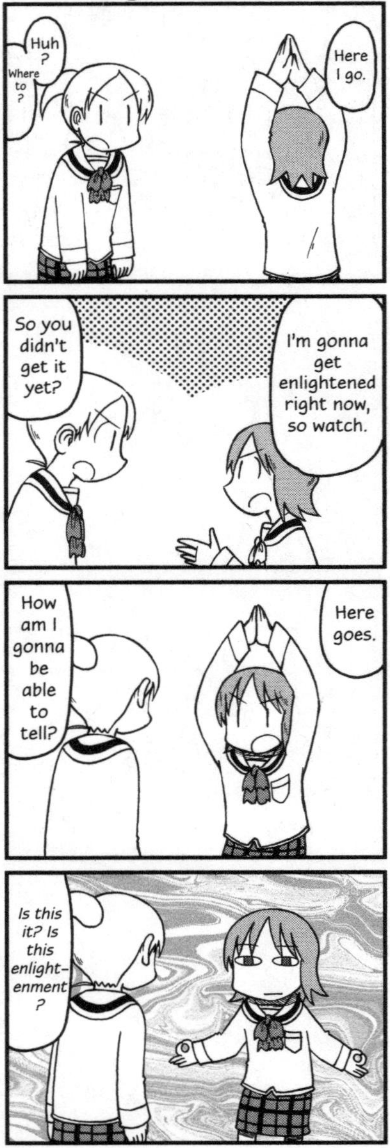
Here I go.
Huh? Where to?
I'm gonna get enlightened right now, so watch.
So you didn't get it yet?
Here goes.
How am I gonna be able to tell?
Is this it? Is this enlightenment?

enlightenment is...

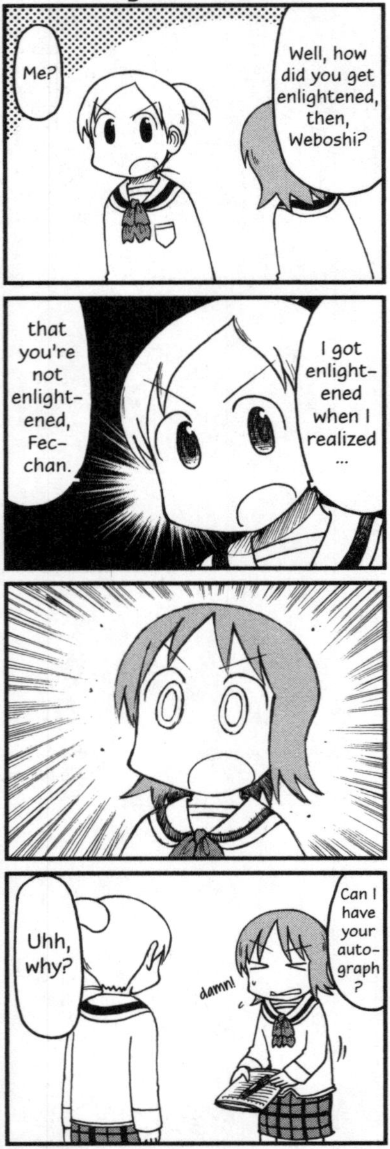
Well, how did you get enlightened, then, Weboshi?
Me?
I got enlightened when I realized...
that you're not enlightened, Fec-chan.
Can I have your autograph?
damn!
Uhh, why?

enlightenment is...

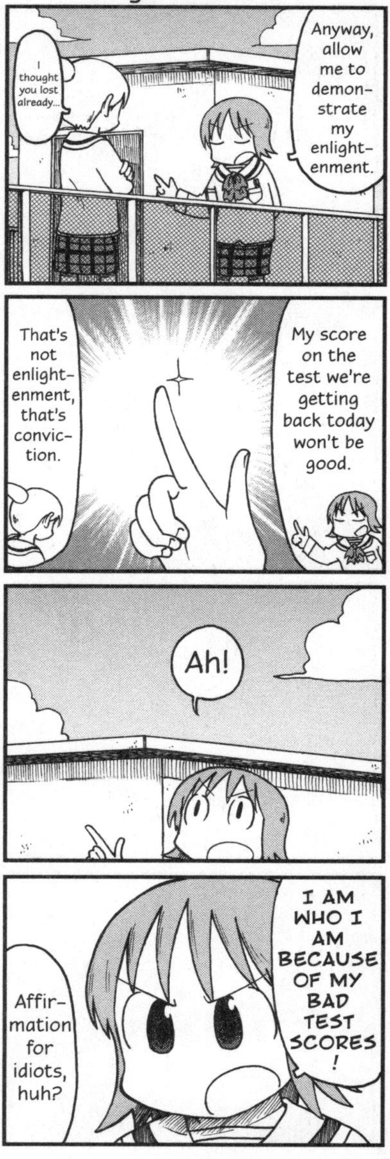

Anyway, allow me to demonstrate my enlightenment.
I thought you lost already...
My score on the test we're getting back today won't be good.
That's not enlightenment, that's conviction.
Ah!
I AM WHO I AM BECAUSE OF MY BAD TEST SCORES!
Affirmation for idiots, huh?

enlightenment is...

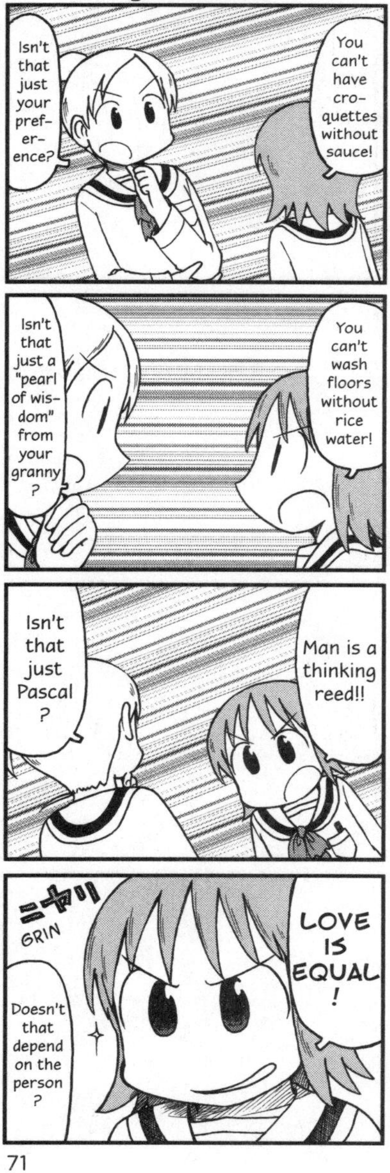

You can't have croquettes without sauce!
Isn't that just your preference?
You can't wash floors without rice water!
Isn't that just a "pearl of wisdom" from your granny?
Man is a thinking reed!!
Isn't that just Pascal?
LOVE IS EQUAL!
ニヤリ
GRIN
Doesn't that depend on the person?

visitation

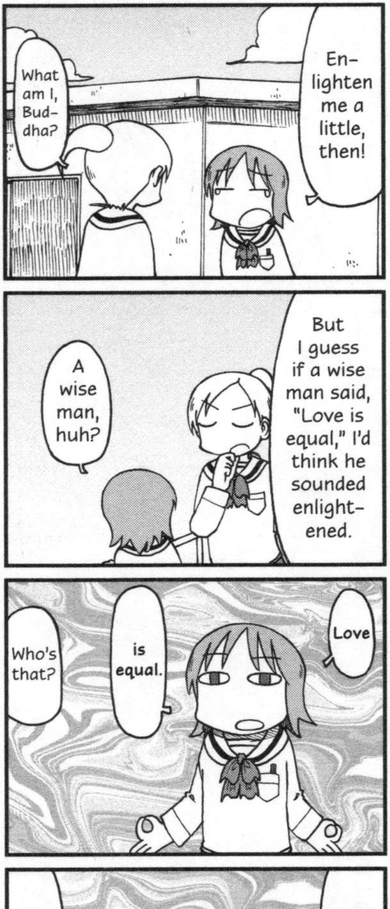
Enlighten me a little, then!
What am I, Buddha?
But I guess if a wise man said, "Love is equal," I'd think he sounded enlightened.
A wise man, huh?
Love
is equal.
Who's that?
Hello, I'm the Formulary of Adjudications.*
That's not a person.

*legal code of the Kamakura shogunate

she's saying "hmm," but she's not thinking about anything

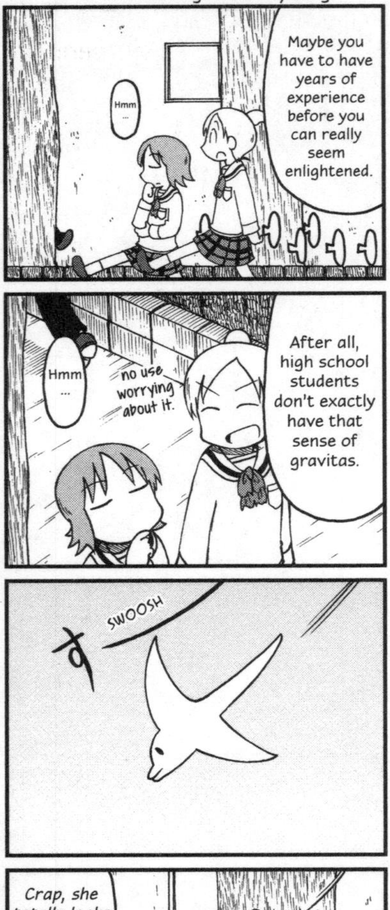
Maybe you have to have years of experience before you can really seem enlightened.
Hmm ...
After all, high school students don't exactly have that sense of gravitas.
no use worrying about it.
Hmm ...
SWOOSH
す
hmm...
Crap, she totally looks enlightened right now...

chapter 181: end

chapter 182

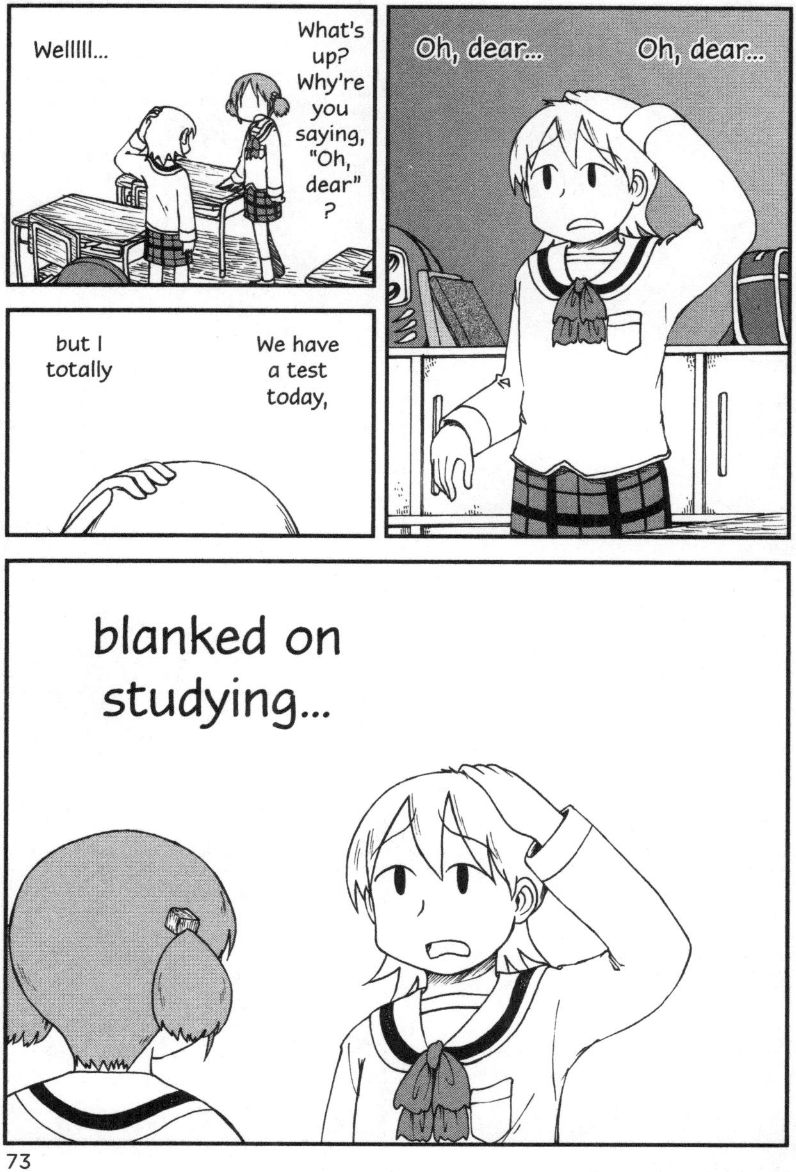
Oh, dear...
Oh, dear...
What's up? Why're you saying, "Oh, dear"?
Welllll...
We have a test today,
but I totally
blanked on studying...

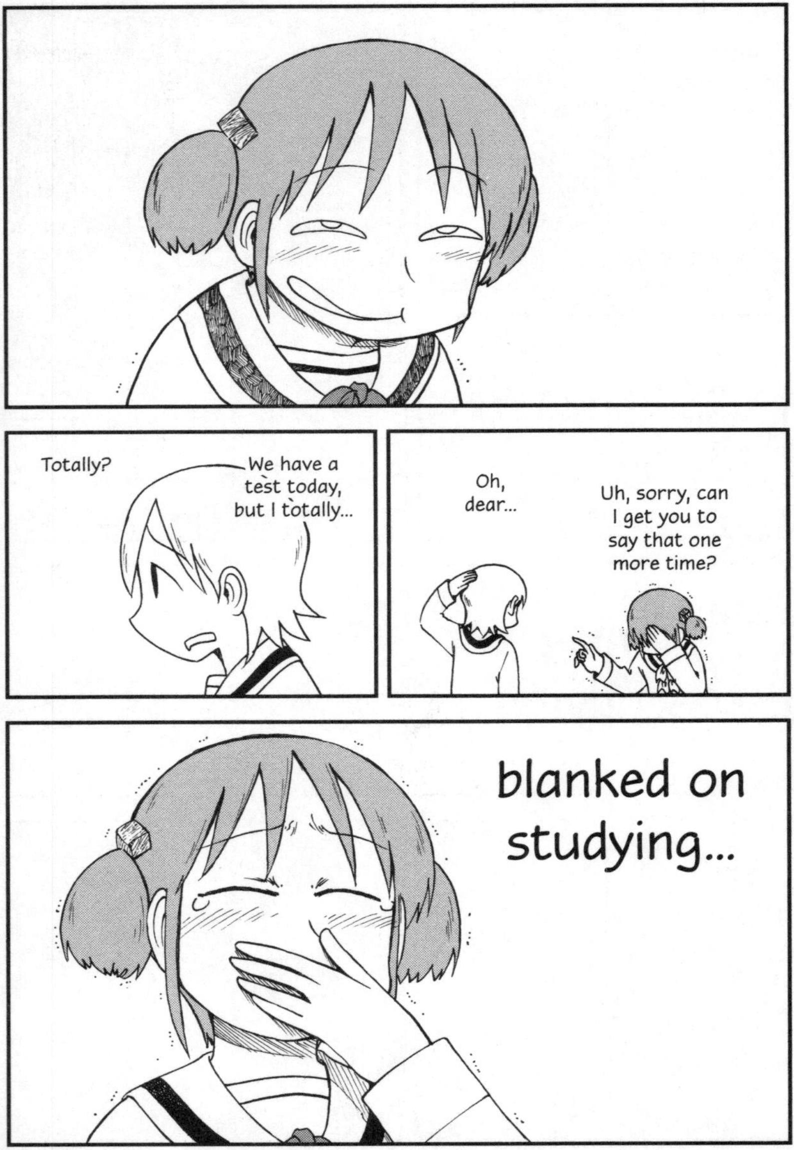
Uh, sorry, can I get you to say that one more time?
Oh, dear...
We have a test today, but I totally...
Totally?
blanked on studying...

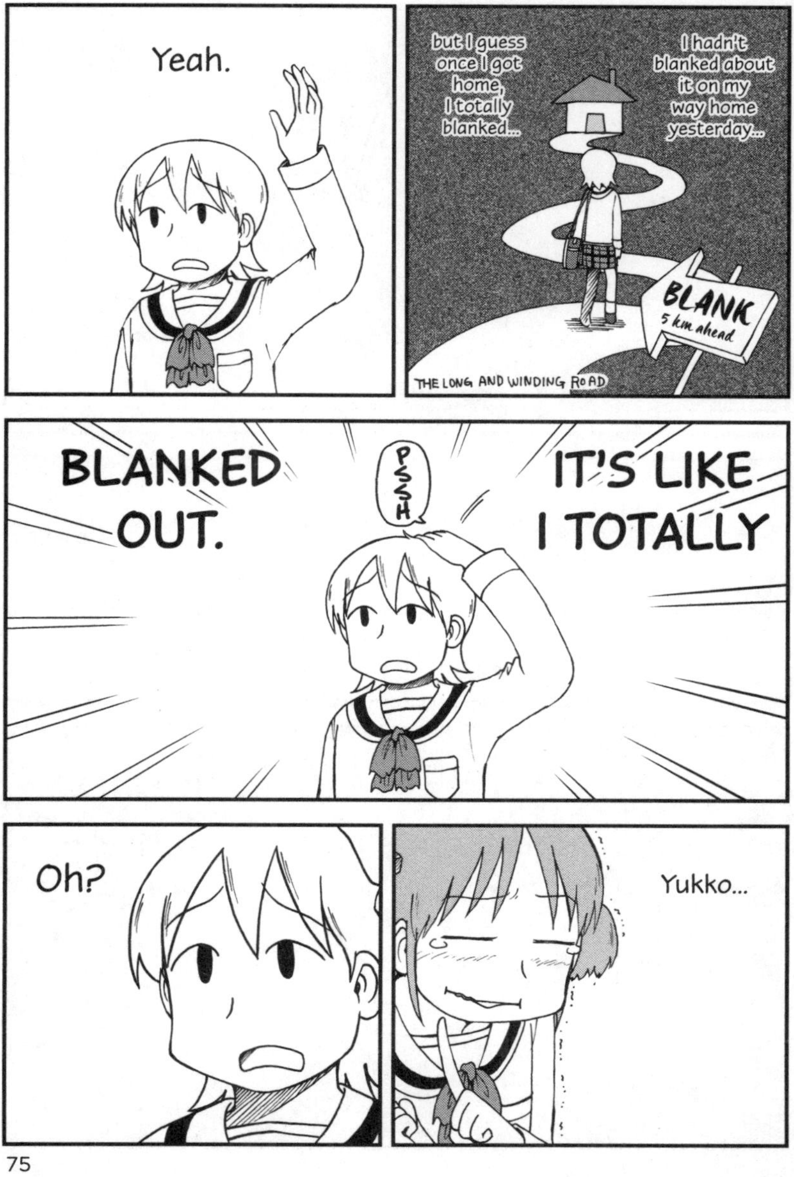
I hadn't blanked about it on my way home yesterday...
but I guess once I got home, I totally blanked...
BLANK
5 km ahead
THE LONG AND WINDING ROAD
Yeah.
IT'S LIKE I TOTALLY
PSSH
BLANKED OUT.
Yukko...
Oh?

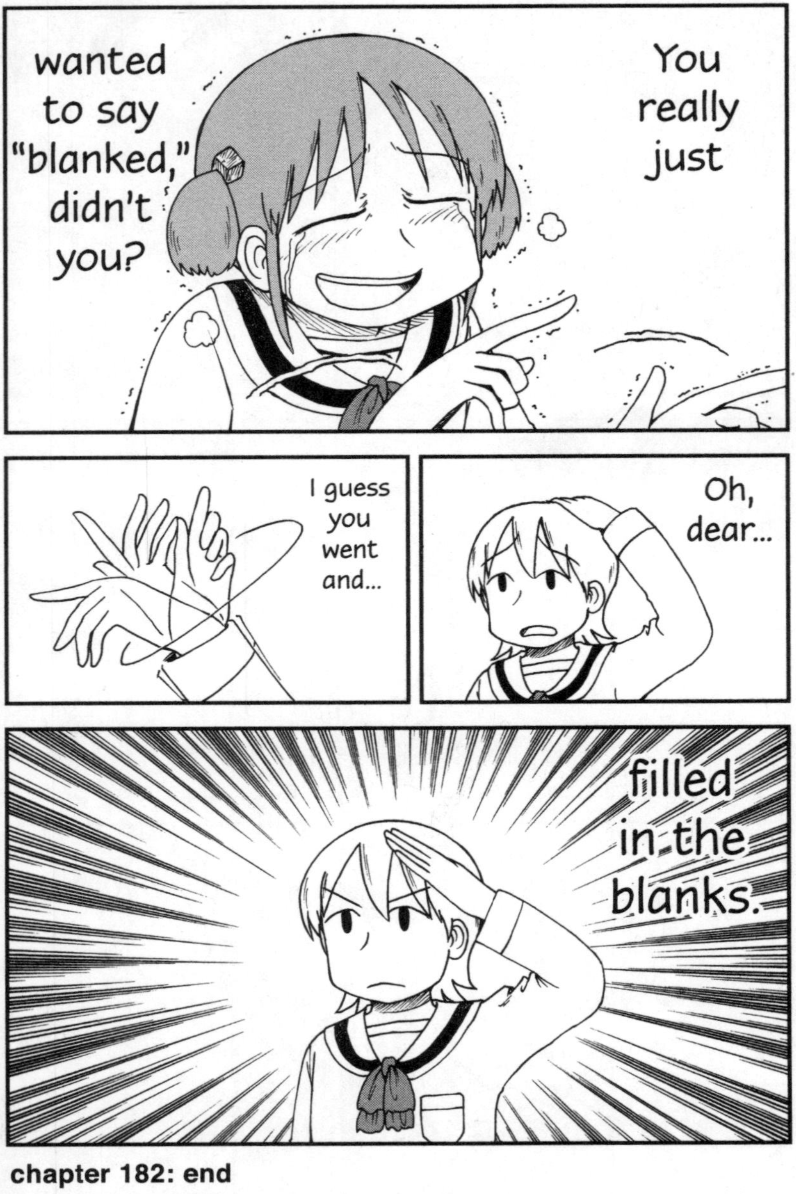
You really just
wanted to say "blanked," didn't you?
Oh, dear...
I guess you went and...
filled in the blanks.

chapter 182: end

chapter 183

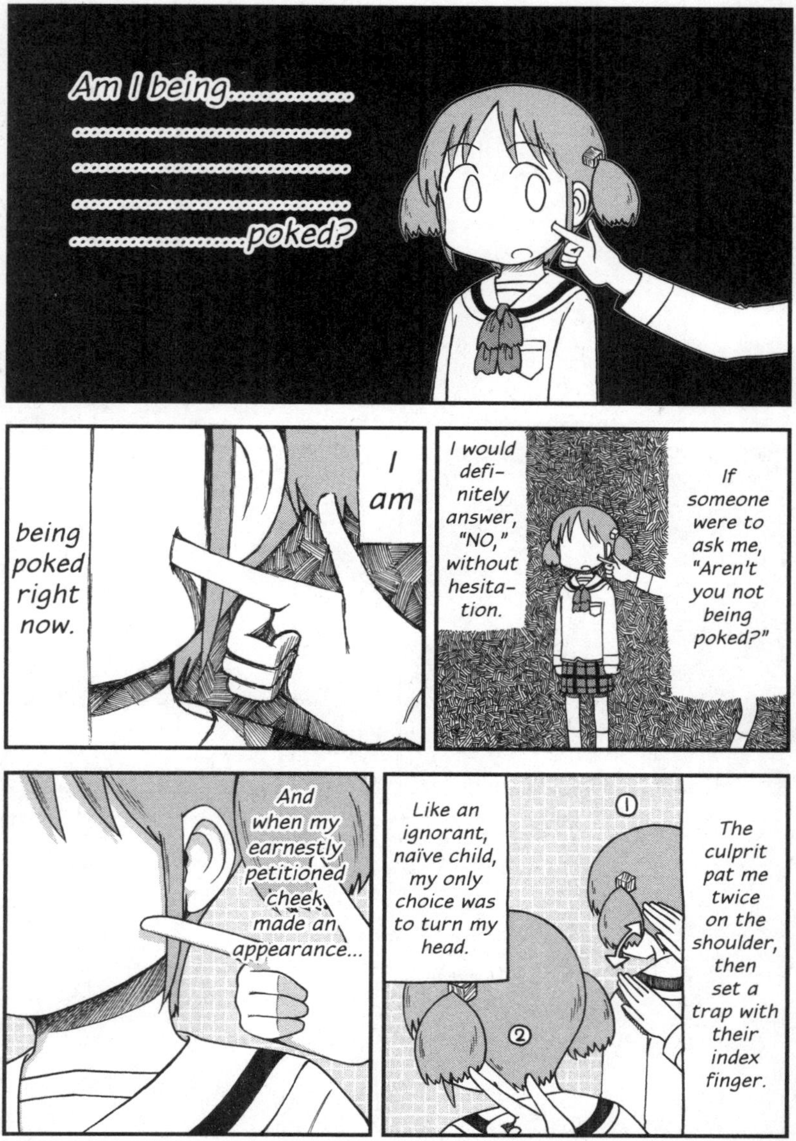

Am I being..................
....
....
....
................................poked?
If someone were to ask me, "Aren't you not being poked?"
I would definitely answer, "NO," without hesitation.
I am
being poked right now.
The culprit pat me twice on the shoulder, then set a trap with their index finger.
①
②
Like an ignorant, naïve child, my only choice was to turn my head.
And when my earnestly petitioned cheek made an appearance...

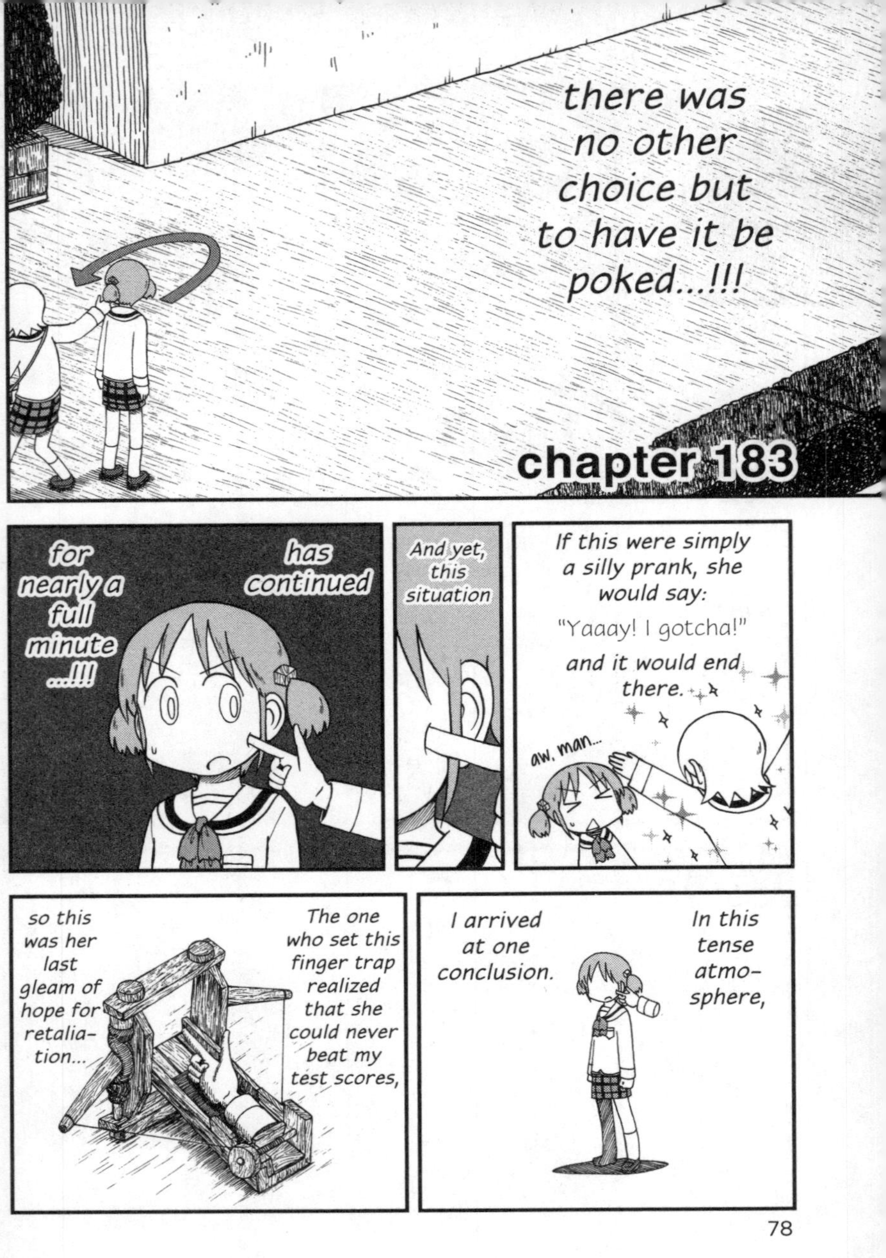
there was no other choice but to have it be poked...!!!
chapter 183
If this were simply a silly prank, she would say:
"Yaaay! I gotcha!"
and it would end there.
aw, man...
And yet, this situation
has continued
for nearly a full minute ...!!!
In this tense atmo-sphere,
I arrived at one conclusion.
The one who set this finger trap realized that she could never beat my test scores,
so this was her last gleam of hope for retalia-tion...

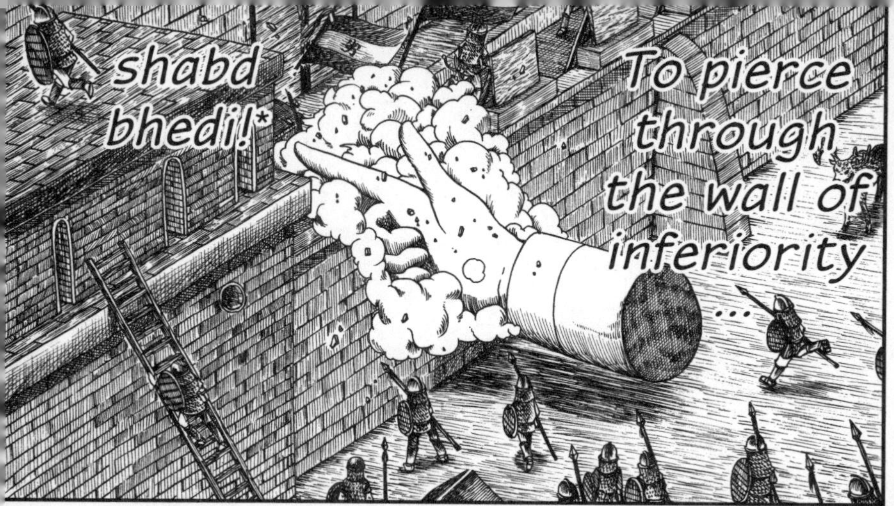
To pierce through the wall of inferiority ...
shabd bhedi!*

*archery technique used by Prithviraj to hit a target based on sound alone

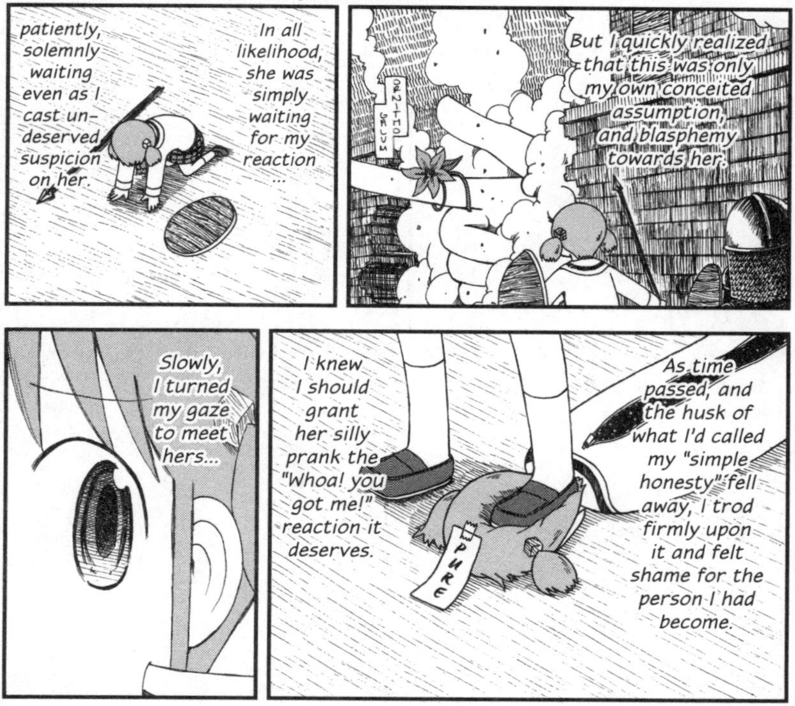
But I quickly realized that this was only my own conceited assumption, and blasphemy towards her.
ORNITHOGALUM
In all likelihood, she was simply waiting for my reaction ...
patiently, solemnly waiting even as I cast un-deserved suspicion on her.
As time passed, and the husk of what I'd called my "simple honesty" fell away, I trod firmly upon it and felt shame for the person I had become.
PURE
I knew I should grant her silly prank the "Whoa! you got me!" reaction it deserves.
Slowly, I turned my gaze to meet hers...

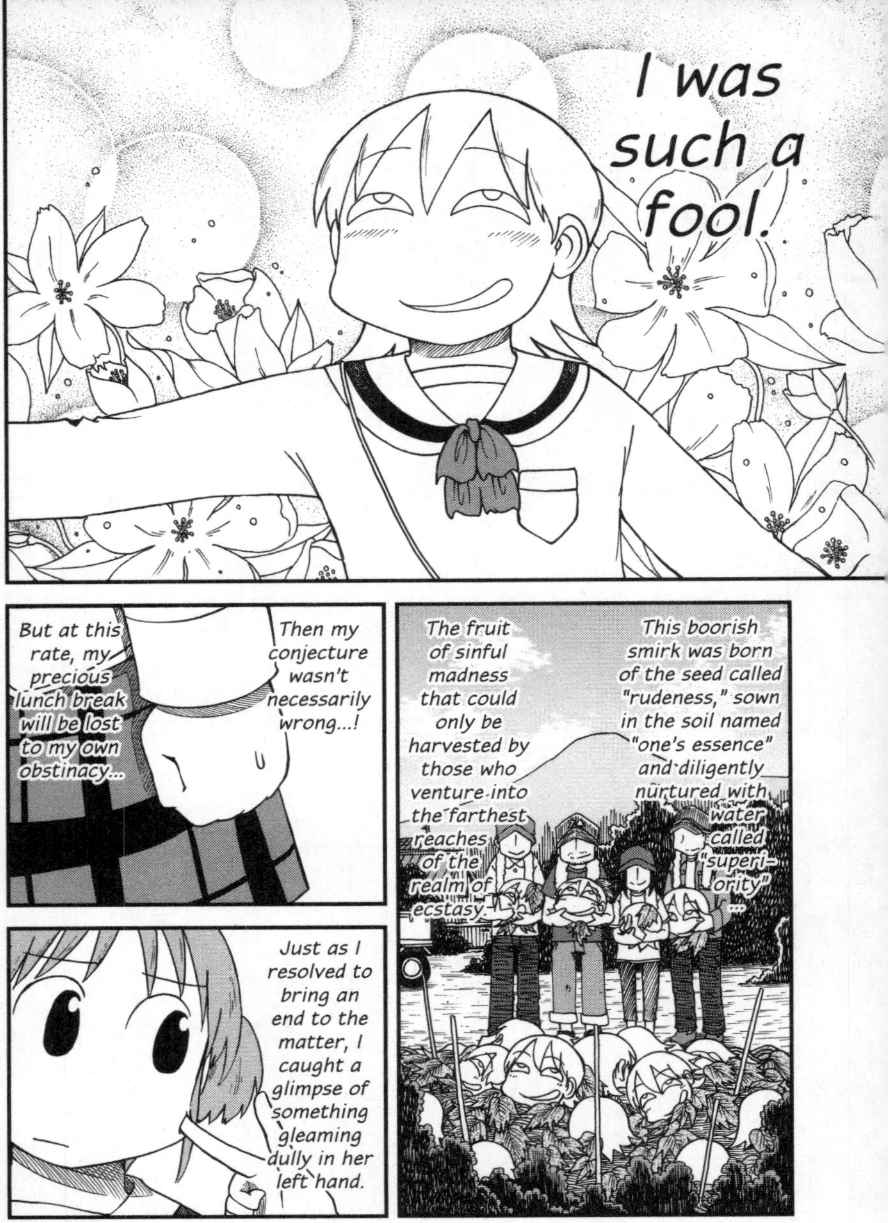

I was such a fool.
This boorish smirk was born of the seed called "rudeness," sown in the soil named "one's essence" and diligently nurtured with water called "superiority"...
The fruit of sinful madness that could only be harvested by those who venture into the farthest reaches of the realm of ecstasy.
Then my conjecture wasn't necessarily wrong...!
But at this rate, my precious lunch break will be lost to my own obstinacy...
Just as I resolved to bring an end to the matter, I caught a glimpse of something gleaming dully in her left hand.

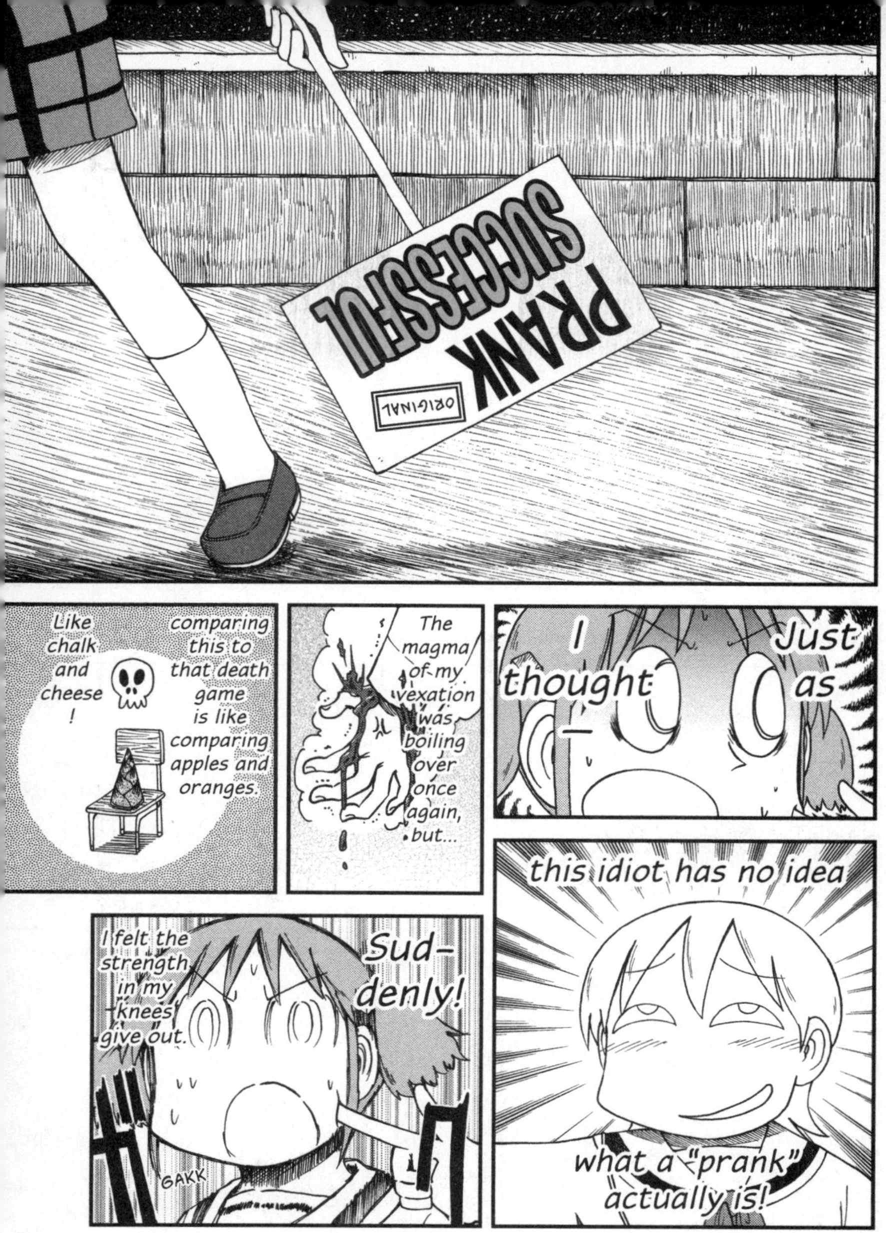
PRANK SUCCESSFUL
ORIGINAL
Just as I thought—
The magma of my vexation was boiling over once again, but...
comparing this to that death game is like comparing apples and oranges.
Like chalk and cheese!
this idiot has no idea what a "prank" actually is!
Sud-denly!
I felt the strength in my knees give out.
GAKK

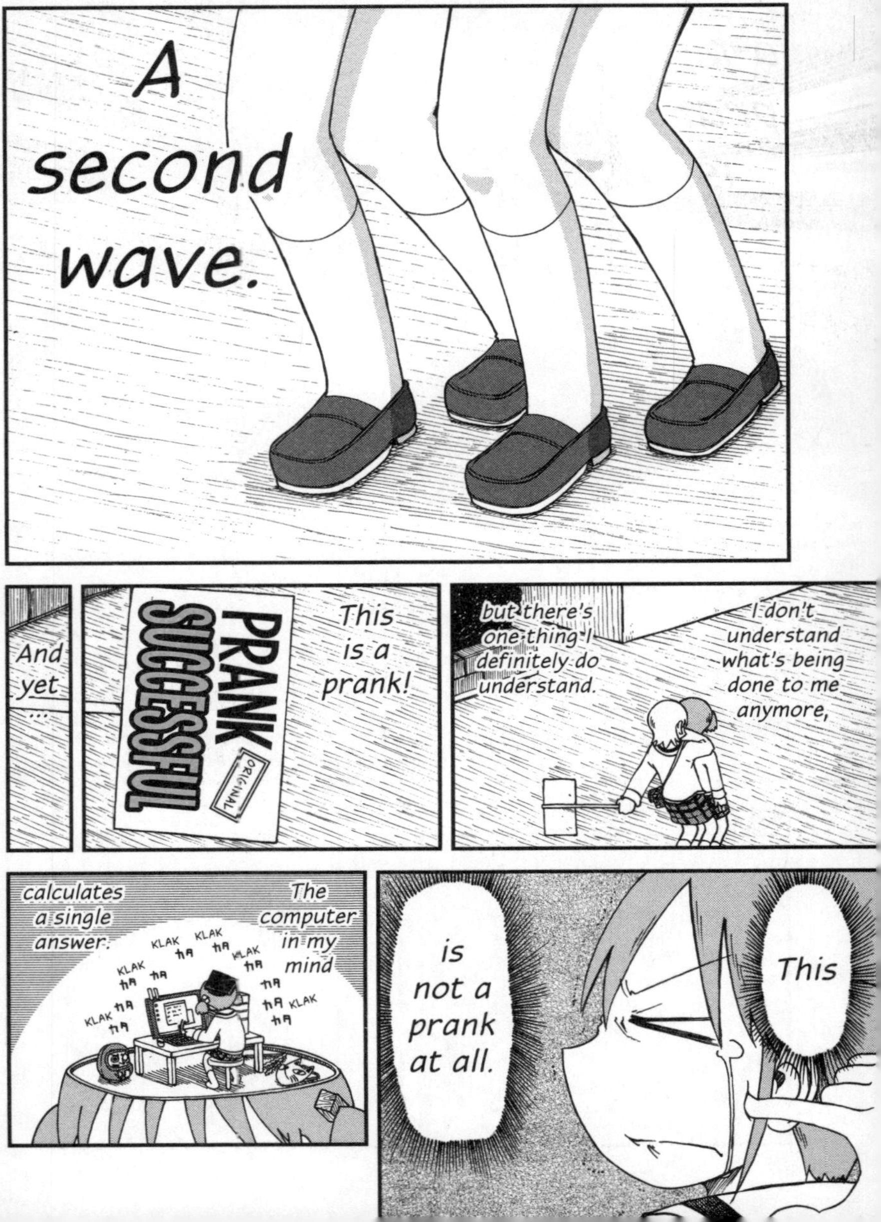
A second wave.
I don't understand what's being done to me anymore,
but there's one thing I definitely do understand.
This is a prank!
PRANK SUCCESSFUL
ORIGINAL
And yet ...
This
is not a prank at all.
The computer in my mind
calculates a single answer.
KLAK KLAK KLAK KLAK KLAK KLAK

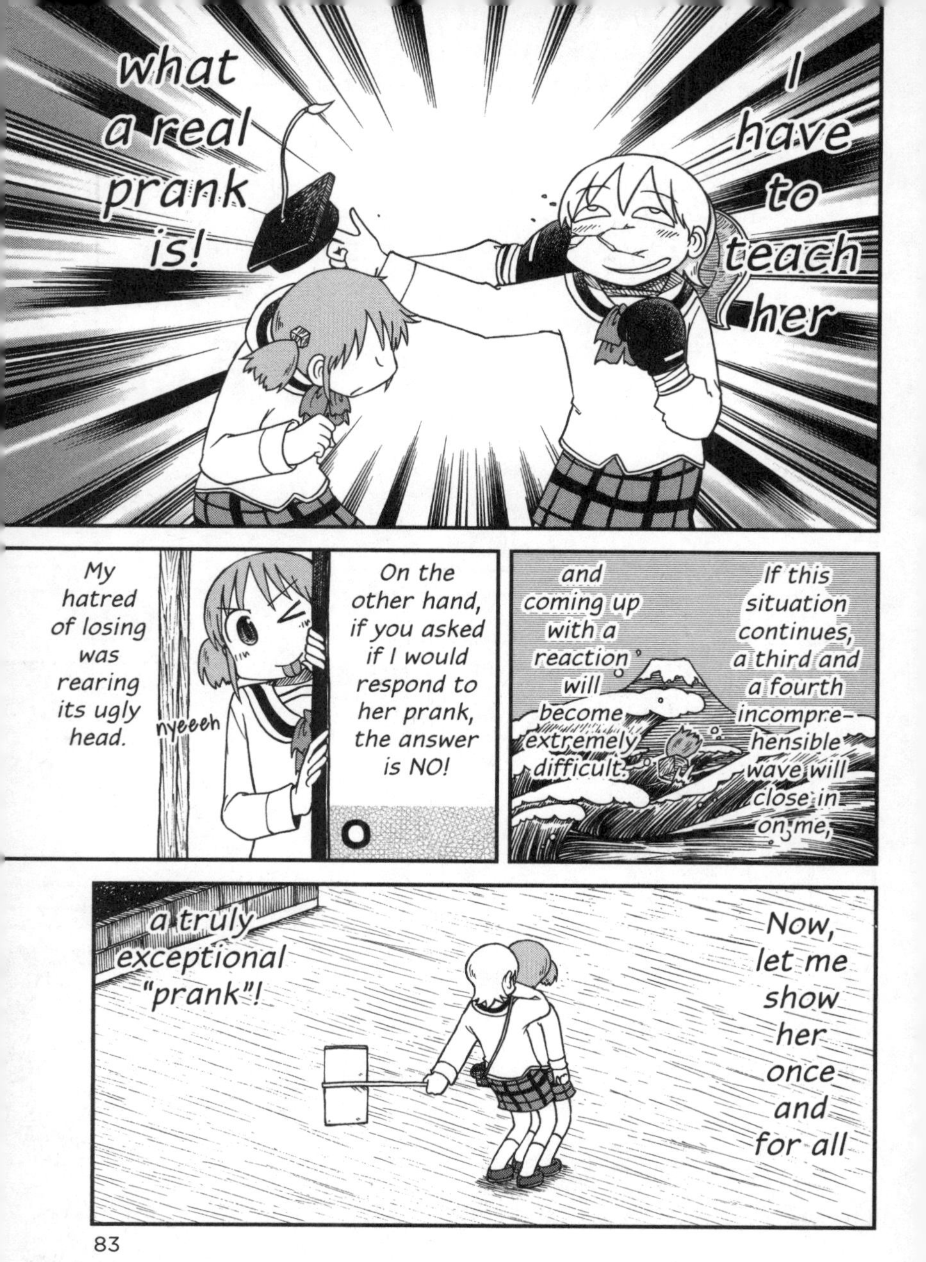
I have to teach her
what a real prank is!
If this situation continues, a third and a fourth incompre-hensible wave will close in on me,
and coming up with a reaction will become extremely difficult.
On the other hand, if you asked if I would respond to her prank, the answer is NO!
My hatred of losing was rearing its ugly head.
nyeeeh
Now, let me show her once and for all
a truly exceptional "prank"!

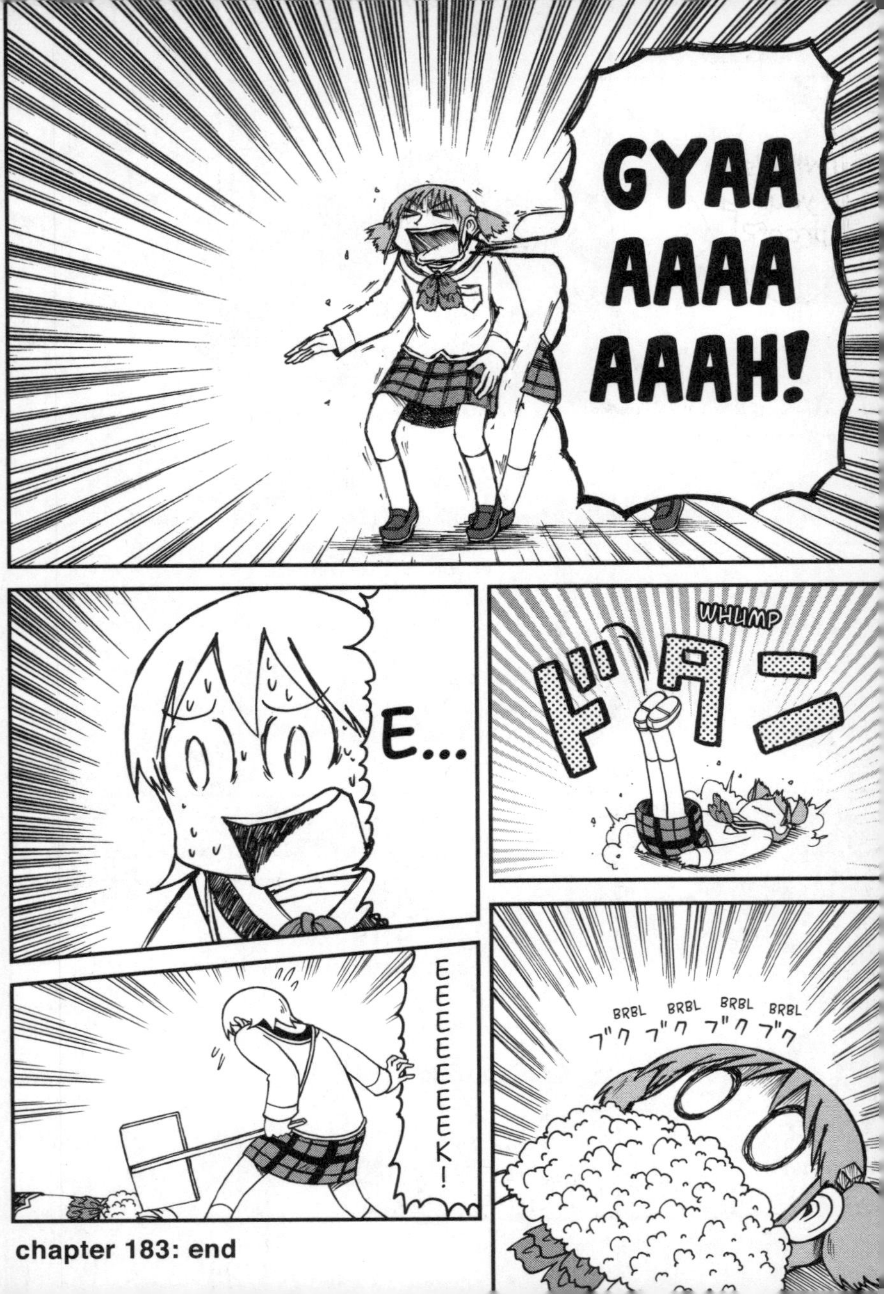
GYAA AAAA AAAH!
WHUMP
ドターン
E...
BRBL BRBL BRBL BRBL
ブクブクブクブク
EEEEEEEK!

chapter 183: end

chapter 184

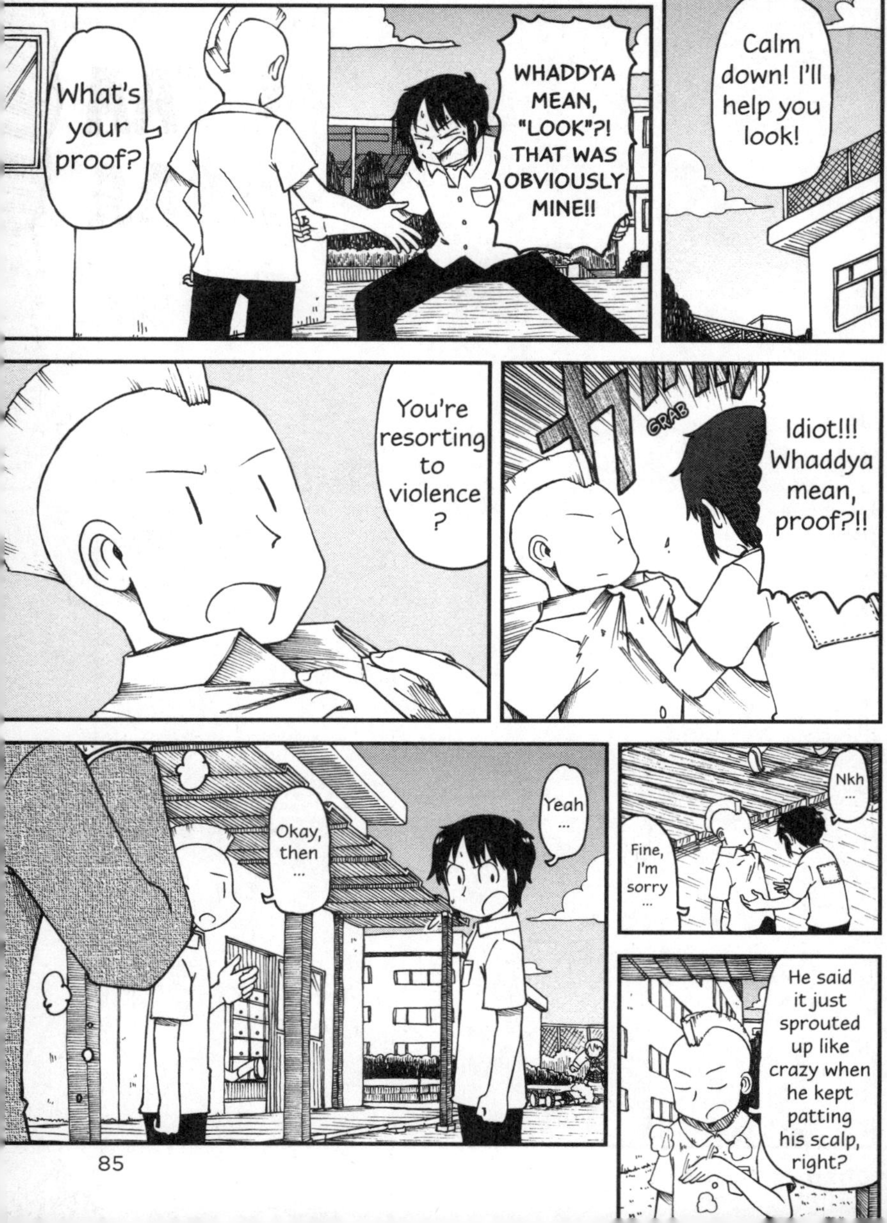
Calm down! I'll help you look!
WHADDYA MEAN, "LOOK"?! THAT WAS OBVIOUSLY MINE!!
What's your proof?
GRAB
Idiot!!! Whaddya mean, proof?!!
You're resorting to violence?
Nkh...
Fine, I'm sorry...
He said it just sprouted up like crazy when he kept patting his scalp, right?
Yeah...
Okay, then...

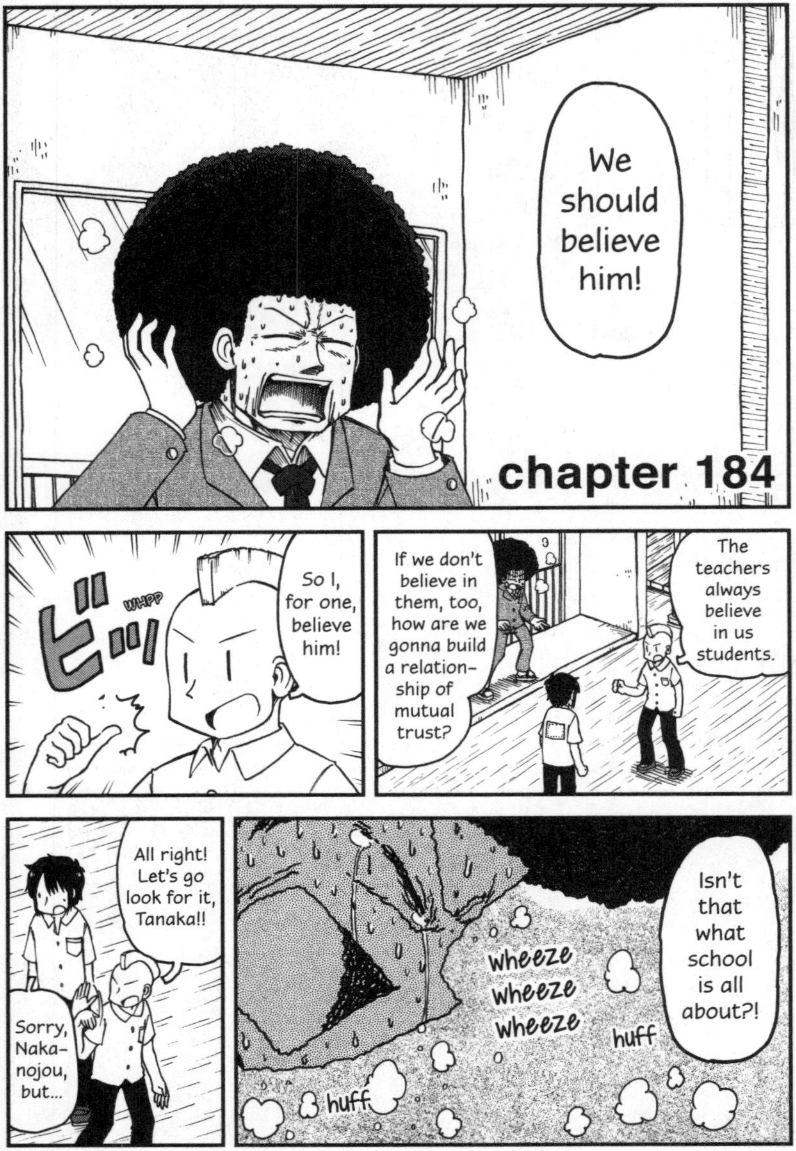
We should believe him!
chapter 184
The teachers always believe in us students.
If we don't believe in them, too, how are we gonna build a relation-ship of mutual trust?
ビッ
WHPP
So I, for one, believe him!
Isn't that what school is all about?!
wheeze wheeze wheeze
huff
huff
All right! Let's go look for it, Tanaka!!
Sorry, Naka-nojou, but...

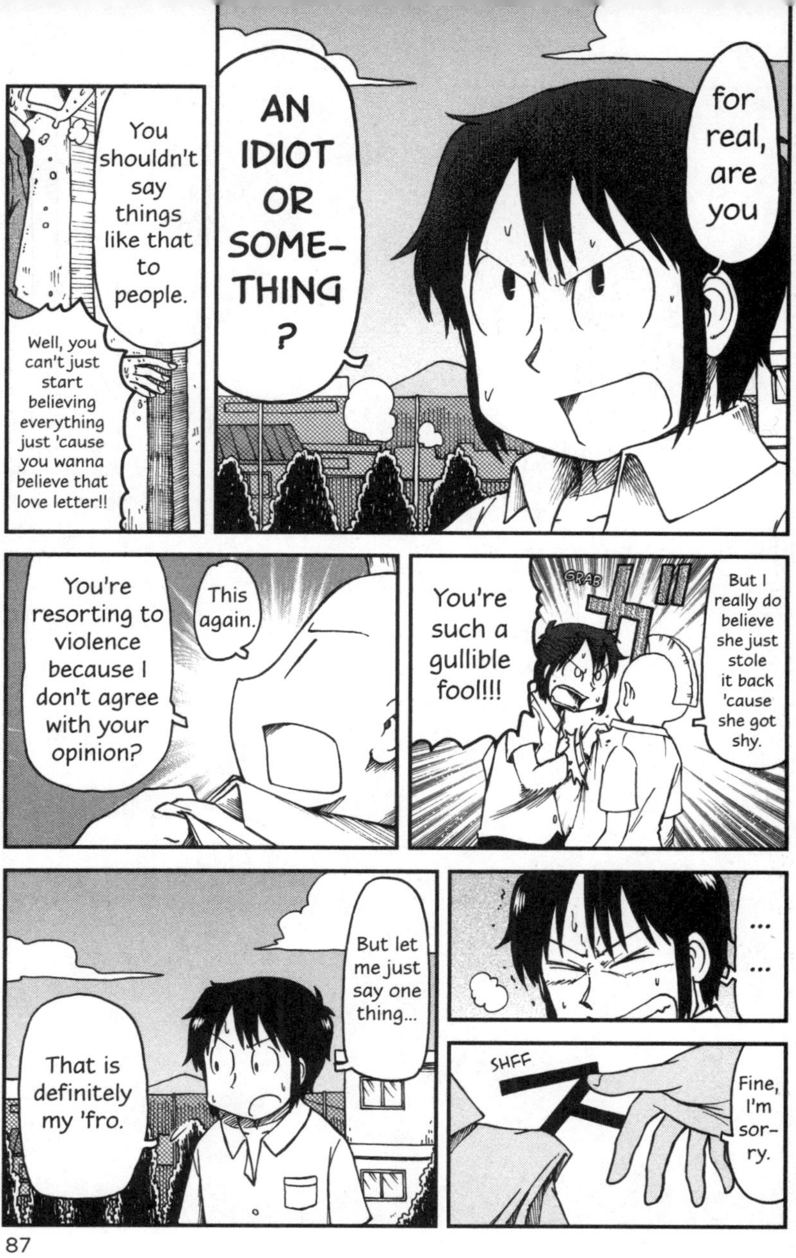
for real, are you
AN IDIOT OR SOME-THING?
You shouldn't say things like that to people.
Well, you can't just start believing everything just 'cause you wanna believe that love letter!!
GRAB
But I really do believe she just stole it back 'cause she got shy.
You're such a gullible fool!!!
This again.
You're resorting to violence because I don't agree with your opinion?
… …
SHFF
Fine, I'm sor-ry.
But let me just say one thing...
That is definitely my 'fro.

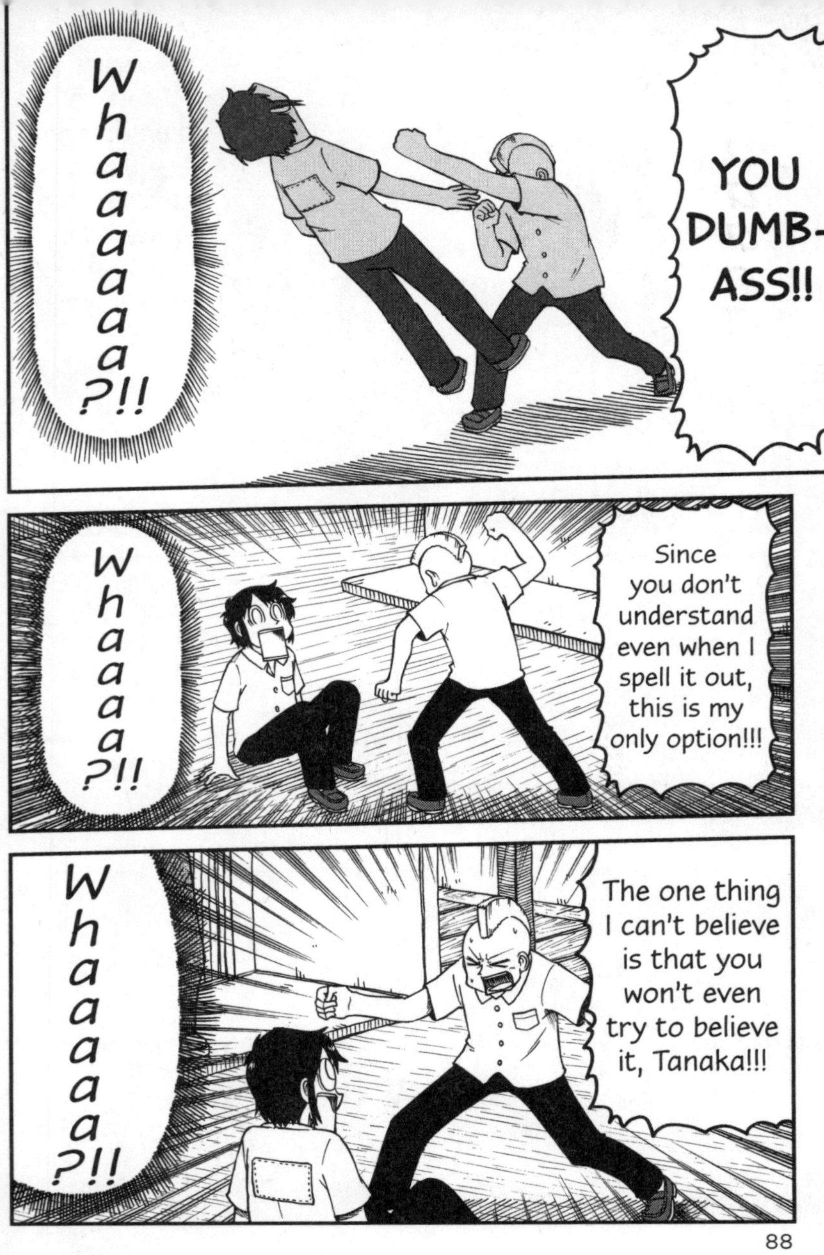
YOU DUMB-ASS!!
Whaaaaaaa?!!
Since you don't understand even when I spell it out, this is my only option!!!
Whaaaaaa?!!
The one thing I can't believe is that you won't even try to believe it, Tanaka!!!
Whaaaaaaa?!!

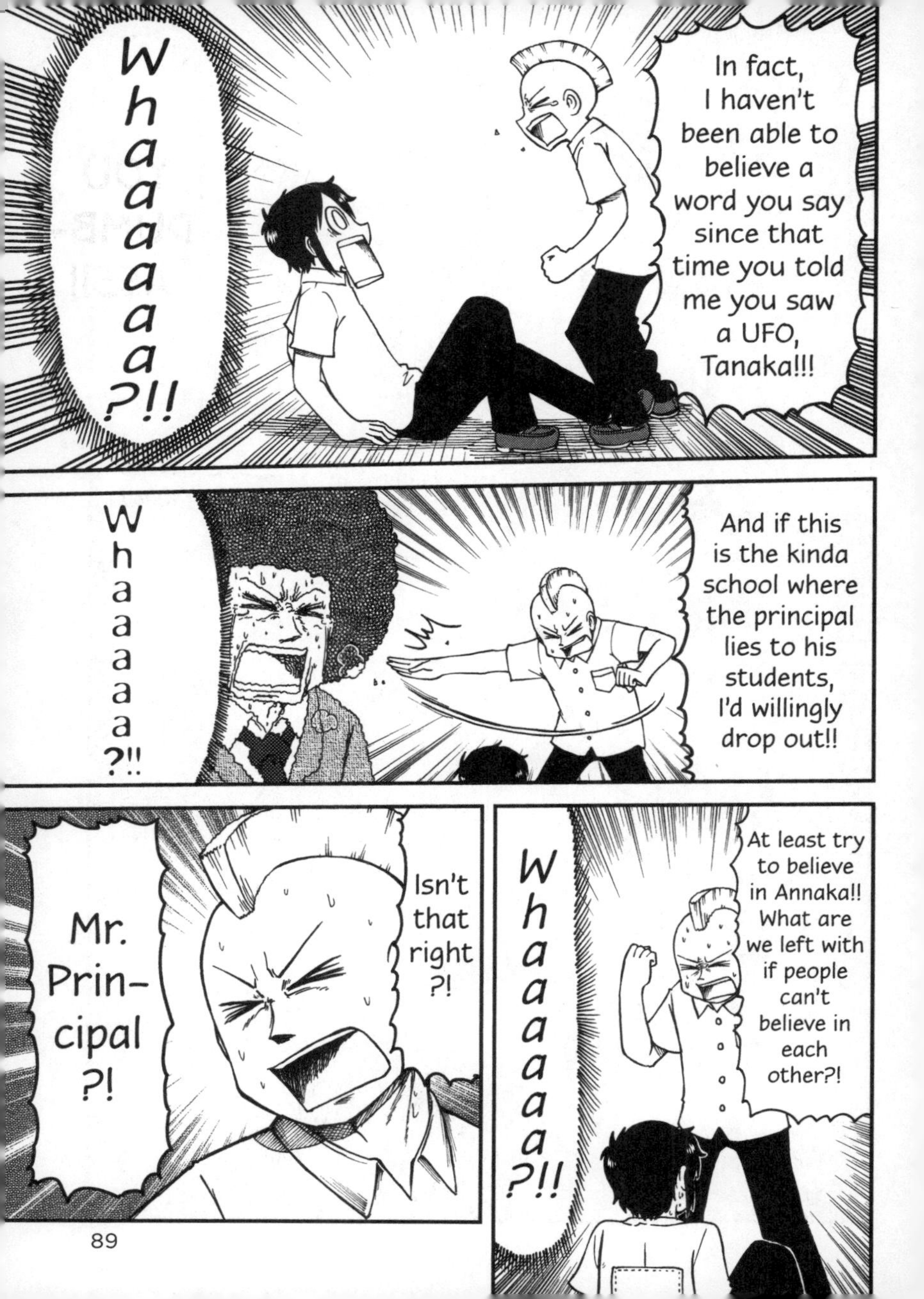

In fact, I haven't been able to believe a word you say since that time you told me you saw a UFO, Tanaka!!!
Whaaaaaaa?!!
And if this is the kinda school where the principal lies to his students, I'd willingly drop out!!
Whaaaaaaa?!!
At least try to believe in Annaka!! What are we left with if people can't believe in each other?!
Whaaaaaaa?!!
Isn't that right?!
Mr. Prin-cipal?!

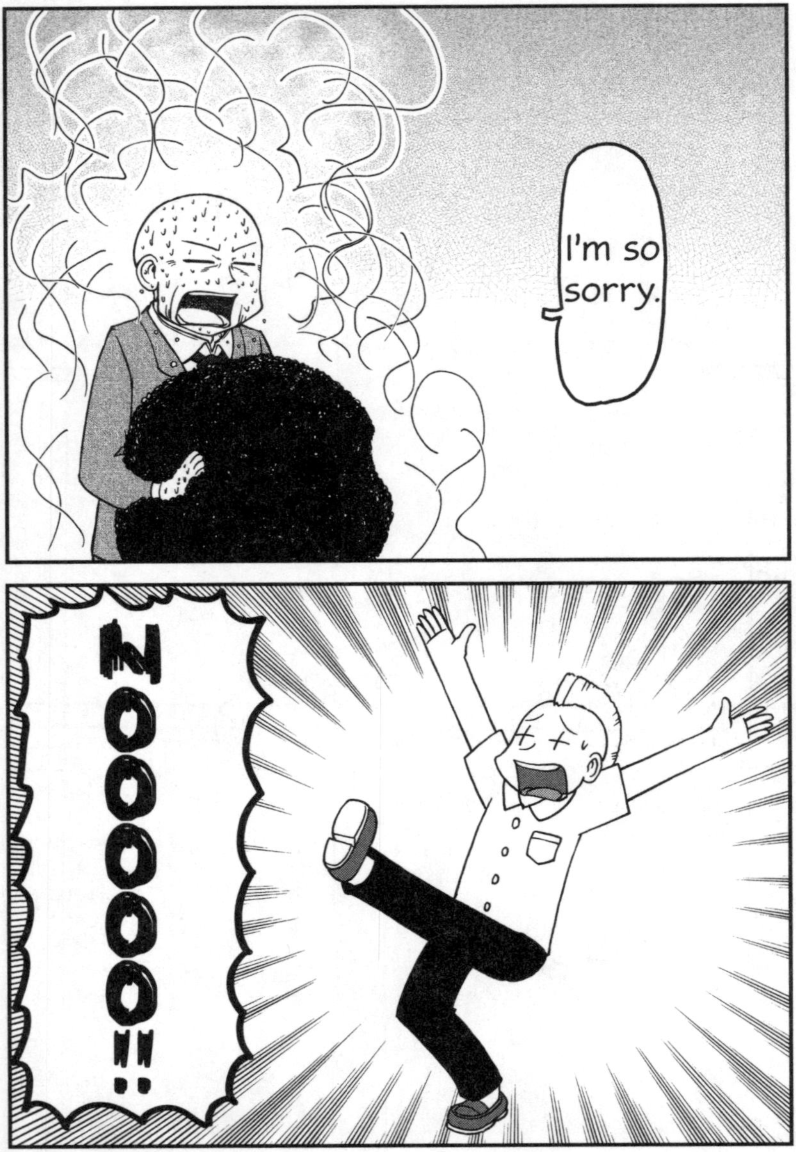
I'm so sorry.
NOOOOO!!

chapter 184: end

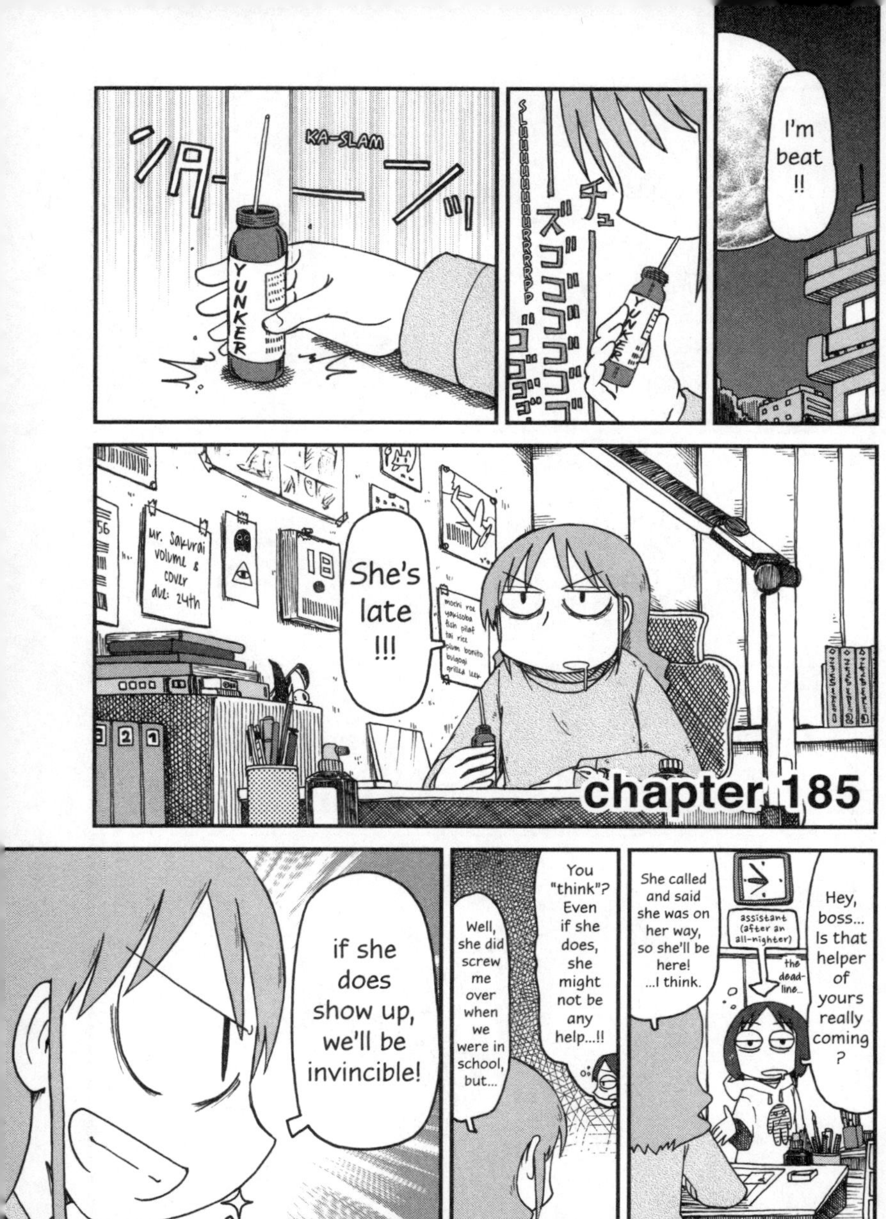
I'm beat !!
SLUUUUUURRRRPP
KA-SLAM
She's late !!!
mochi roe yakisoba fish pilaf tai rice plum bonito bulgogi grilled leek
Mr. Sakurai volume 8 cover due: 24th
chapter 185
Hey, boss... Is that helper of yours really coming?
assistant (after an all-nighter)
the deadline...
She called and said she was on her way, so she'll be here! ...I think.
You "think"? Even if she does, she might not be any help...!!
Well, she did screw me over when we were in school, but...
if she does show up, we'll be invincible!
GRIN

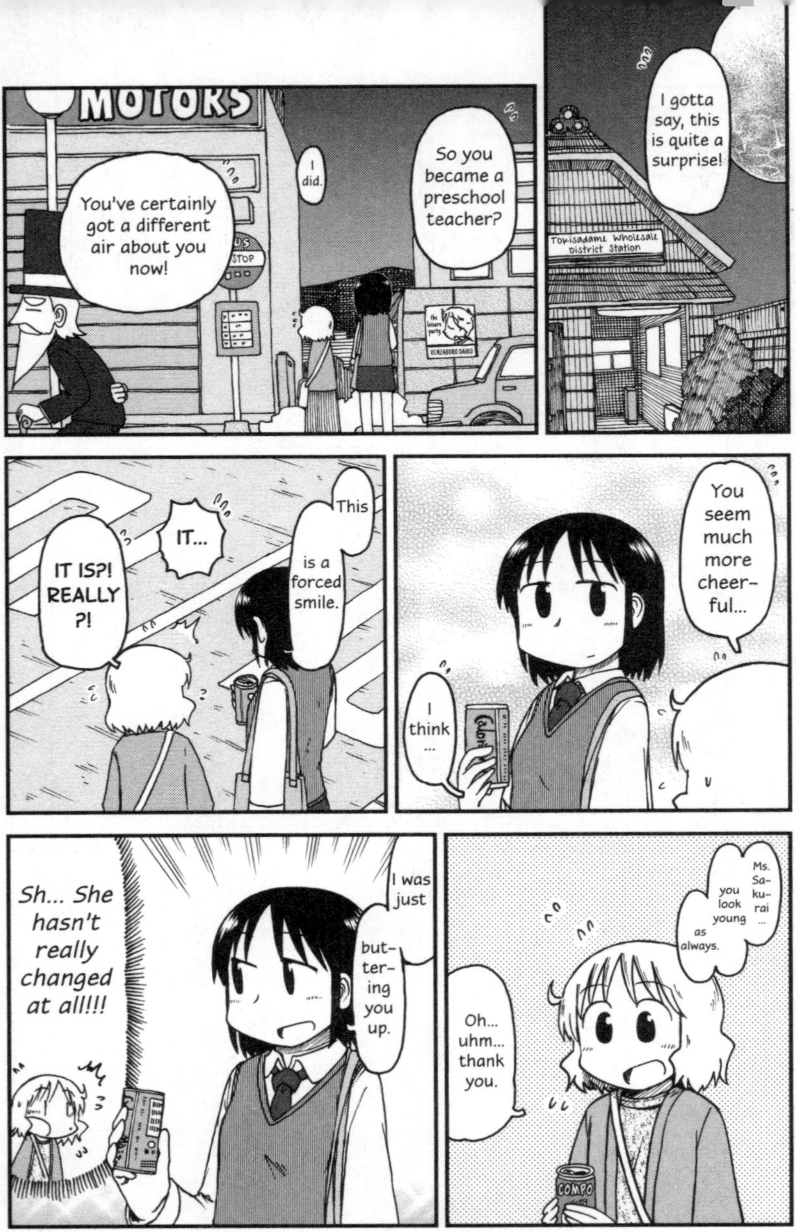
I gotta say, this is quite a surprise!
Tokisadame Wholesale District Station
MOTORS
So you became a preschool teacher?
I did.
You've certainly got a different air about you now!
BUS STOP
the leisure party
KENZABURO DAIKU
You seem much more cheerful...
I think...
This is a forced smile.
IT...
IT IS?! REALLY?!
Ms. Sakurai... you look young as always.
Oh... uhm... thank you.
COMPO
I was just buttering you up.
Sh... She hasn't really changed at all!!!!

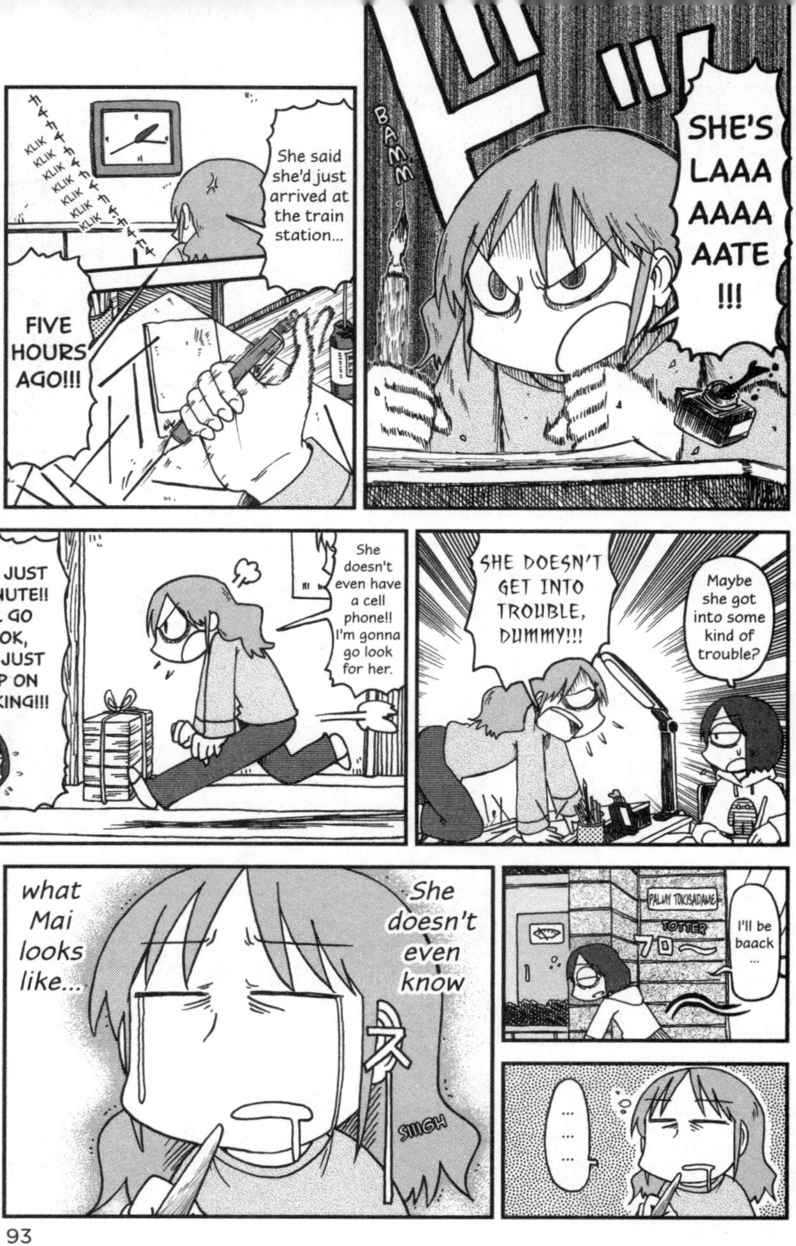
BAMM
SHE'S LAAAAAAAAATE!!!
She said she'd just arrived at the train station...
KLIK KLIK KLIK KLIK KLIK KLIK KLIK
FIVE HOURS AGO!!!
Maybe she got into some kind of trouble?
SHE DOESN'T GET INTO TROUBLE, DUMMY!!!
She doesn't even have a cell phone!! I'm gonna go look for her.
WAIT JUST A MINUTE!! I'LL GO LOOK, YOU JUST KEEP ON WORKING!!!
PALMY TOKISADAME
I'll be baack...
TOTTER
... ...
She doesn't even know
what Mai looks like...
SIIGH

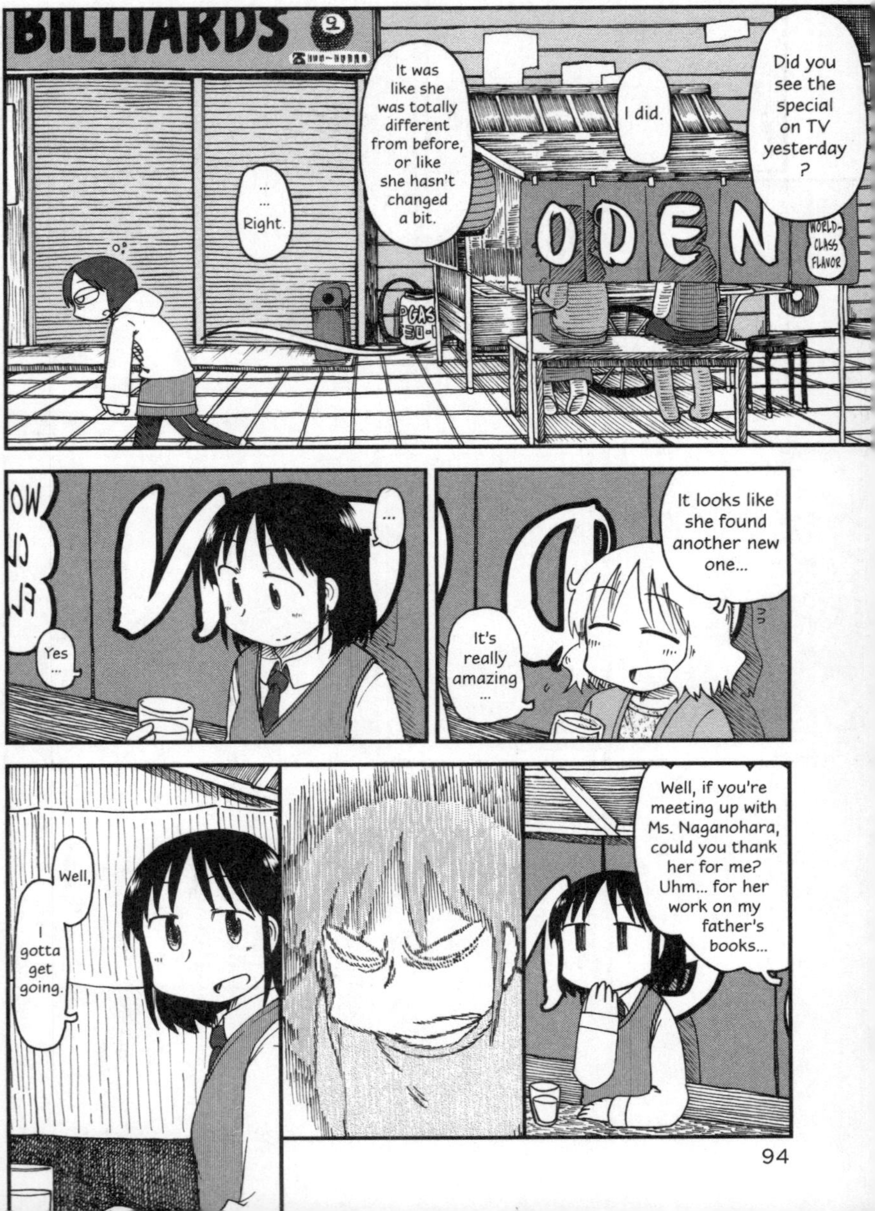
BILLIARDS
ODEN
WORLD-CLASS FLAVOR
Did you see the special on TV yesterday?
I did.
It was like she was totally different from before, or like she hasn't changed a bit.
... ... Right.
It looks like she found another new one...
It's really amazing...
...
Yes...
Well, if you're meeting up with Ms. Naganohara, could you thank her for me? Uhm... for her work on my father's books...
Well,
I gotta get going.

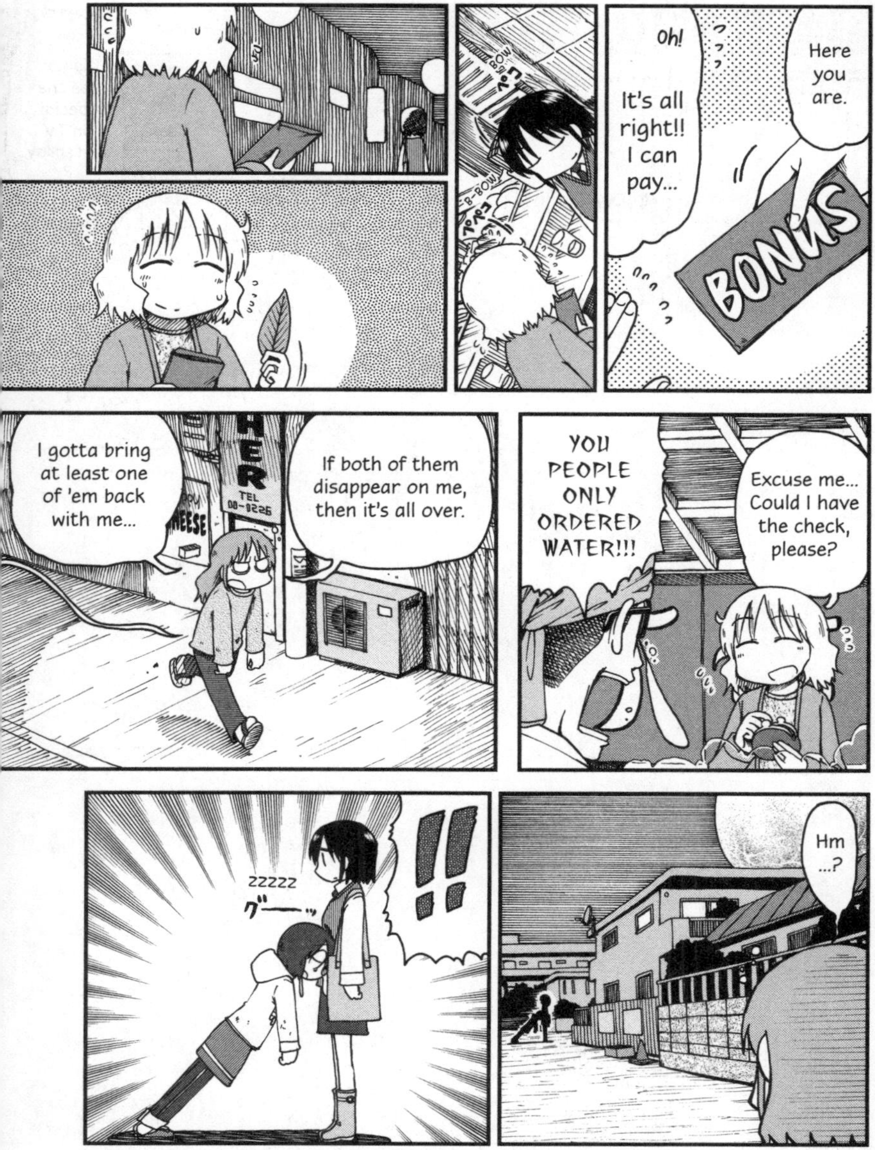

Here you are.
Oh! It's all right!! I can pay...
BONUS
Excuse me... Could I have the check, please?
YOU PEOPLE ONLY ORDERED WATER!!!
If both of them disappear on me, then it's all over.
I gotta bring at least one of 'em back with me...
Hm ...?
!!
ZZZZZ
グー…

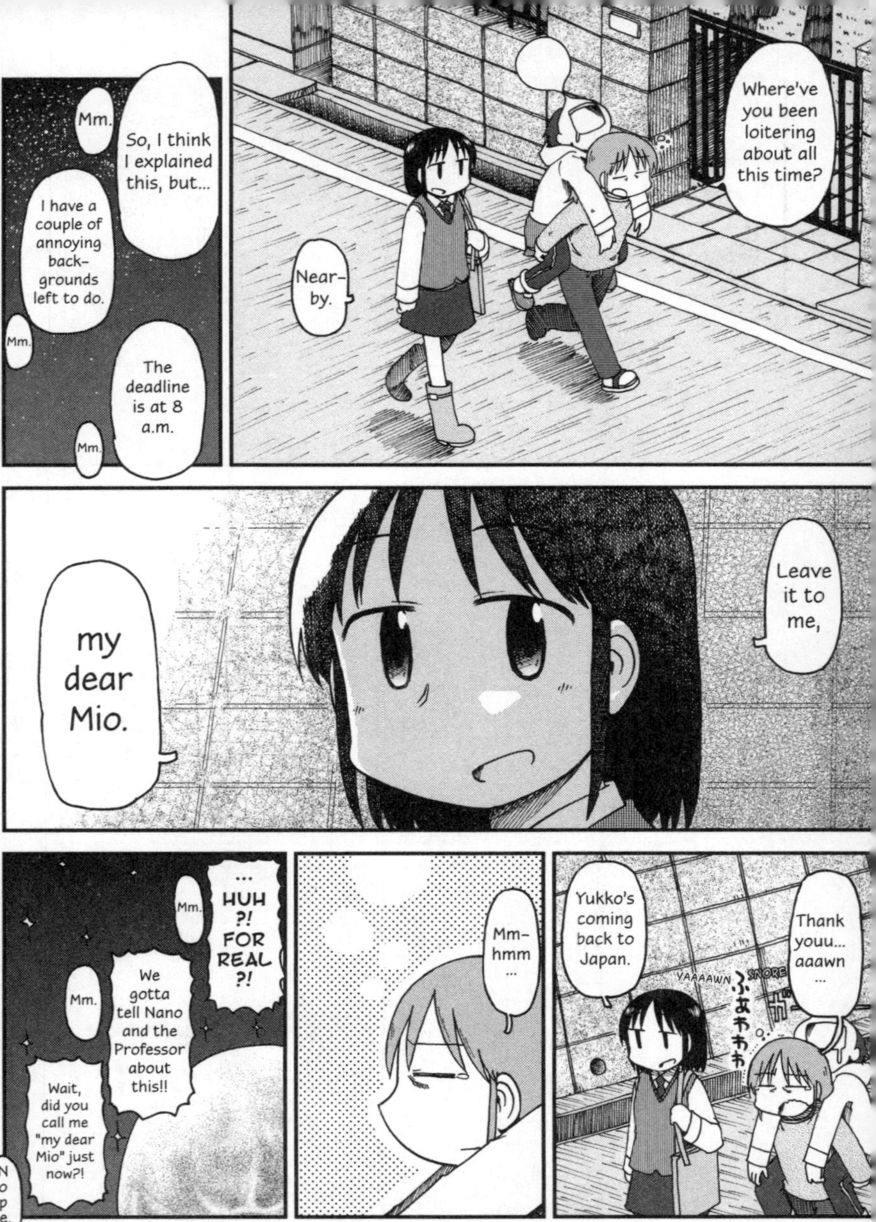
Where've you been loitering about all this time?
Near-by.
So, I think I explained this, but...
Mm.
I have a couple of annoying back-grounds left to do.
Mm.
The deadline is at 8 a.m.
Mm.
Leave it to me,
my dear Mio.
Thank youu... aaawn...
SNORE
YAAAAWN
Yukko's coming back to Japan.
Mm-hmm...
...HUH?! FOR REAL?!
Mm.
We gotta tell Nano and the Professor about this!!
Mm.
Wait, did you call me "my dear Mio" just now?!
Nope.

chapter 185: end

surprise box

It's totally gonna surprise you, so you gotta open it!
As long as I prepare myself, I'm sure I can react calmly to whatever's inside!
WAH !!
WAAAAAAAAH!!!
IT'S A SHARK FIN!!

chapter 186

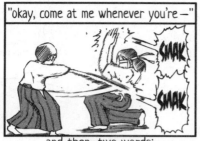

"okay, come at me whenever you're—"

SMAK
SMAK
and then, two words:
HEH.
I see.

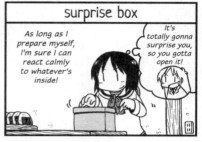

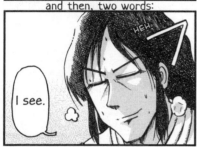

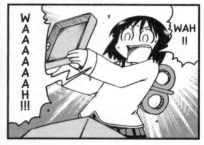

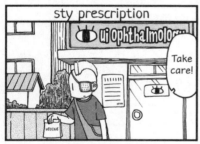

sty prescription

ui ophthalmology
Take care!
MEDICINE
THE EYE DOCTOR GAVE ME A SUPPOSITORY!!!
THE EYE DOCTOR GAVE ME A SUPPOSITORY!!!

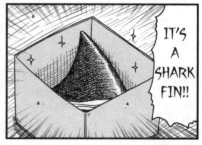

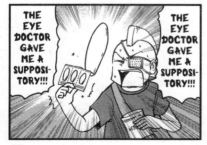

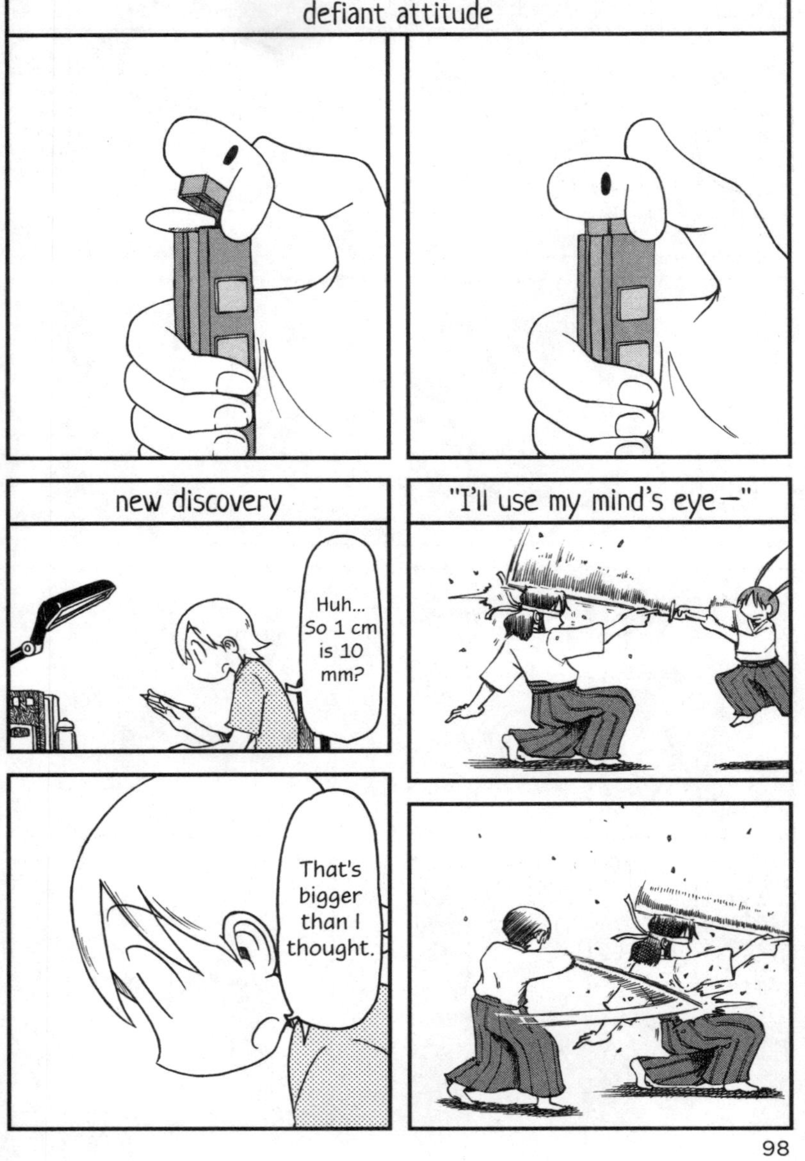
defiant attitude
"I'll use my mind's eye—"
new discovery
Huh... So 1 cm is 10 mm?
That's bigger than I thought.

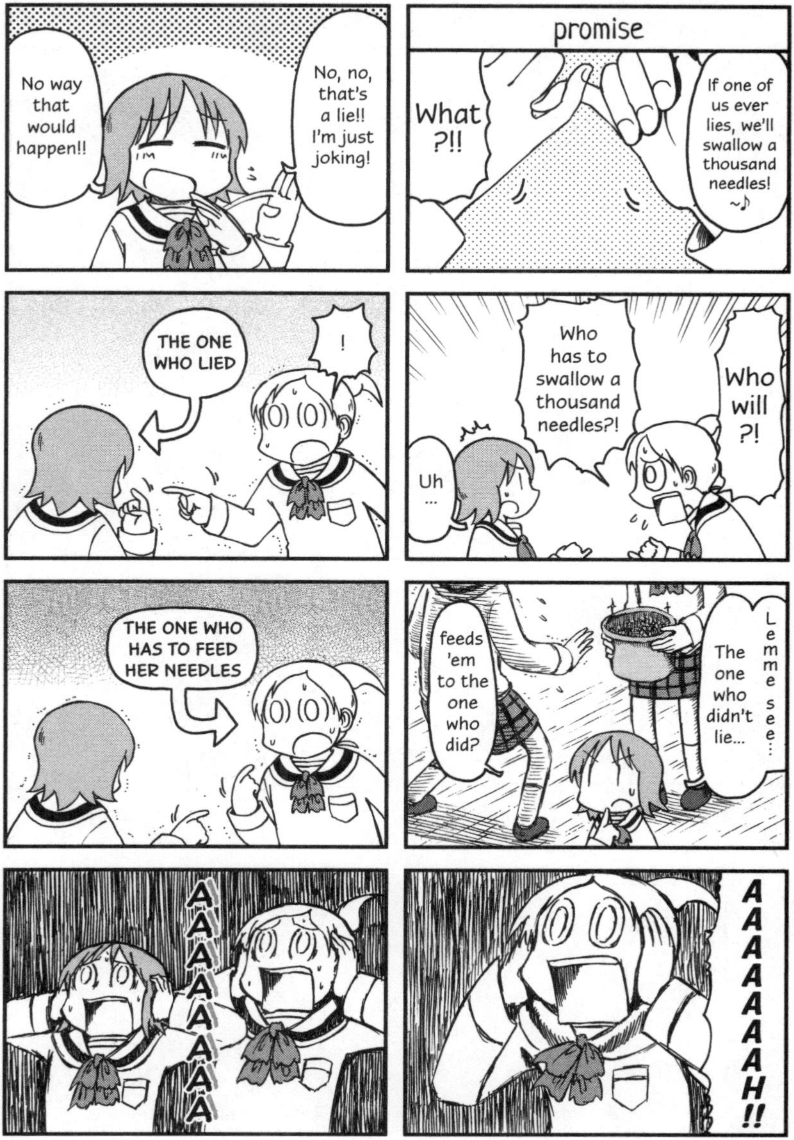
promise
If one of us ever lies, we'll swallow a thousand needles! ~♪
What ?!!
Who will ?!
Who has to swallow a thousand needles?!
Uh ...
Lemme see...
The one who didn't lie...
feeds 'em to the one who did?
AAAAAAAH!!
No, no, that's a lie!! I'm just joking!
No way that would happen!!
!
THE ONE WHO LIED
THE ONE WHO HAS TO FEED HER NEEDLES
AAAAAAAA

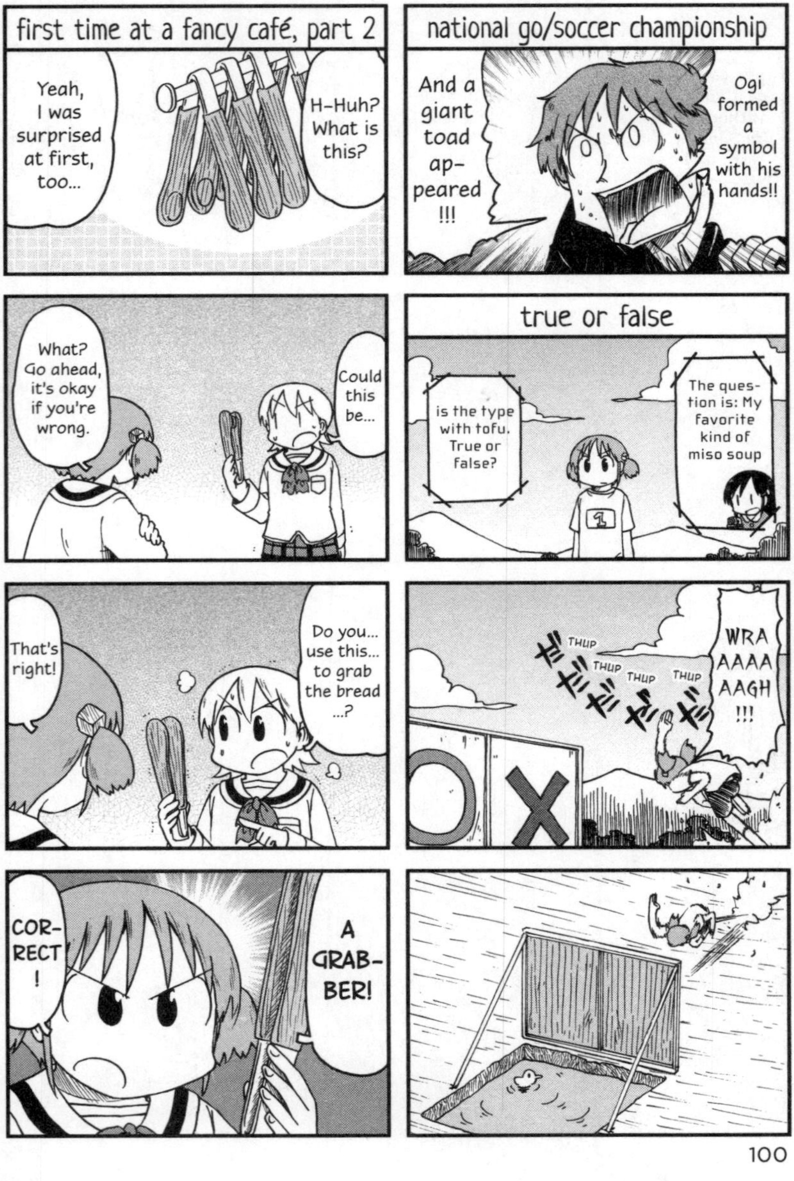
national go/soccer championship
Ogi formed a symbol with his hands!!
And a giant toad ap-peared!!!
true or false
The ques-tion is: My favorite kind of miso soup
is the type with tofu. True or false?
WRA AAAA AAGH!!!
THUP
THUP
THUP
THUP
first time at a fancy café, part 2
H-Huh? What is this?
Yeah, I was surprised at first, too...
Could this be...
What? Go ahead, it's okay if you're wrong.
Do you... use this... to grab the bread ...?
That's right!
A GRAB-BER!
COR-RECT!

a simple misunderstanding

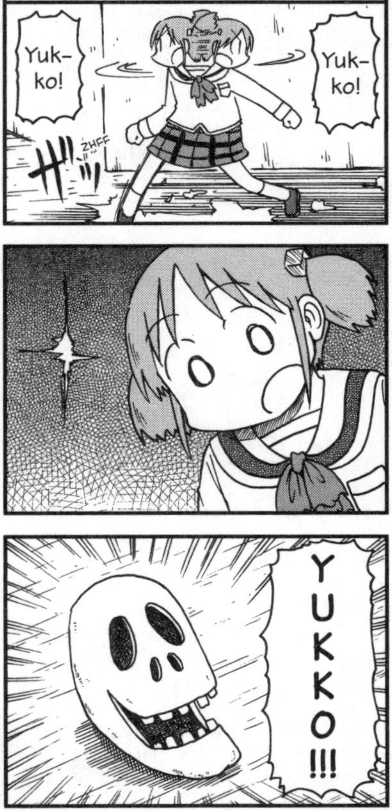
Yuk-ko!
ZHFF
Yuk-ko!
YUKKO!!!

principal vs. vice principal: temporary truce version

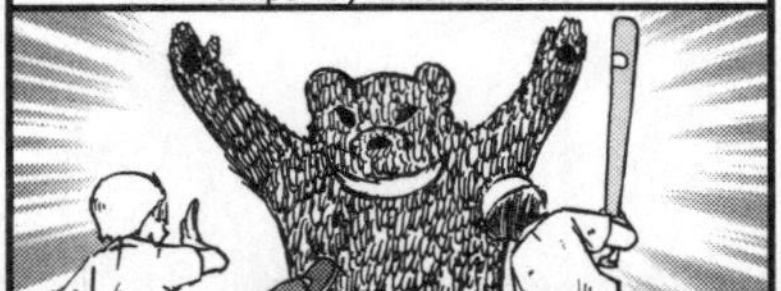

first time at a fancy café, part 3

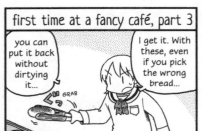

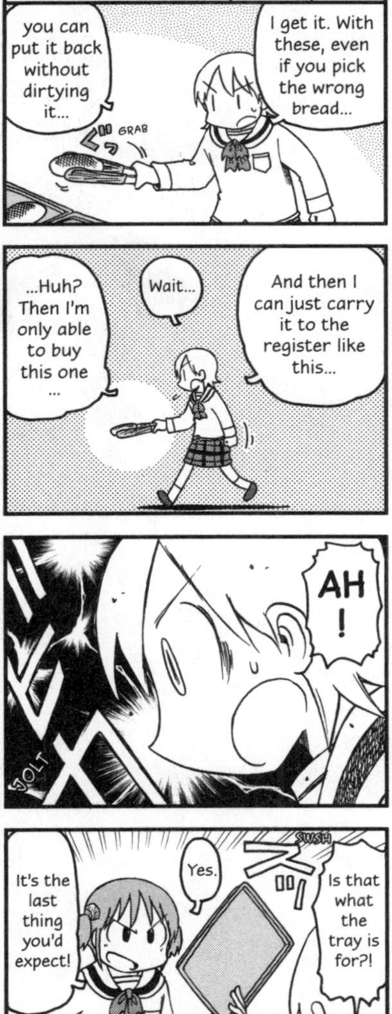
I get it. With these, even if you pick the wrong bread...
you can put it back without dirtying it...
GRAB
And then I can just carry it to the register like this...
Wait...
...Huh? Then I'm only able to buy this one ...
AH!
JOLT
SWSH
Is that what the tray is for?!
Yes.
It's the last thing you'd expect!

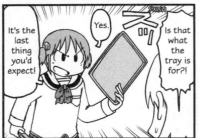

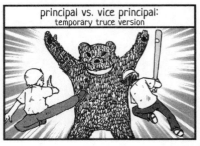

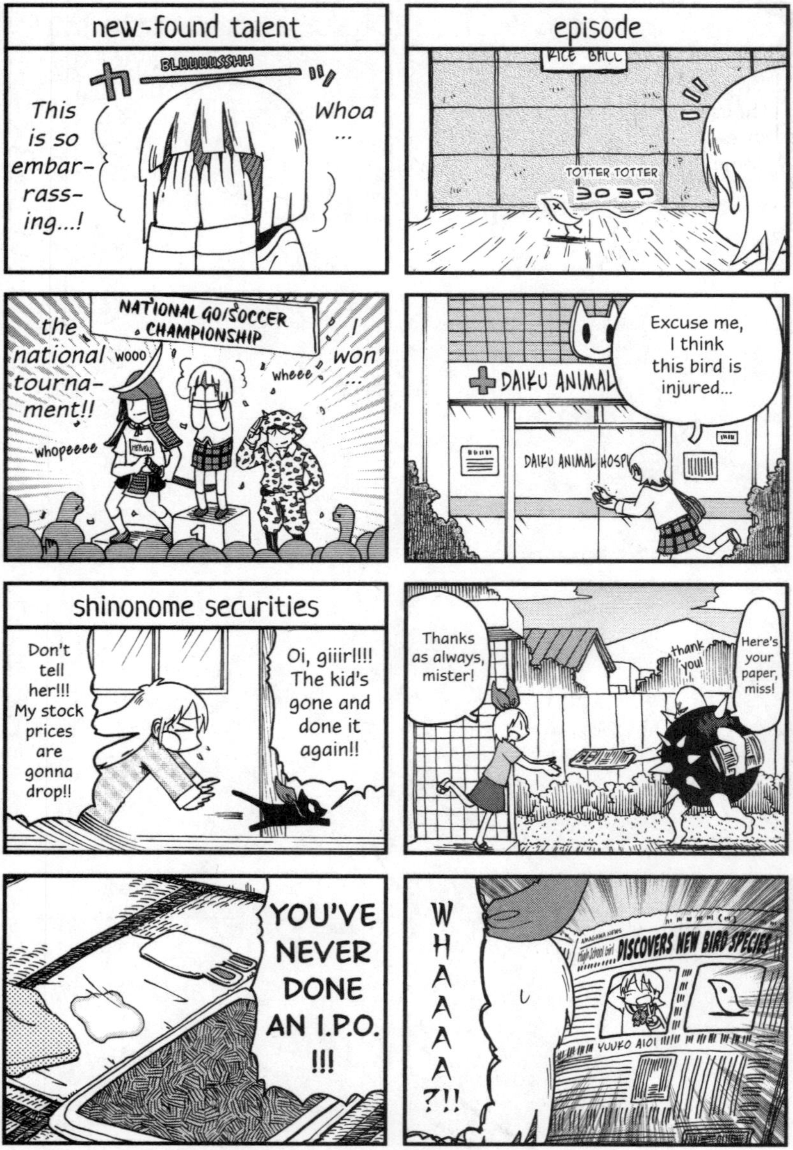
episode
RICE BALL
TOTTER TOTTER
DAIKU ANIMAL
Excuse me, I think this bird is injured...
DAIKU ANIMAL HOSP
Here's your paper, miss!
thank you!
Thanks as always, mister!
High School Girl DISCOVERS NEW BIRD SPECIES
YUUKO AIOI
WHAAAAA?!!
new-found talent
BLUUUUSSHH
Whoa...
This is so embarrassing...!
NATIONAL GO/SOCCER CHAMPIONSHIP
I won...
wheee
the national tournament!!
wooo
whopeeee
shinonome securities
Oi, giiir!!!! The kid's gone and done it again!!
Don't tell her!!! My stock prices are gonna drop!!
YOU'VE NEVER DONE AN I.P.O. !!!

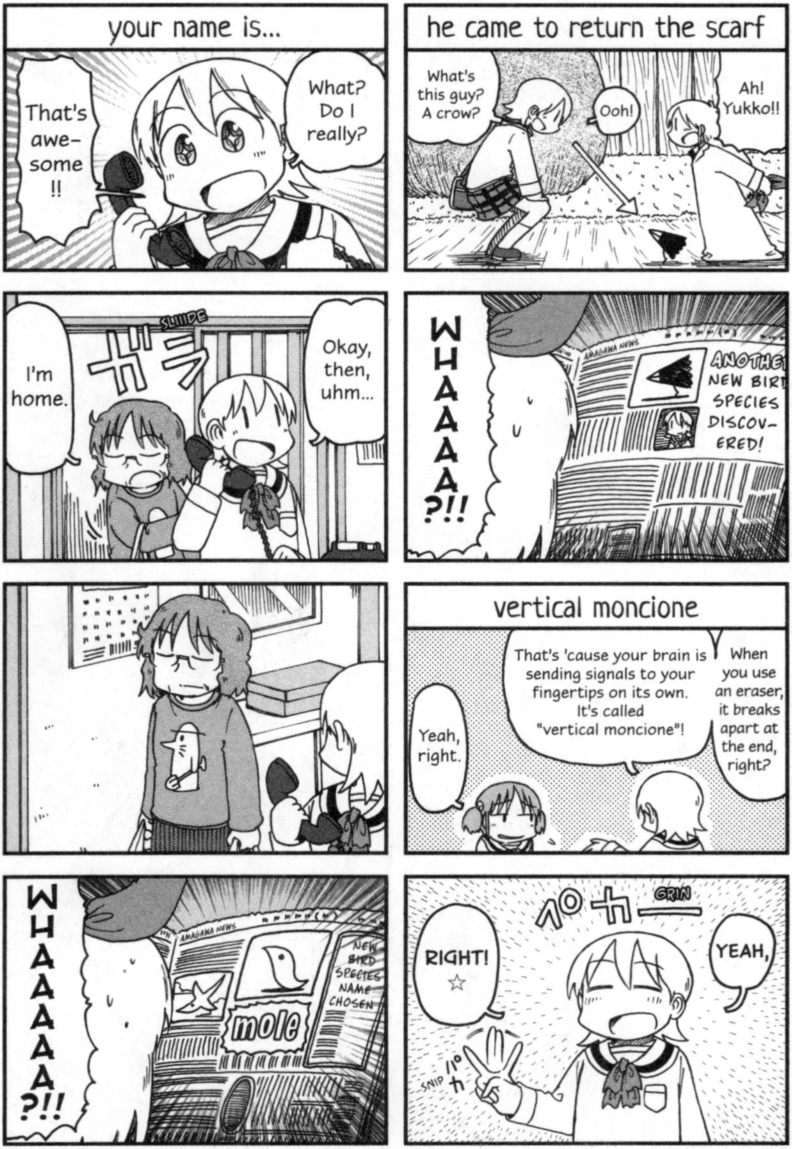
he came to return the scarf
Ah! Yukko!!
Ooh!
What's this guy? A crow?
WHAAAAA?!!
AMAGAWA NEWS
ANOTHE NEW BIR SPECIES DISCOV-ERED!
vertical moncione
When you use an eraser, it breaks apart at the end, right?
That's 'cause your brain is sending signals to your fingertips on its own. It's called "vertical moncione"!
Yeah, right.
GRIN
YEAH,
RIGHT! ☆
SNIP
your name is...
What? Do I really?
That's awe-some !!
Okay, then, uhm...
SLIIIDE
ガラ
I'm home.
...
..
...
WHAAAAAA?!!
AMAGAWA NEWS
NEW BIRD SPECIES NAME CHOSEN
mole

vertical moncione

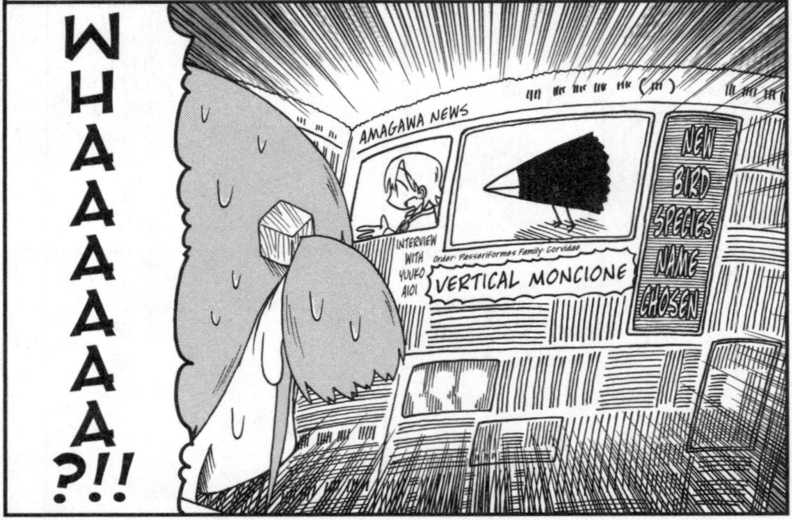
WHAAAAAAA?!!
AMAGAWA NEWS
NEW BIRD SPECIES NAME CHOSEN
INTERVIEW WITH YUUKO AIOI
Order: Passeriformes Family: Corvidae
VERTICAL MONCIONE

inside story

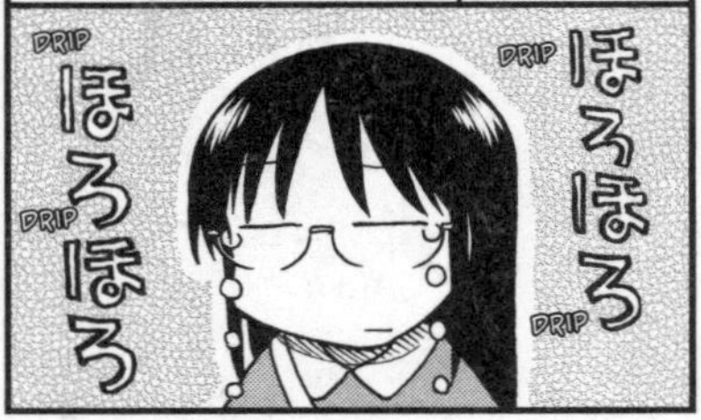
DRIP ほろほろ DRIP
DRIP ほろほろ DRIP

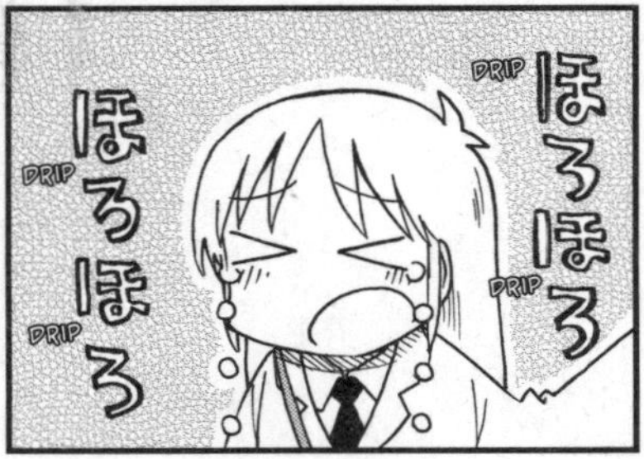
DRIP ほろほろ DRIP
DRIP ほろほろ DRIP

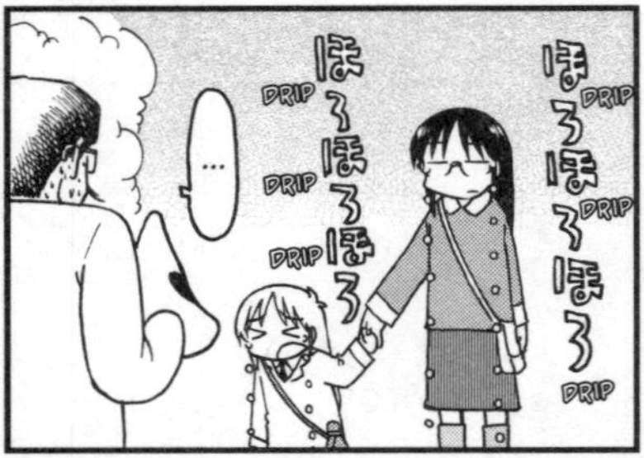
ほろほろほろ DRIP DRIP DRIP
ほろほろほろ DRIP DRIP DRIP
...

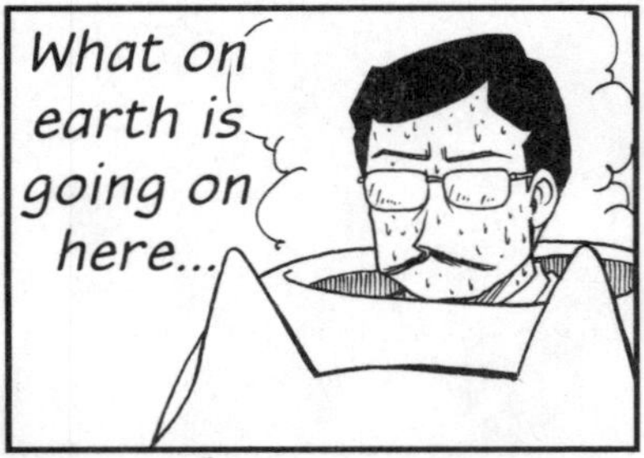
What on earth is going on here...

the path where light shines

I....

I can't believe those things I always see were new species...

I FOUND OOOOONE!!

Maybe I should try to find one, too.

WHAAAAA?!!

Wh...

Ahh, this here is an Aioi Special.

105

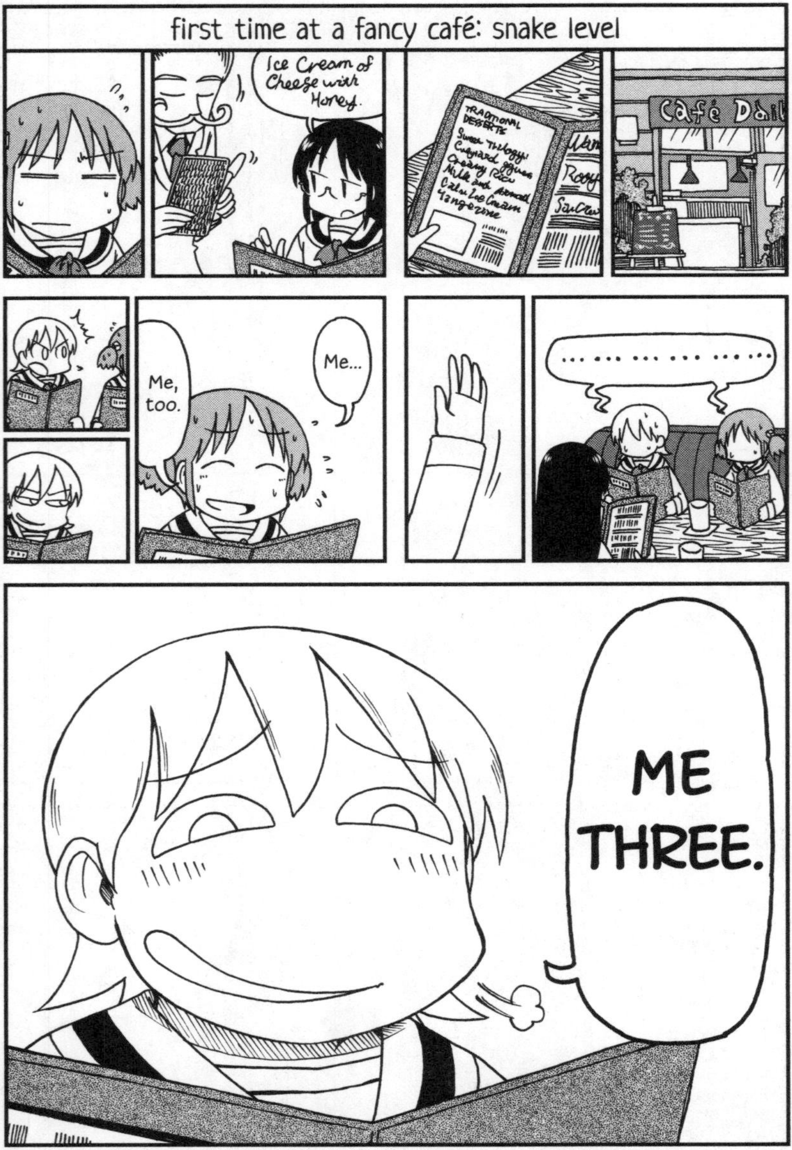
first time at a fancy café: snake level
TRADITIONAL DESSERTS
Ice Cream of Cheese with Honey.
....
Me...
Me, too.
ME THREE.

chapter 187

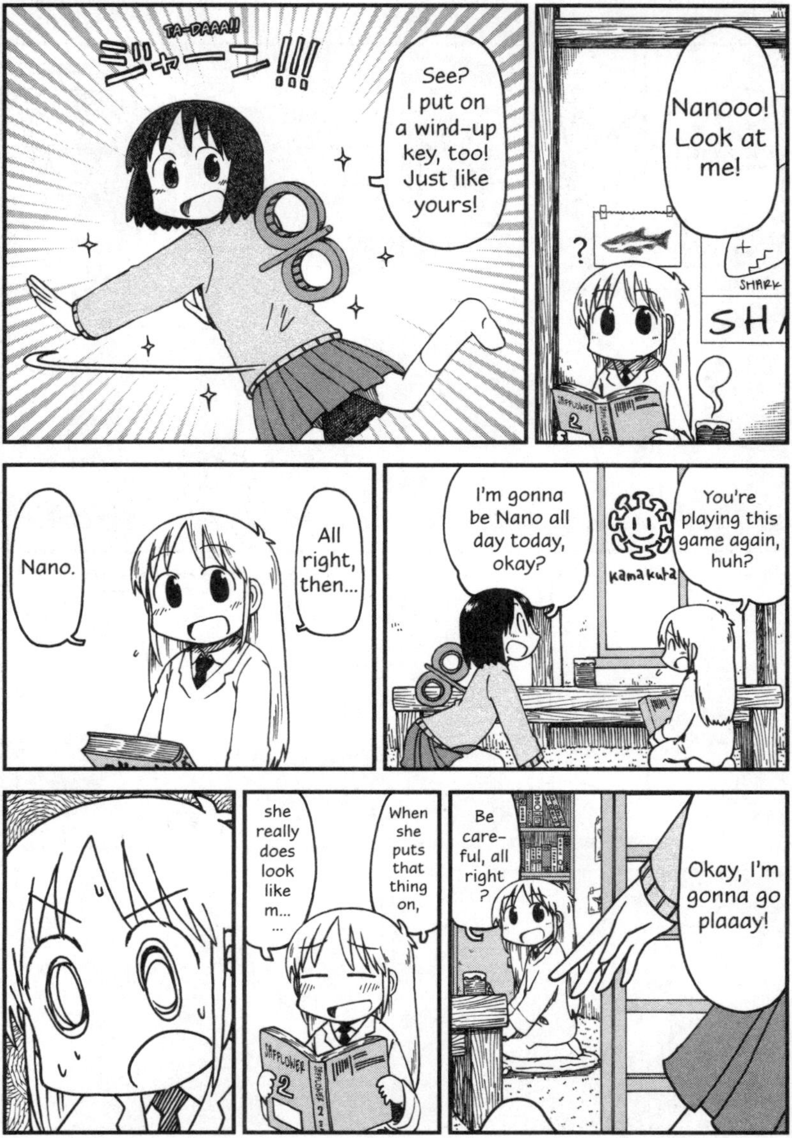
Nanooo! Look at me!
SHARK
SAFFLOWER 2
TA-DAAA!!
ジャーン!!!
See? I put on a wind-up key, too! Just like yours!
You're playing this game again, huh?
I'm gonna be Nano all day today, okay?
kamakura
All right, then...
Nano.
Okay, I'm gonna go plaaay!
Be care-ful, all right?
When she puts that thing on,
she really does look like m... ...
SAFFLOWER 2

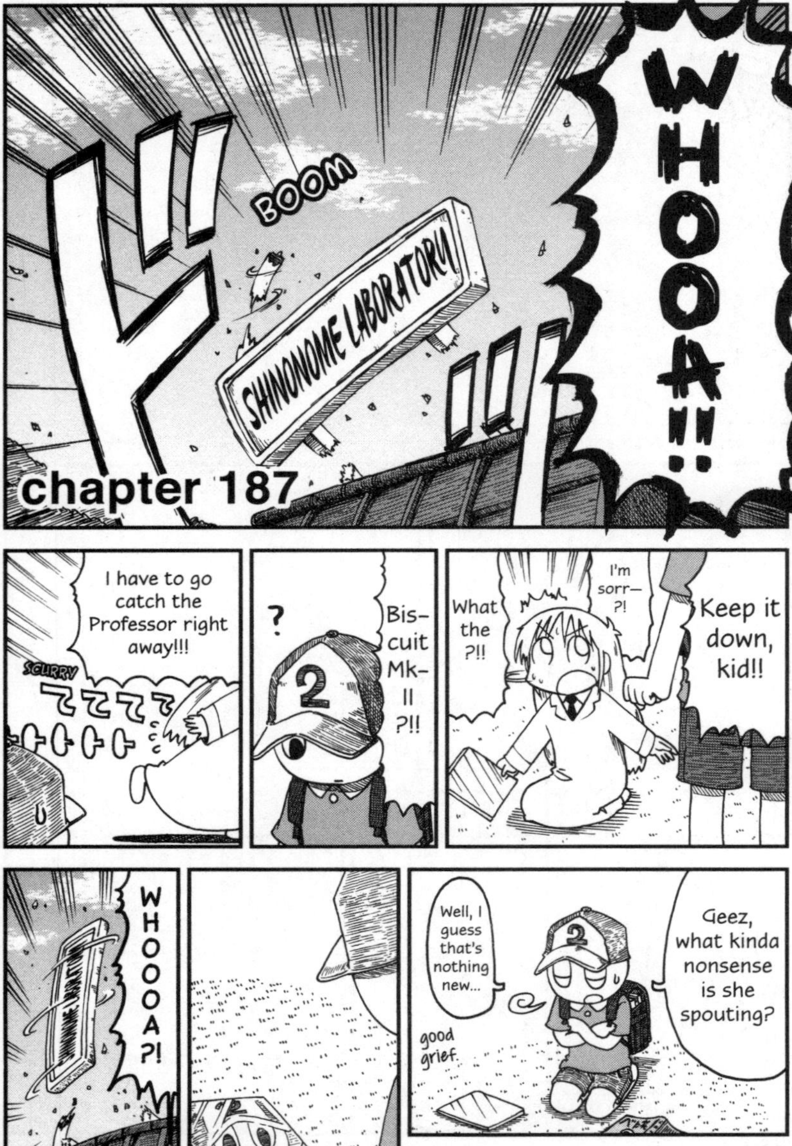
WHOA!!
BOOM
SHINONOME LABORATORY
chapter 187
Keep it down, kid!!
I'm sorr—?!
What the ?!!
Bis-cuit Mk-II ?!!
?
I have to go catch the Professor right away!!!
SCURRY
Geez, what kinda nonsense is she spouting?
Well, I guess that's nothing new...
good grief.
WHOOOOA?!

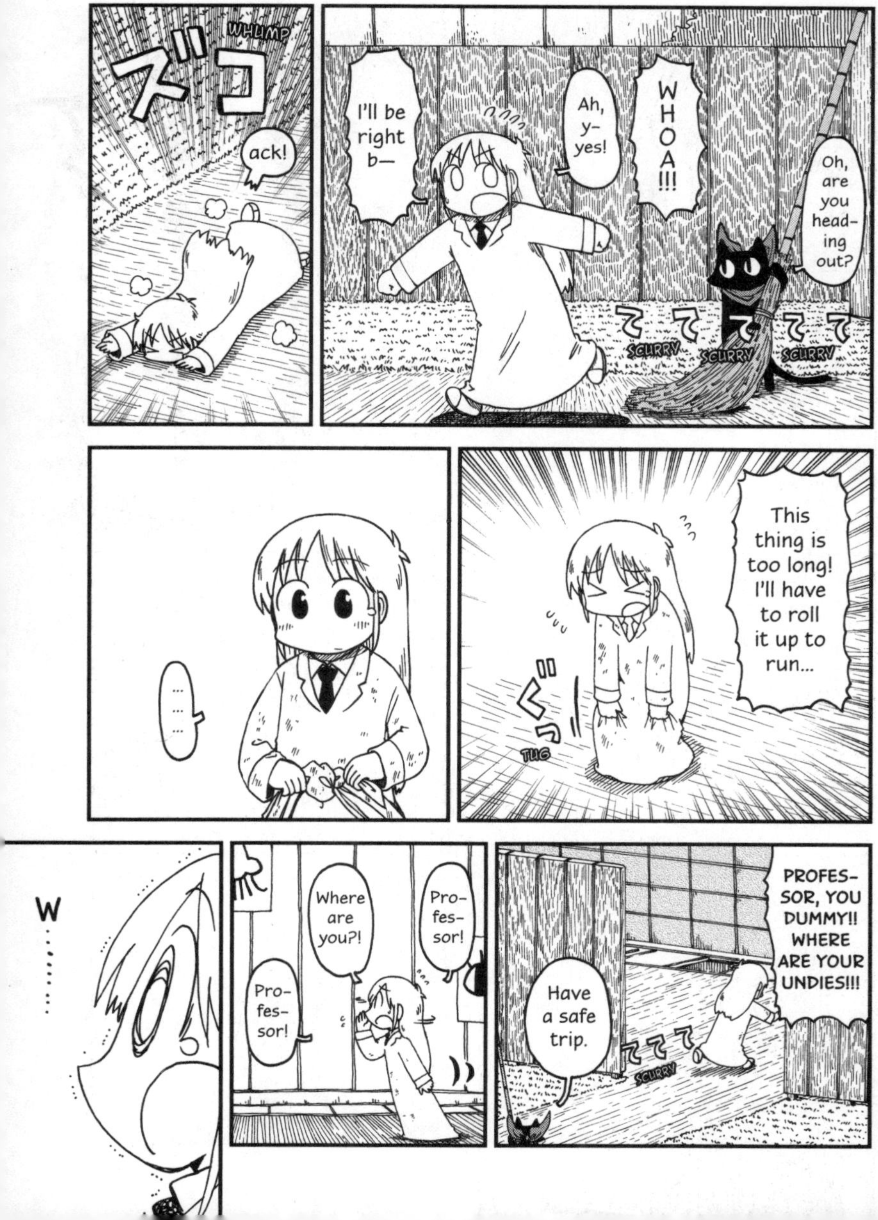
Oh, are you head-ing out?
WHOA!!!
Ah, y- yes!
I'll be right b—
SCURRY
SCURRY
SCURRY
WHUMP
ack!
This thing is too long! I'll have to roll it up to run...
TUG
... ...
PROFES-SOR, YOU DUMMY!! WHERE ARE YOUR UNDIES!!!
Have a safe trip.
SCURRY
Pro-fes-sor!
Where are you?!
Pro-fes-sor!
W.........

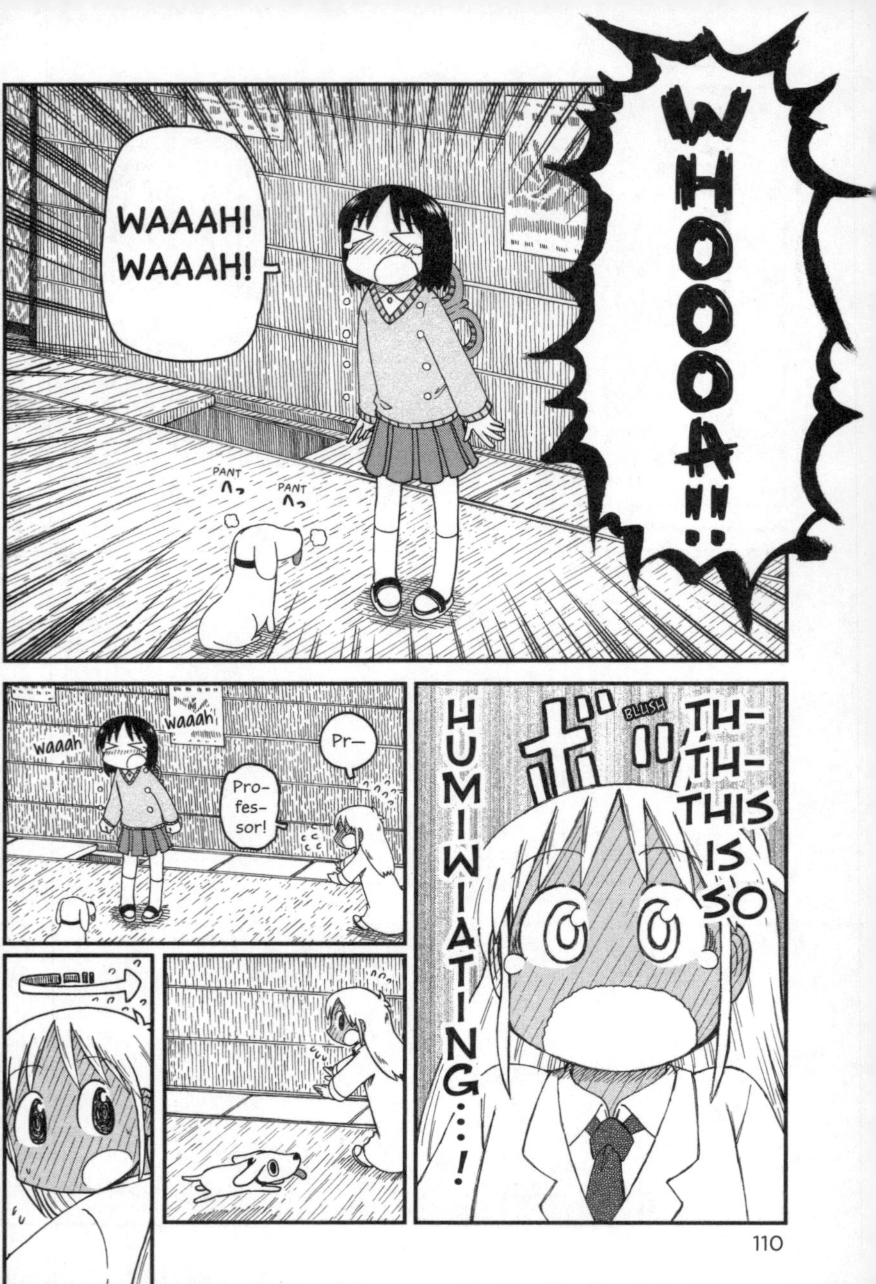
WHOOOOA!!
WAAAH! WAAAH!
PANT
PANT
BLUSH
TH-TH-THIS IS SO
HUMIWIATING...!
waaah
waaah
Pr—
Pro-fes-sor!

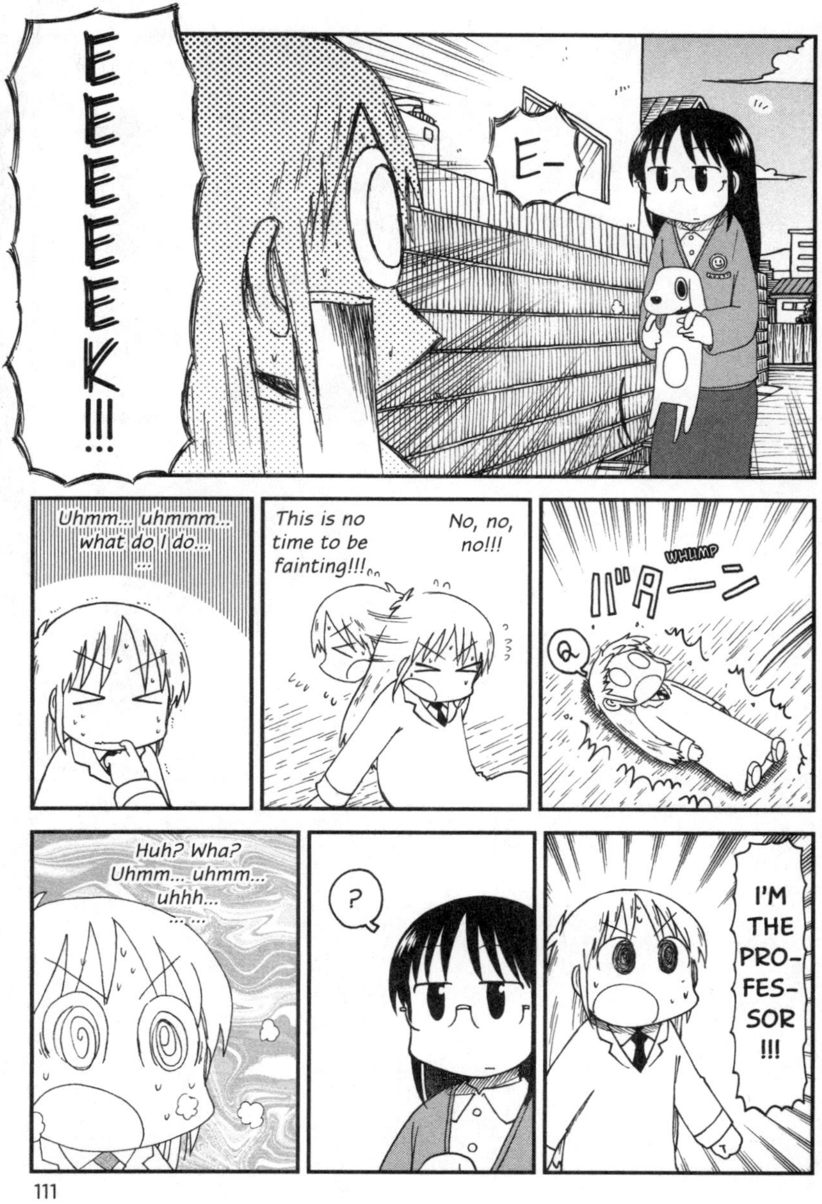
E–
EEEEEK!!!
WHUMP
バターン
No, no, no!!!
This is no time to be fainting!!!
Uhmm... uhmmm... what do I do... ...
I'M THE PRO-FES-SOR!!!
?
Huh? Wha? Uhmm... uhmm... uhhh... ... ...

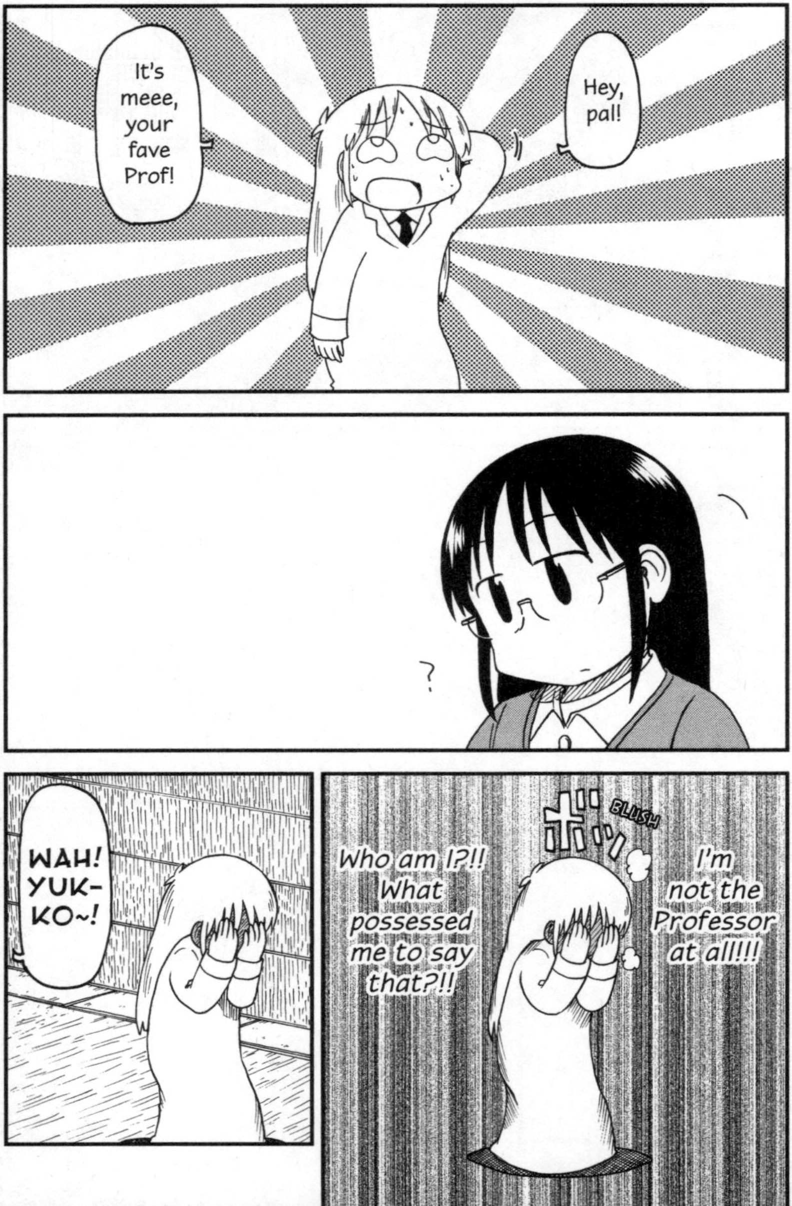
Hey, pal!
It's meee, your fave Prof!
?
ボッ
BLUSH
I'm not the Professor at all!!!
Who am I?!! What possessed me to say that?!!
WAH! YUKKO~!

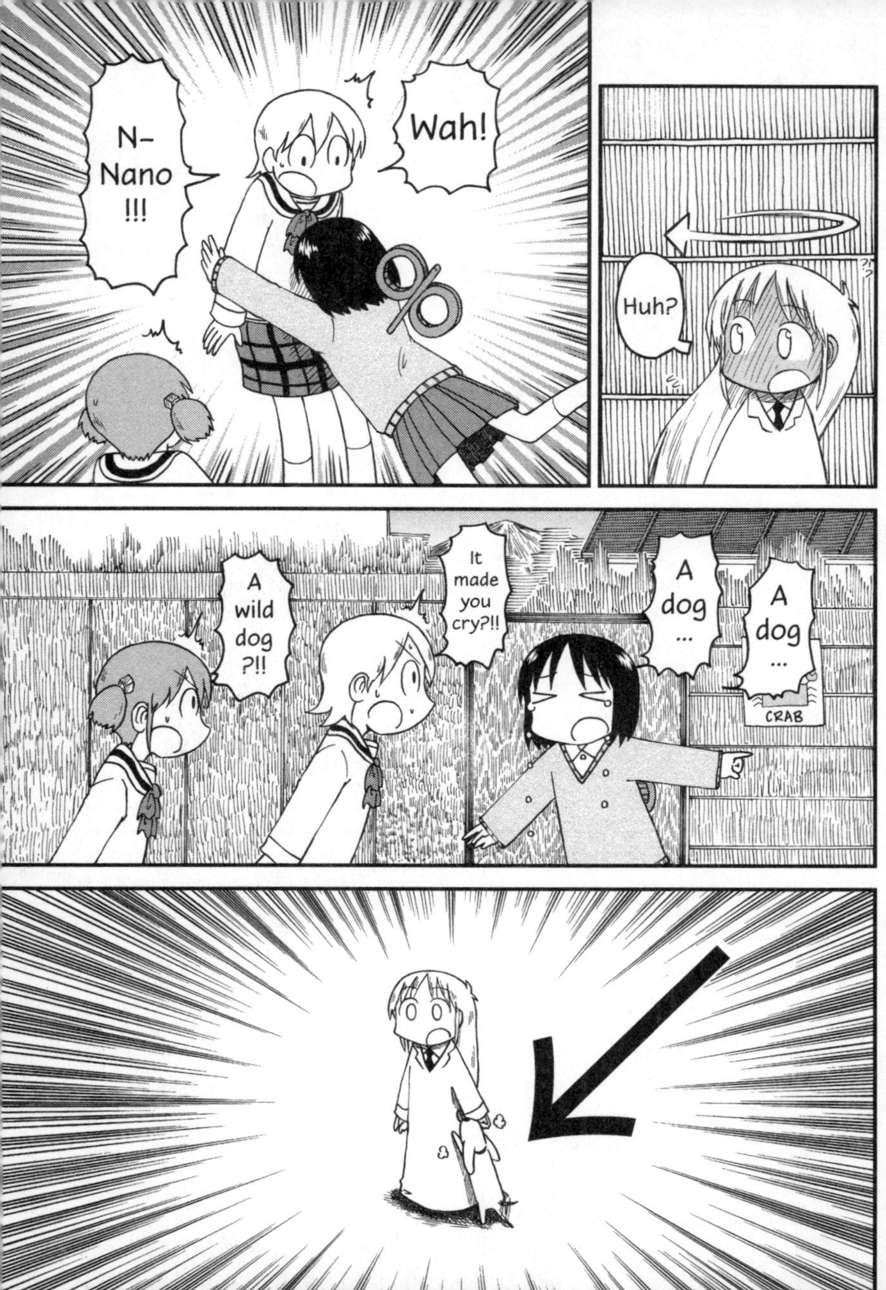

Huh?
Wah!
N- Nano !!!
A dog ...
A dog ...
CRAB
It made you cry?!!
A wild dog ?!!

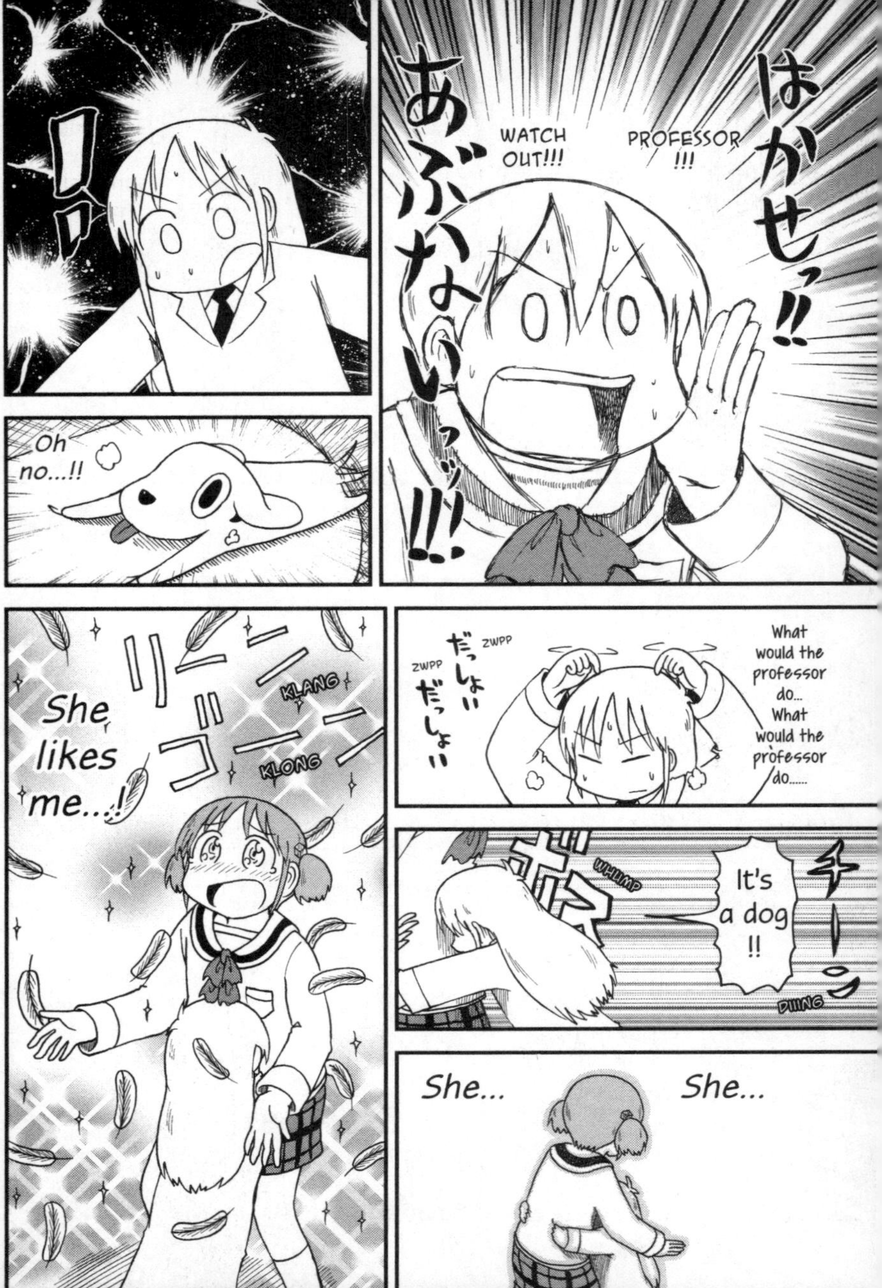
はかせっ!!
PROFESSOR !!!
あぶないぃっ!!!
WATCH OUT!!!
Oh no...!!
What would the professor do... What would the professor do......
だっしょい
ZWPP
だっしょい
ZWPP
It's a dog !!
WHUMP
DIIING
KLANG
KLONG
She likes me...!
She...
She...

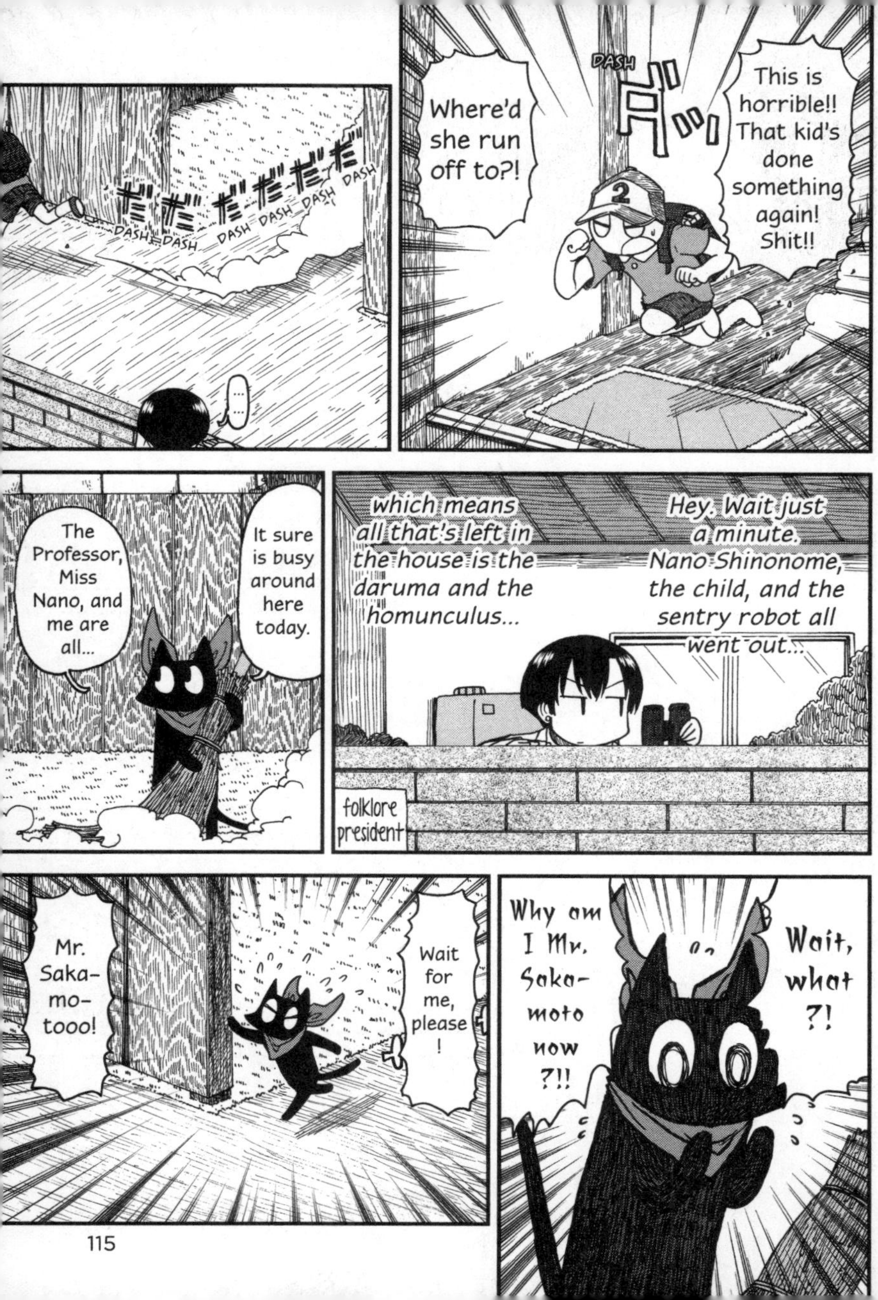
This is horrible!! That kid's done something again! Shit!!
DASH
Where'd she run off to?!
DASH DASH DASH DASH DASH DASH
......
Hey. Wait just a minute. Nano Shinonome, the child, and the sentry robot all went out...
which means all that's left in the house is the daruma and the homunculus...
folklore president
It sure is busy around here today.
The Professor, Miss Nano, and me are all...
Wait, what?!
Why am I Mr. Sakamoto now?!!
Wait for me, please!
Mr. Sakamotooo!

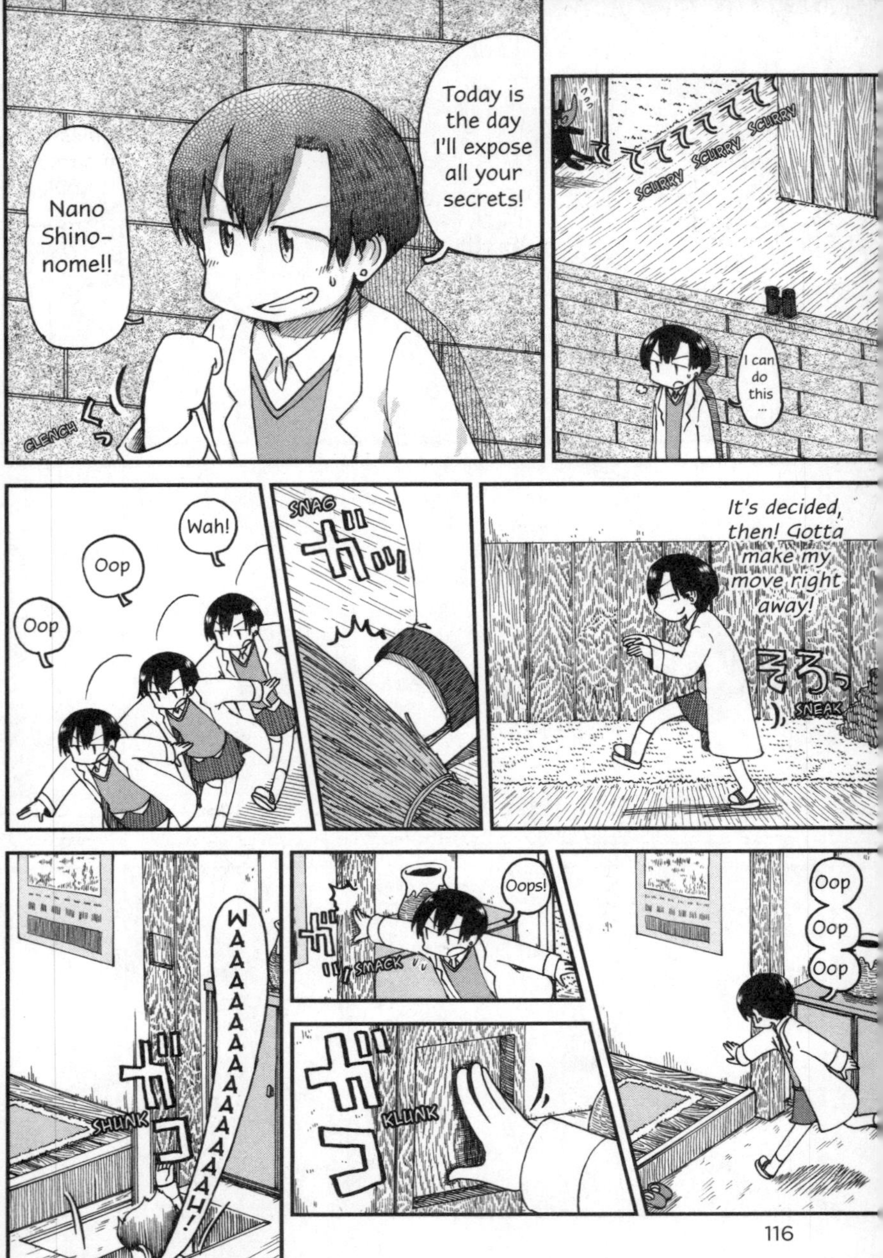
SCURRY SCURRY SCURRY
I can do this ...
Today is the day I'll expose all your secrets!
Nano Shino-nome!!
CLENCH
It's decided, then! Gotta make my move right away!
SNEAK
SNAG
Wah!
Oop
Oop
Oop
Oop
Oop
Oops!
SMACK
KLUNK
WAAAAAAAAAAAAAAAAH!
SHUNK

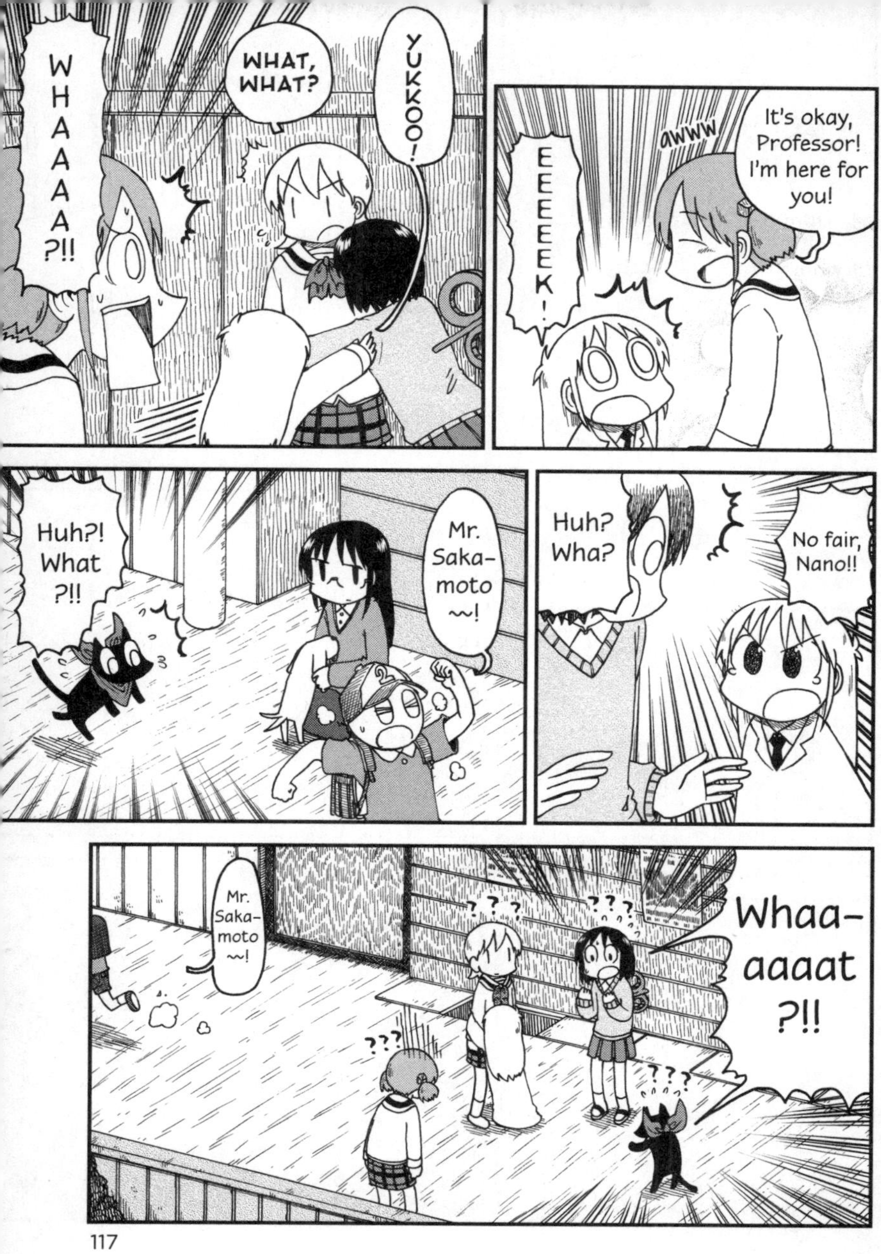
It's okay, Professor! I'm here for you!
awww
EEEEEEK!!
YUKKOO!
WHAT, WHAT?
WHAAAAAA?!!
No fair, Nano!!
Huh? Wha?
Mr. Saka-moto ~!
Huh?! What ?!!
Whaa-aaaat ?!!
???
???
???
???
Mr. Saka-moto ~!

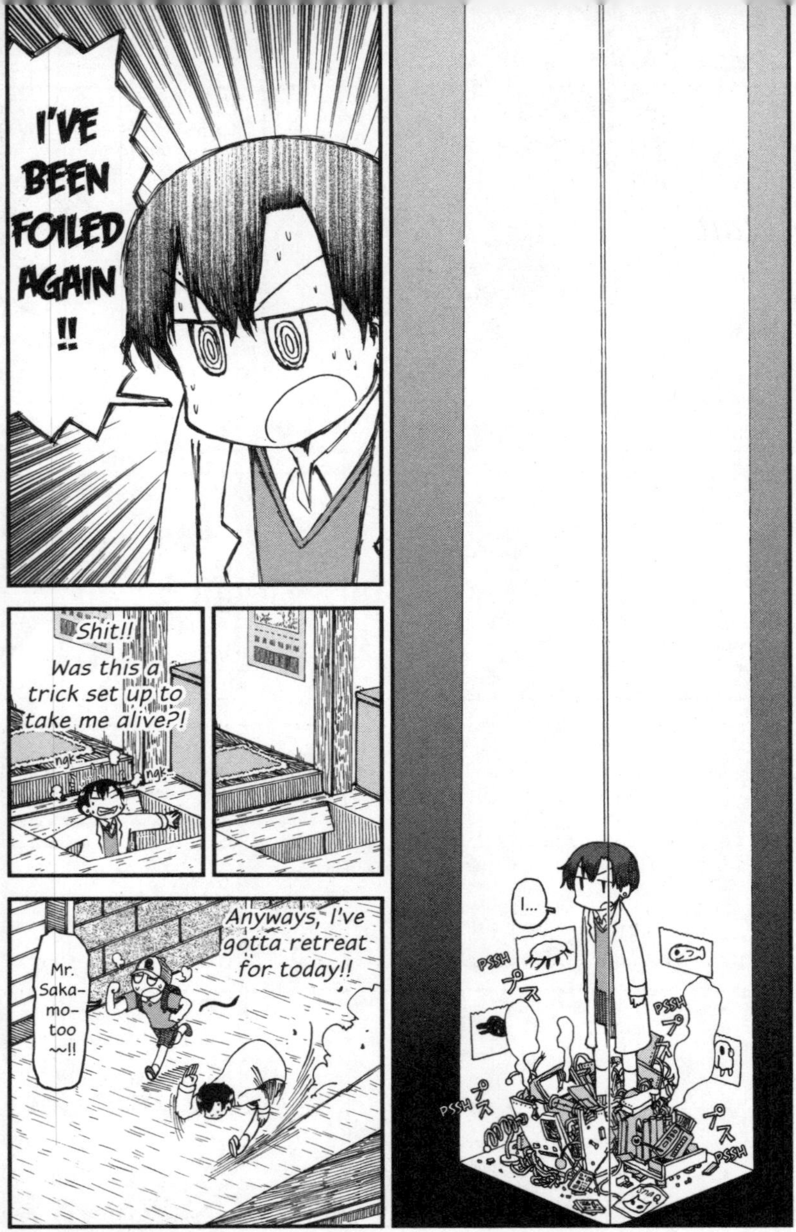
I...
PSSH
パス
PSSH
パス
PSSH
パス
PSSH
パス
I'VE BEEN FOILED AGAIN!!
Shit!! Was this a trick set up to take me alive?!
ngk
ngk
Anyways, I've gotta retreat for today!!
Mr. Saka-mo-too~!!

chapter 187: end

chapter 188

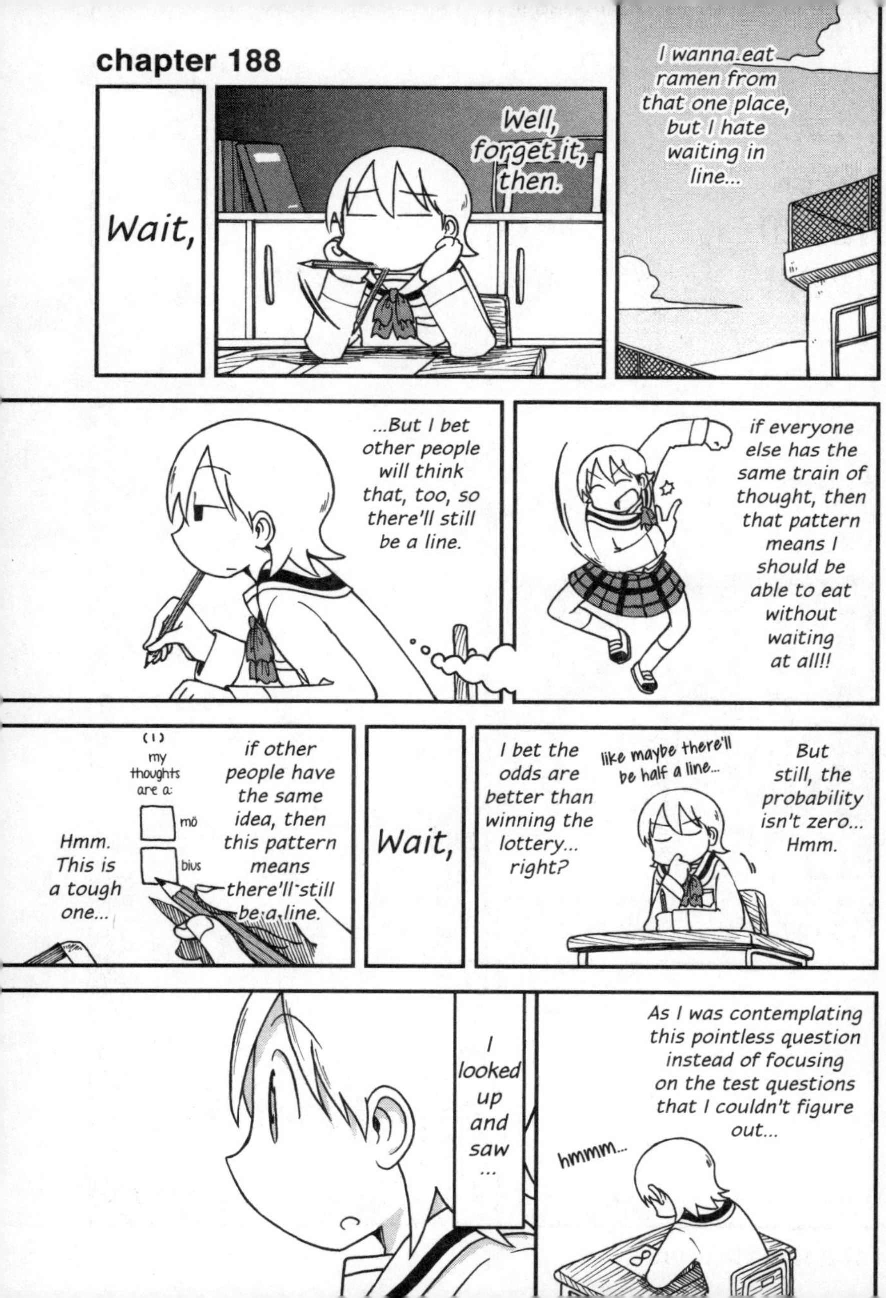
I wanna eat ramen from that one place, but I hate waiting in line...
Well, forget it, then.
Wait,
if everyone else has the same train of thought, then that pattern means I should be able to eat without waiting at all!!
...But I bet other people will think that, too, so there'll still be a line.
But still, the probability isn't zero... Hmm.
like maybe there'll be half a line...
I bet the odds are better than winning the lottery... right?
Wait,
if other people have the same idea, then this pattern means there'll still be a line.
(1)
my thoughts are a:
mö
bius
Hmm. This is a tough one...
As I was contemplating this pointless question instead of focusing on the test questions that I couldn't figure out...
hmmm...
I looked up and saw...

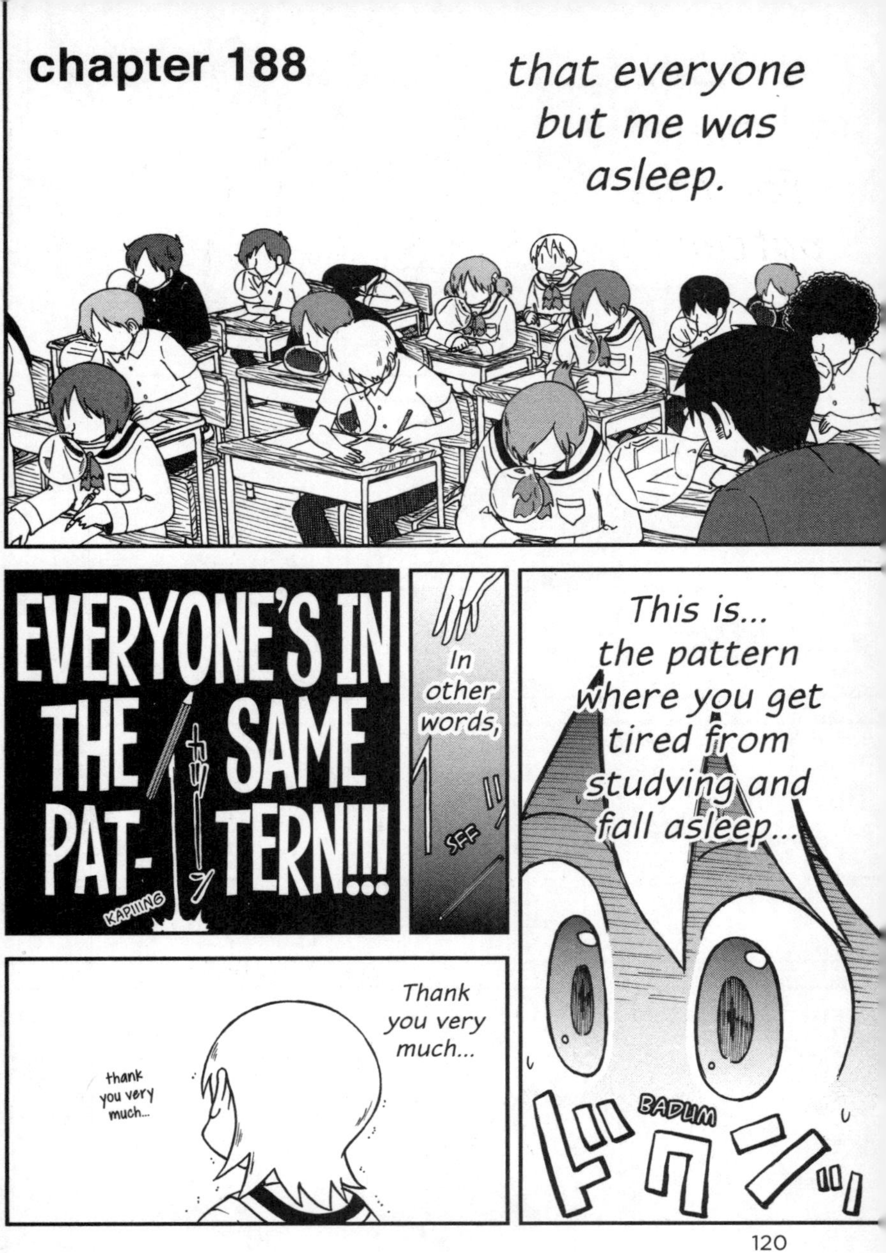
chapter 188
that everyone but me was asleep.
This is... the pattern where you get tired from studying and fall asleep...
BADUM
In other words,
SFF
EVERYONE'S IN THE SAME PAT-TERN!!!
KAPIIING
Thank you very much...
thank you very much...

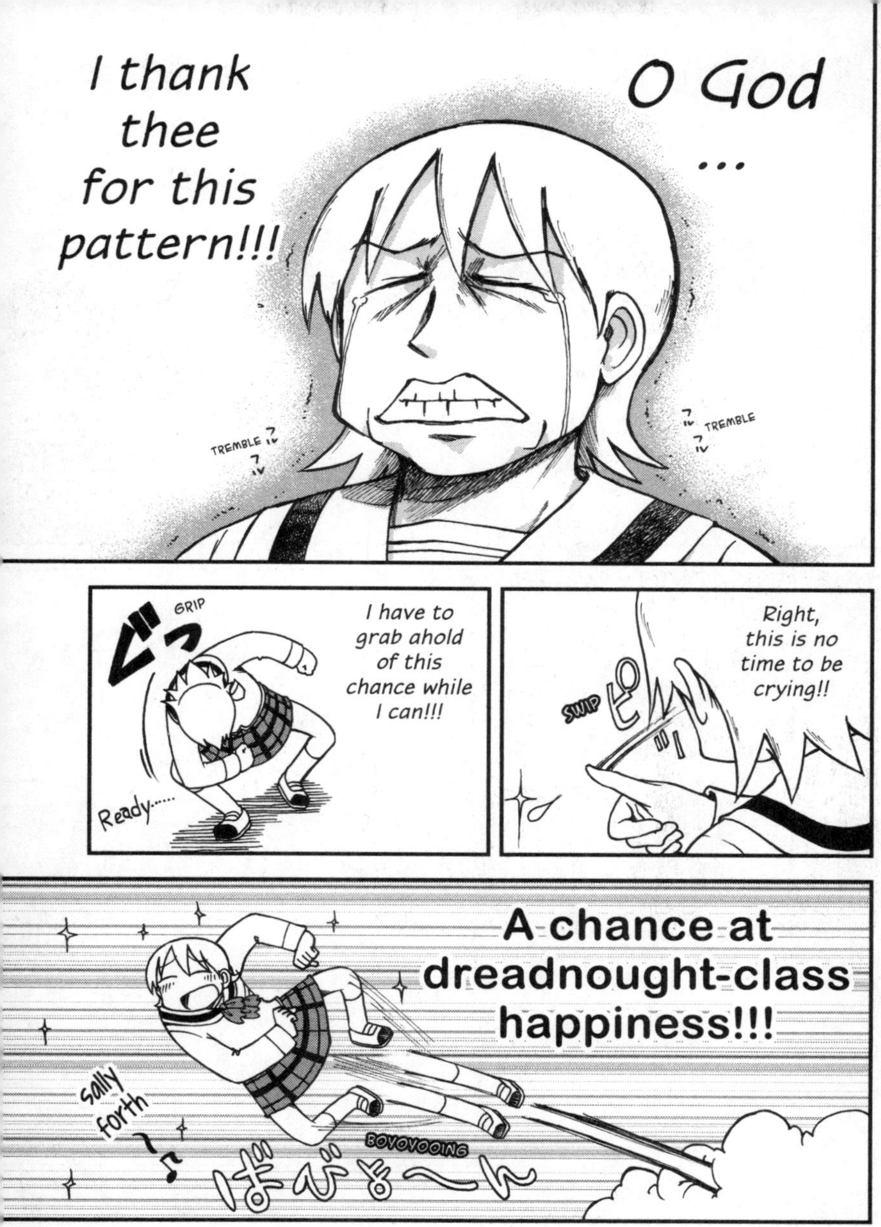
O God
...
I thank thee for this pattern!!!
TREMBLE
TREMBLE
Right, this is no time to be crying!!
SWIP
I have to grab ahold of this chance while I can!!!
GRIP
Ready......
A chance at dreadnought-class happiness!!!
sally forth
BOYOVOOING

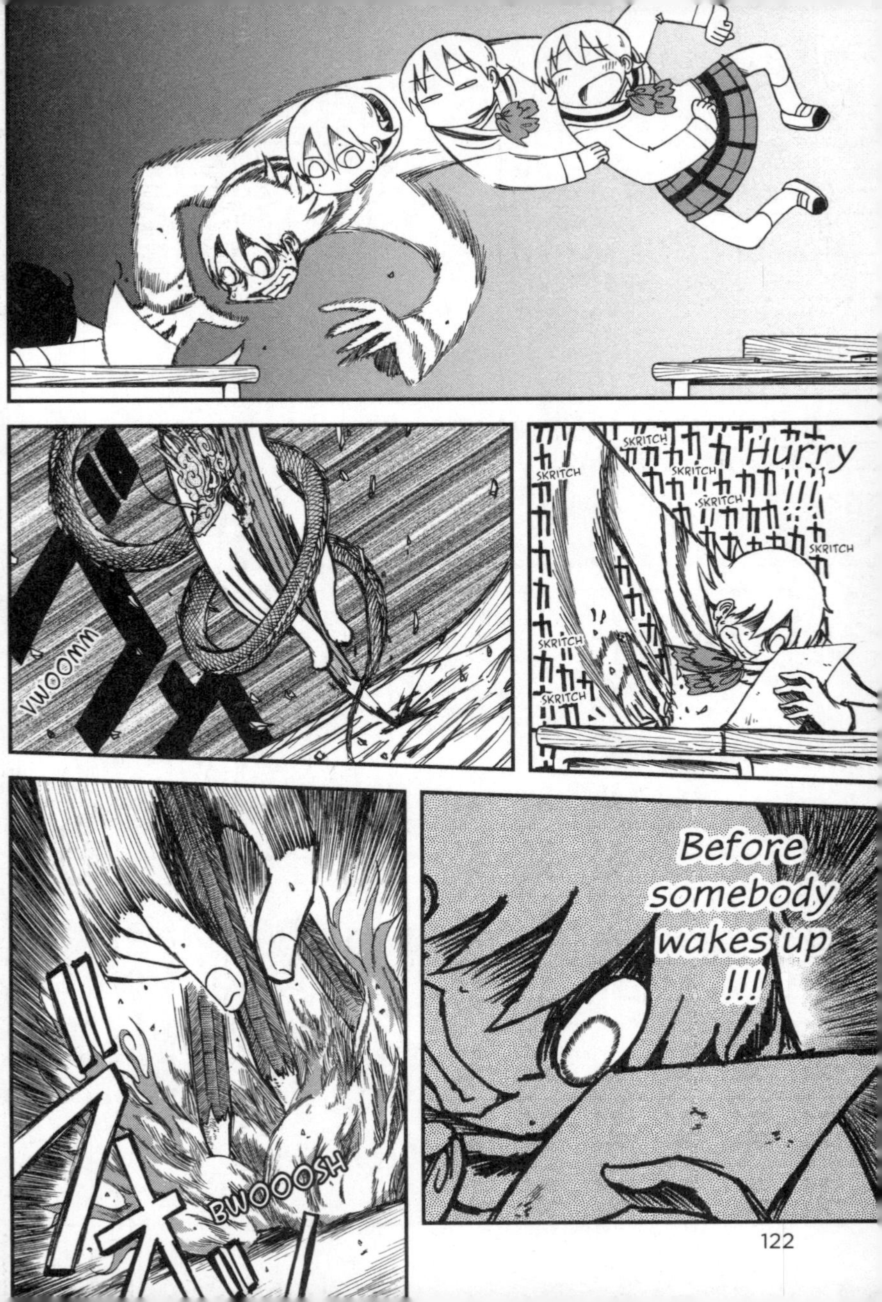
SKRITCH
SKRITCH
Hurry
!!!
SKRITCH
SKRITCH
SKRITCH
SKRITCH
SKRITCH
VWOOMM
Before somebody wakes up !!!
BWOOOSH

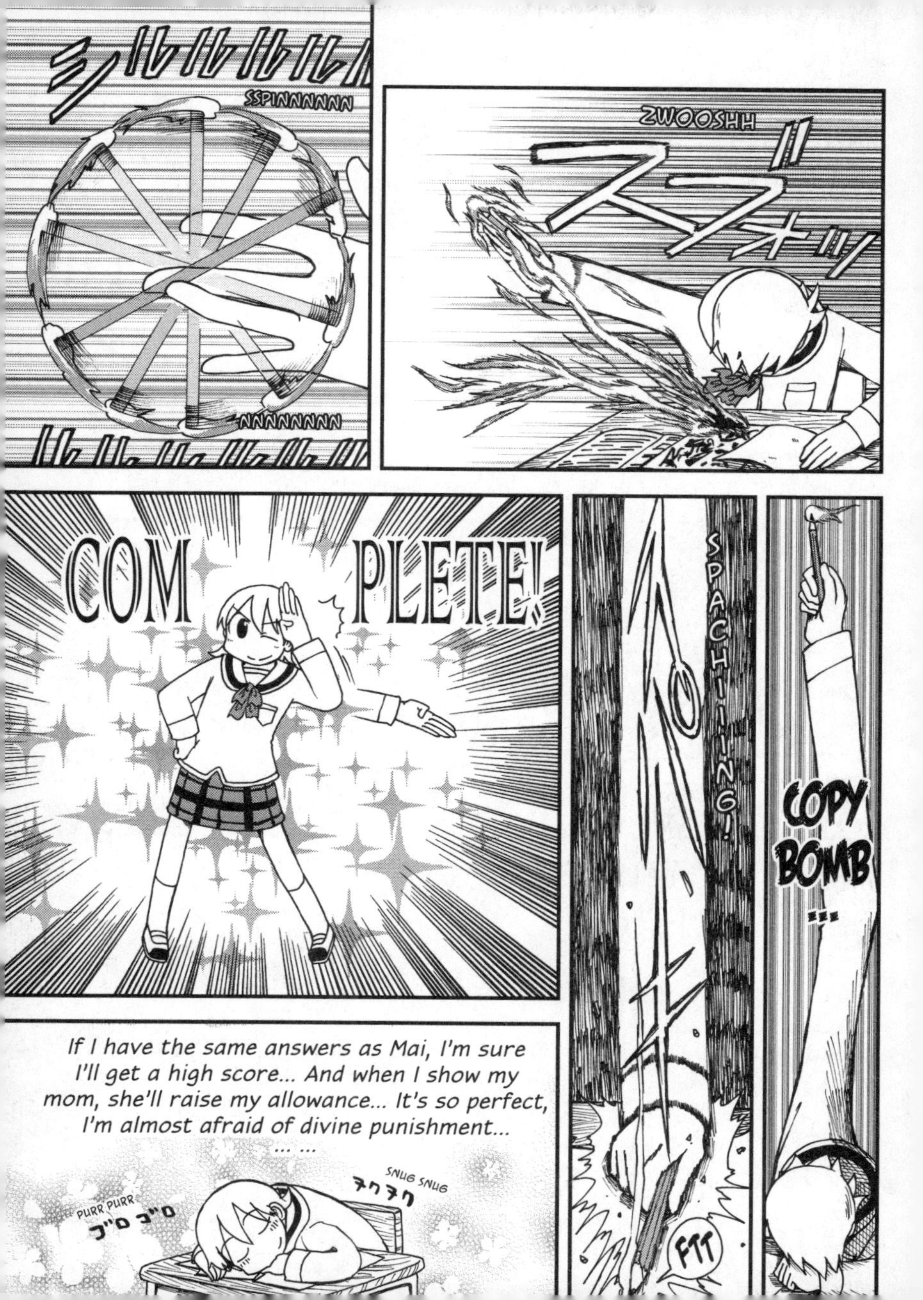
ZWOOSHH
SSPINNNNNNN
NNNNNNNN
COPY BOMB
SPACHIIING!
FTT
COMPLETE!
If I have the same answers as Mai, I'm sure I'll get a high score... And when I show my mom, she'll raise my allowance... It's so perfect, I'm almost afraid of divine punishment...
... ...
SNUG SNUG
ヌクヌク
PURR PURR
ゴロゴロ

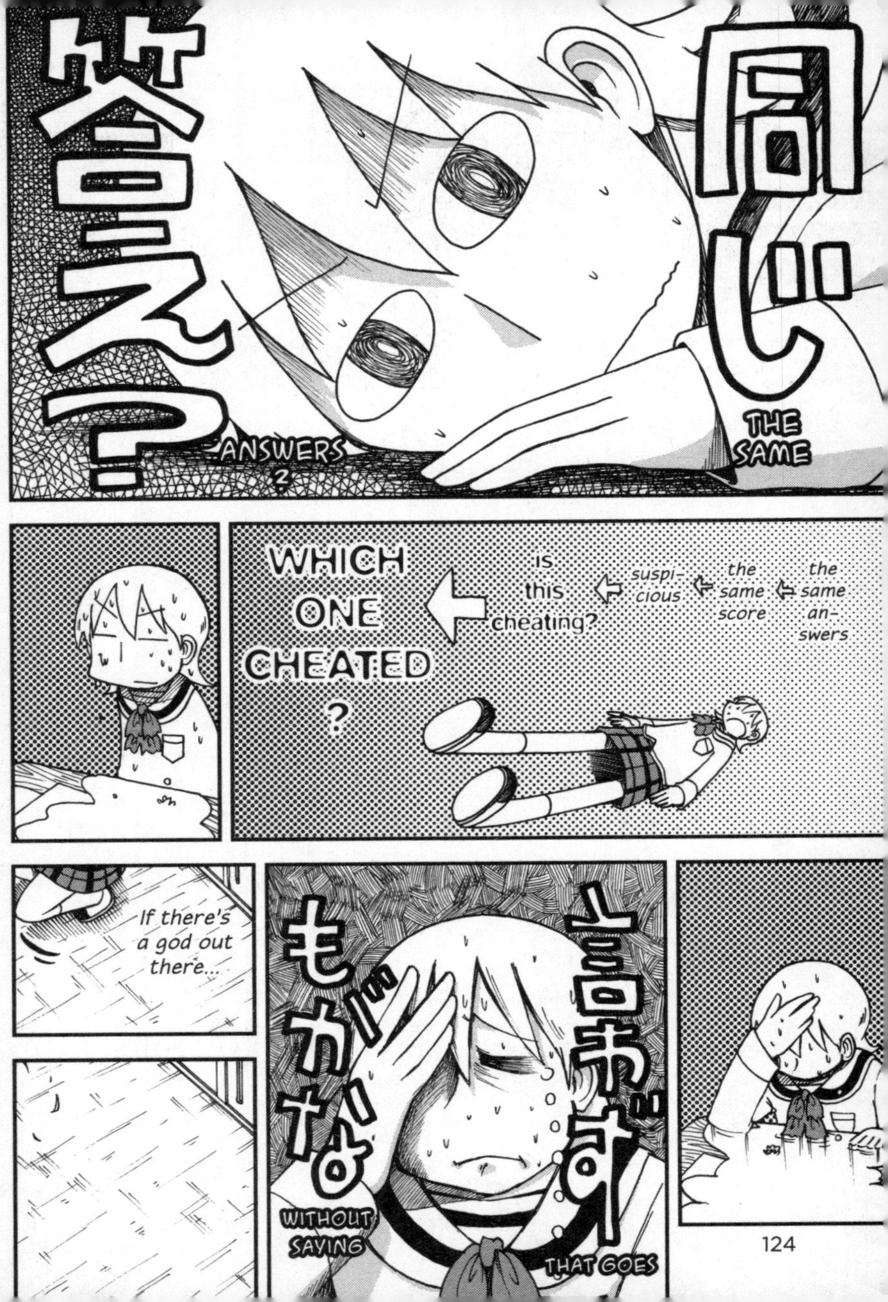

同じ
THE SAME
答え?
ANSWERS?
the same answers
the same score
suspicious
is this cheating?
WHICH ONE CHEATED?
言わずもがな
THAT GOES
WITHOUT SAYING
If there's a god out there...

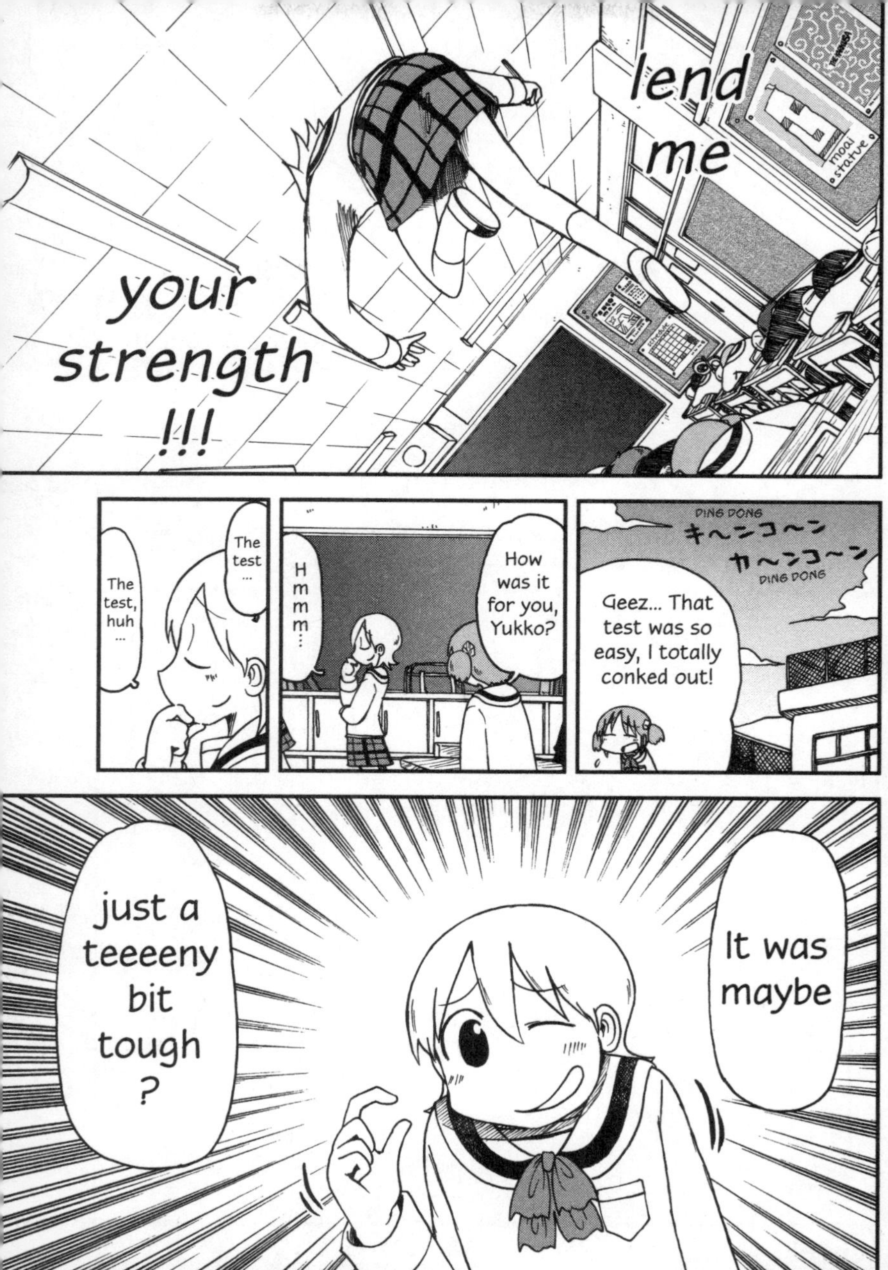
lend me
moai statue
your strength !!!
DING DONG
キ〜ンコ〜ン
カ〜ンコ〜ン
DING DONG
Geez... That test was so easy, I totally conked out!
How was it for you, Yukko?
Hmmm...
The test ...
The test, huh ...
It was maybe
just a teeeeny bit tough ?

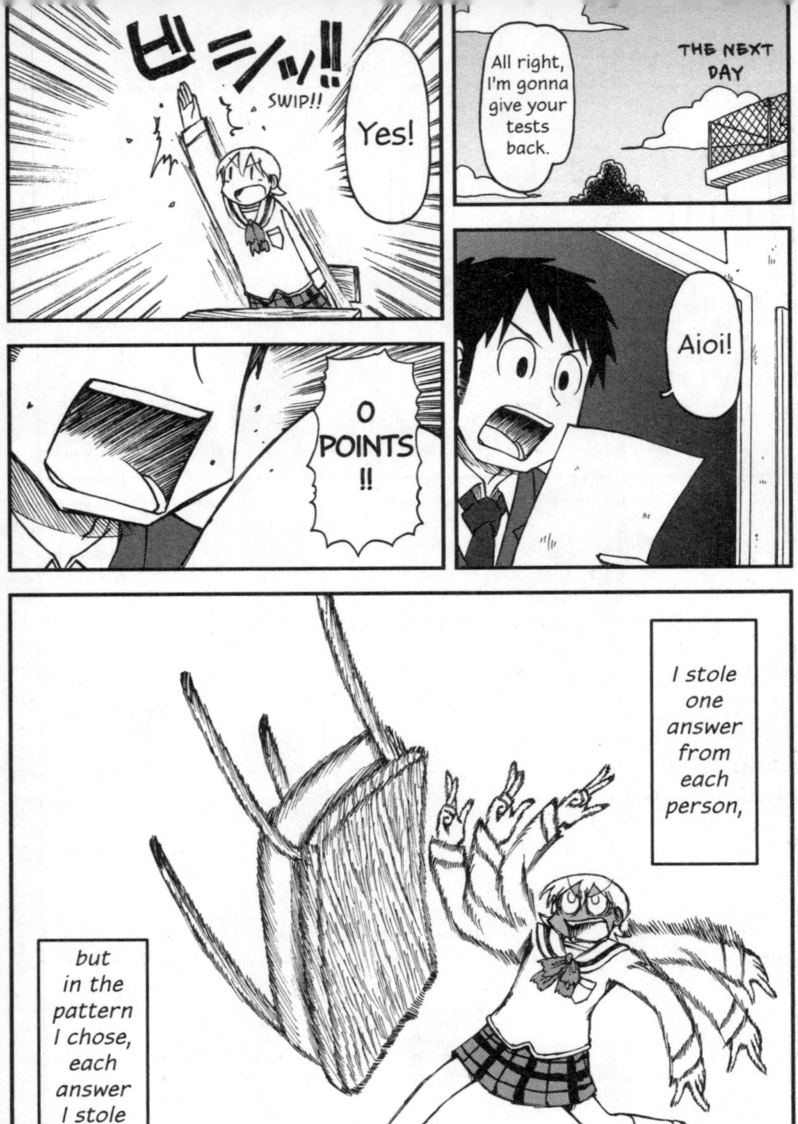
THE NEXT DAY
All right, I'm gonna give your tests back.
Yes!
ビシッ!!
SWIP!!
Aioi!
0 POINTS!!
I stole one answer from each person,
but in the pattern I chose, each answer I stole was wrong!!

chapter 188: end

chapter 189

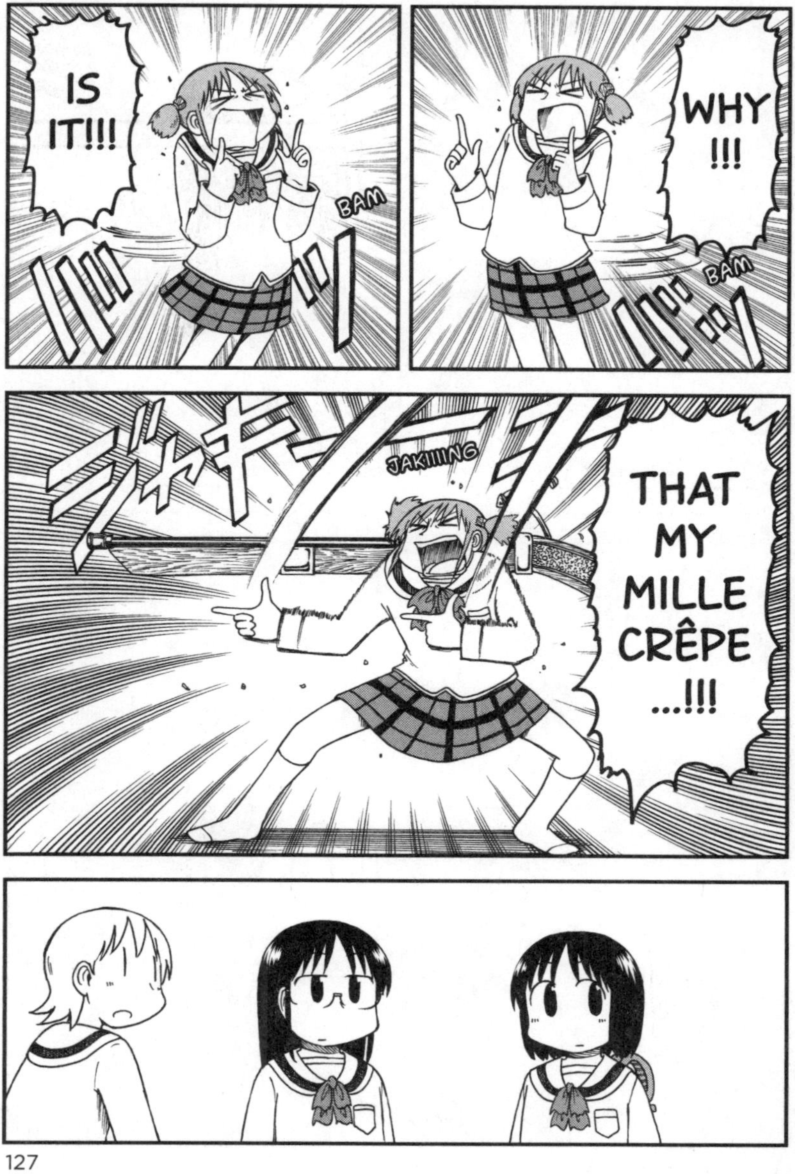
WHY !!!
BAM
IS IT!!!
BAM
ジャキーン
JAKIIIING
THAT MY MILLE CRÊPE ...!!!

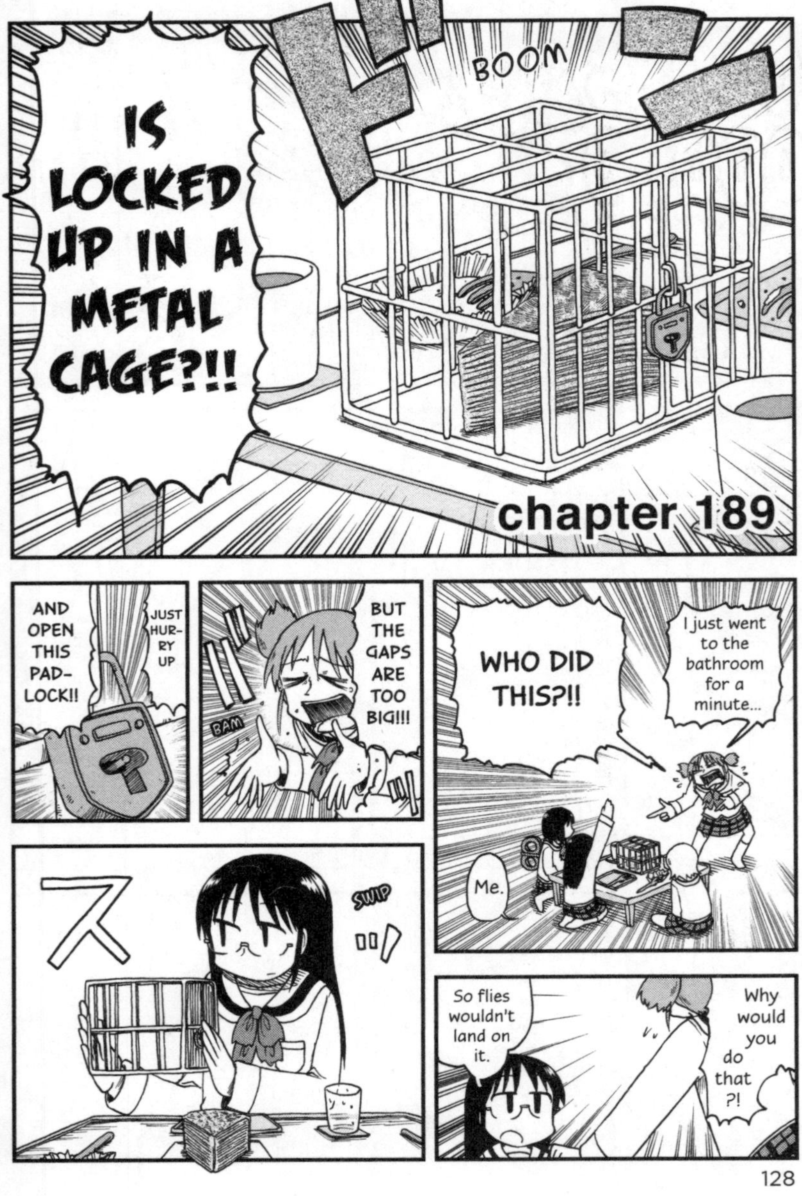

BOOM
IS LOCKED UP IN A METAL CAGE?!!
chapter 189
I just went to the bathroom for a minute...
WHO DID THIS?!!
Me.
Why would you do that?!
So flies wouldn't land on it.
BUT THE GAPS ARE TOO BIG!!!
BAM
JUST HURRY UP
AND OPEN THIS PAD-LOCK!!
ス
SWIP

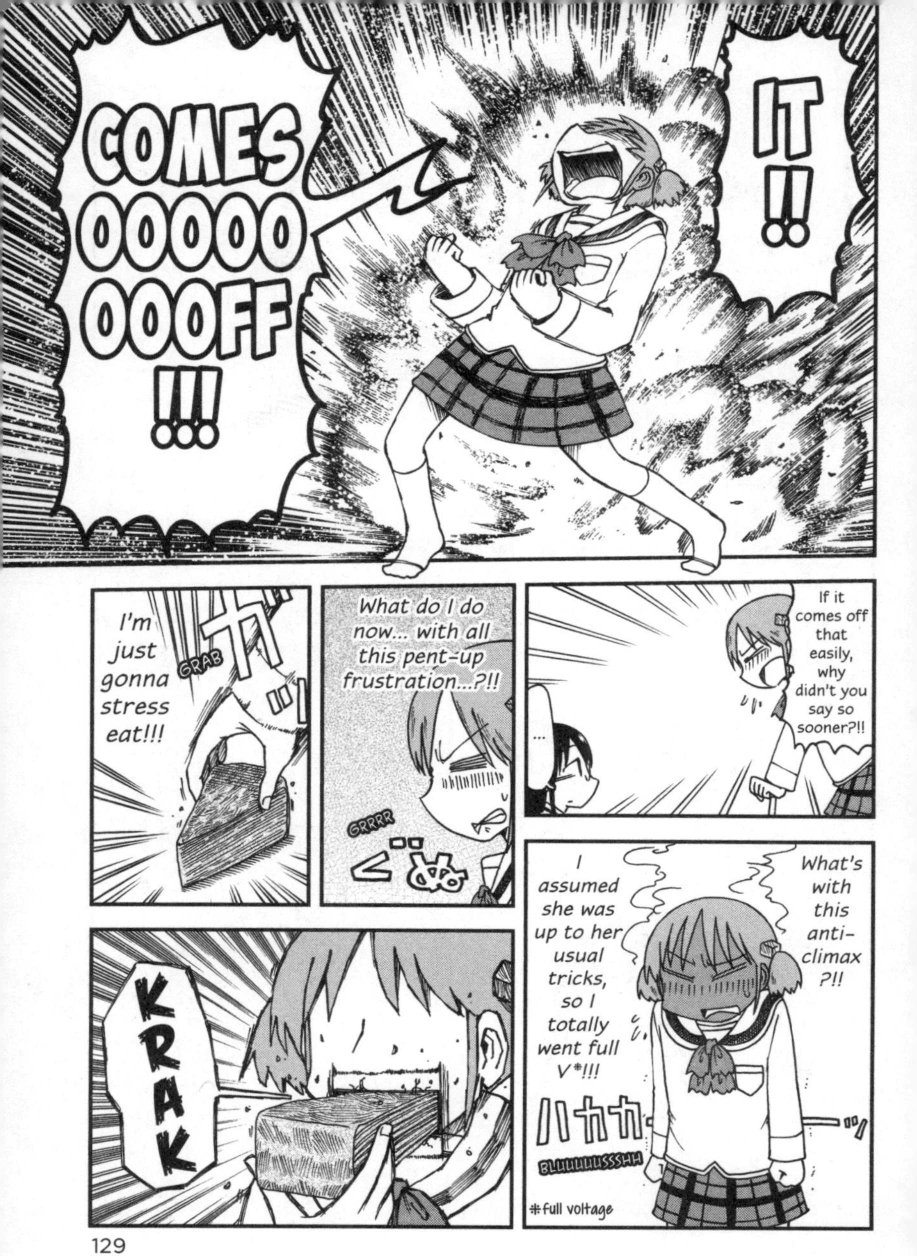
IT!!
COMES OOOOOOOOOFF!!!
If it comes off that easily, why didn't you say so sooner?!!
...
What do I do now... with all this pent-up frustration...?!!
GRRRR
I'm just gonna stress eat!!!
GRAB
What's with this anti-climax?!!
I assumed she was up to her usual tricks, so I totally went full V*!!!
BLUUUUUSSSHH
*full voltage
KRAK

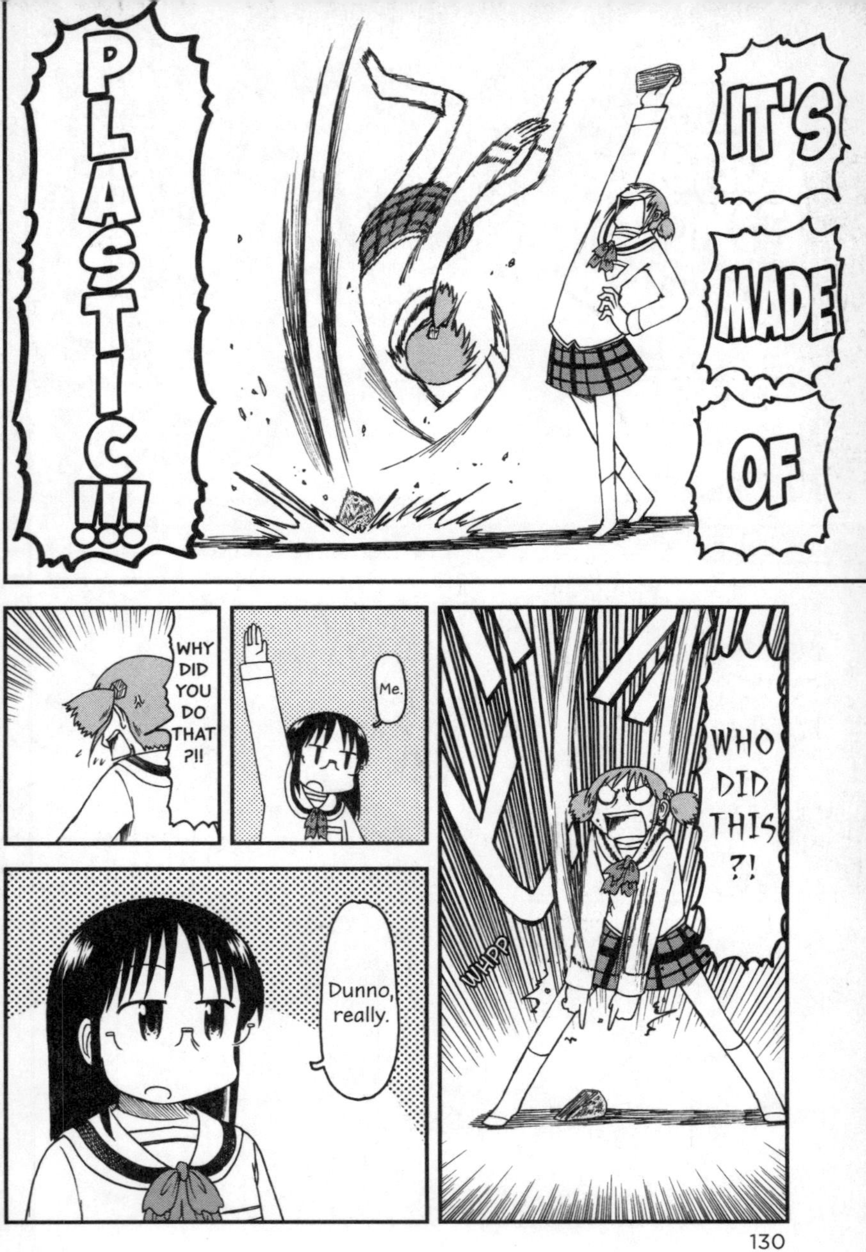

IT'S MADE OF
PLASTIC!!!
WHO DID THIS?!
WHPP
Me.
WHY DID YOU DO THAT?!!
Dunno, really.

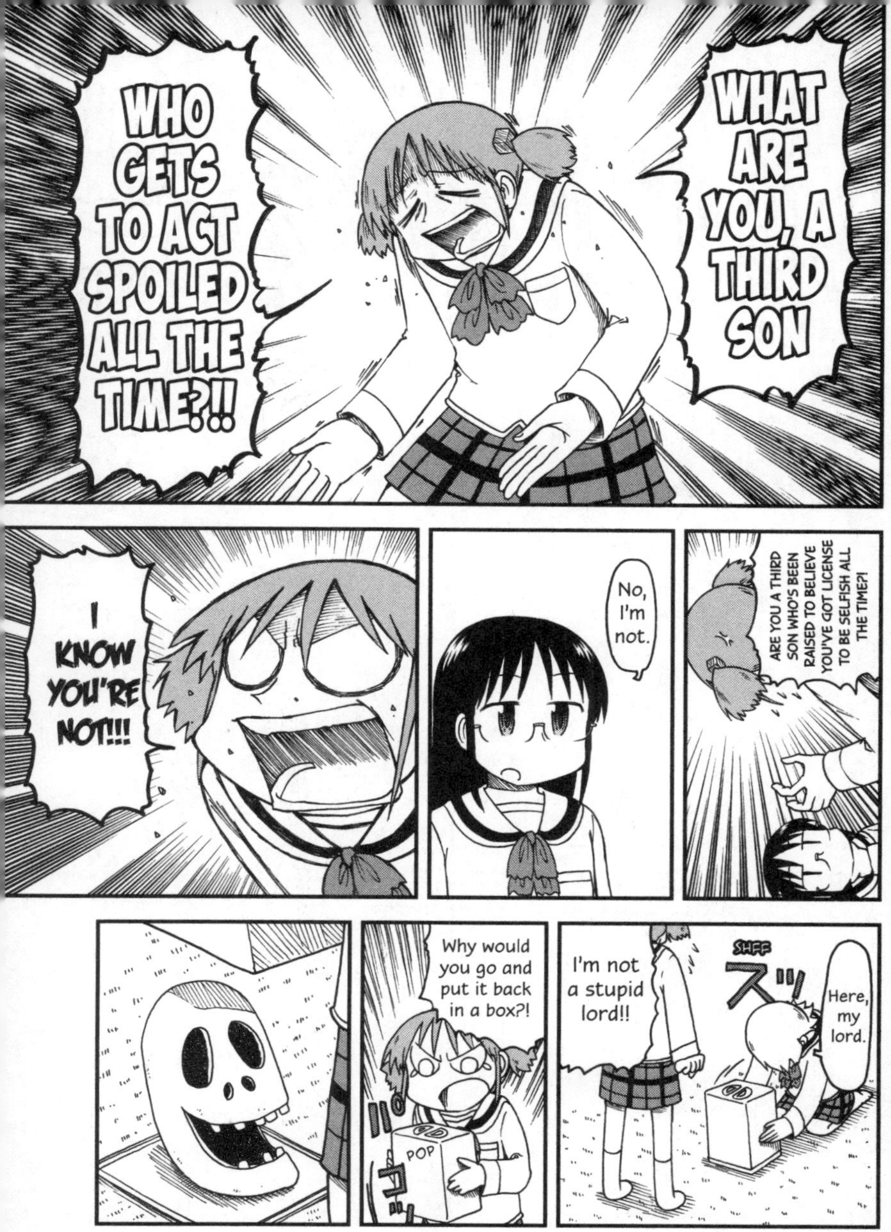
WHAT ARE YOU, A THIRD SON
WHO GETS TO ACT SPOILED ALL THE TIME?!!
ARE YOU A THIRD SON WHO'S BEEN RAISED TO BELIEVE YOU'VE GOT LICENSE TO BE SELFISH ALL THE TIME?!
No, I'm not.
I KNOW YOU'RE NOT!!!
SHFF
Here, my lord.
I'm not a stupid lord!!
Why would you go and put it back in a box?!
POP

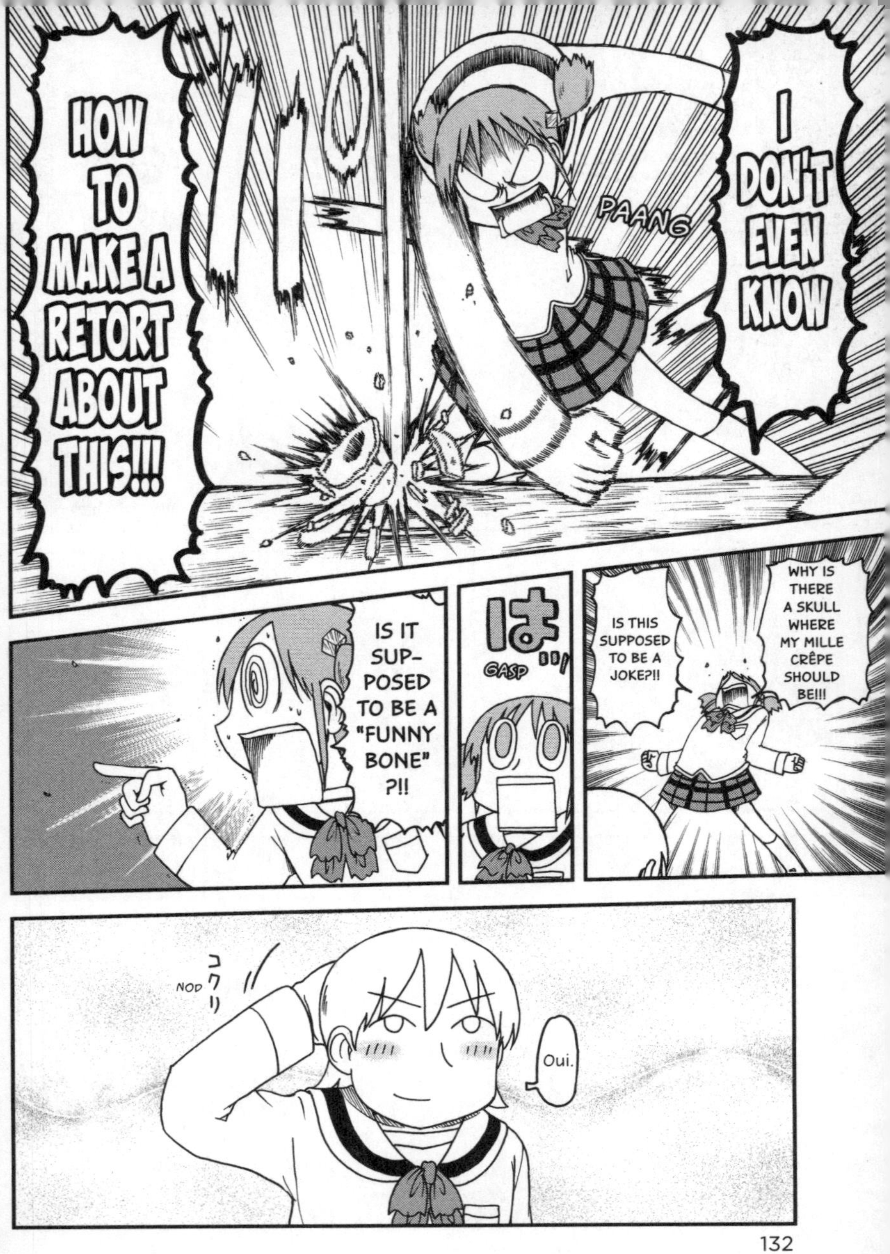
I DON'T EVEN KNOW
PAANG
HOW TO MAKE A RETORT ABOUT THIS!!!
WHY IS THERE A SKULL WHERE MY MILLE CRÊPE SHOULD BE!!!
IS THIS SUPPOSED TO BE A JOKE?!!
は
GASP
IS IT SUP-POSED TO BE A "FUNNY BONE"?!!
コクリ
NOD
Oui.

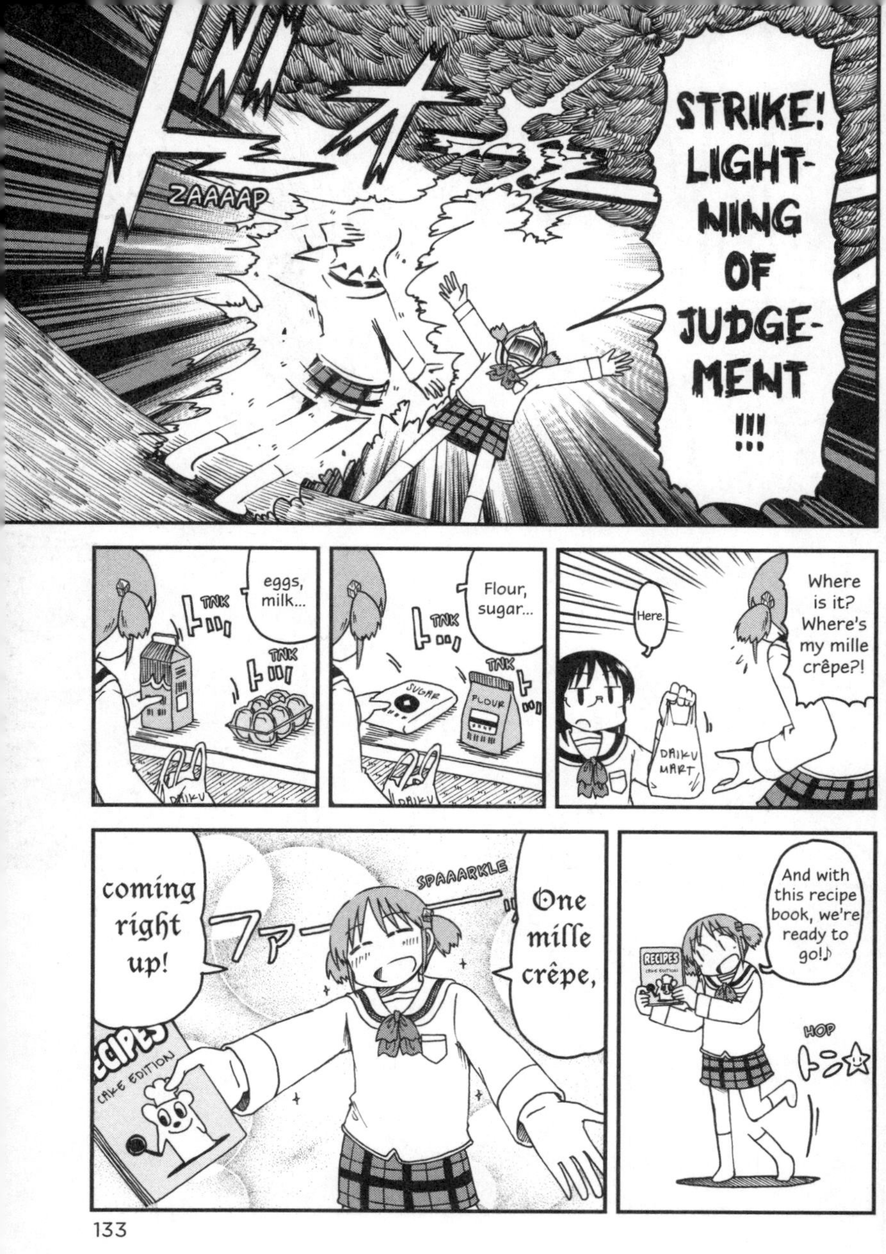
STRIKE! LIGHT-NING OF JUDGE-MENT !!!
ZAAAAP
Where is it? Where's my mille crêpe?!
Here.
DAIKU MART
Flour, sugar...
TNK
TNK
SUGAR
FLOUR
eggs, milk...
TNK
TNK
And with this recipe book, we're ready to go!♪
RECIPES
HOP
One mille crêpe,
coming right up!
SPAAARKLE
RECIPES
CAKE EDITION

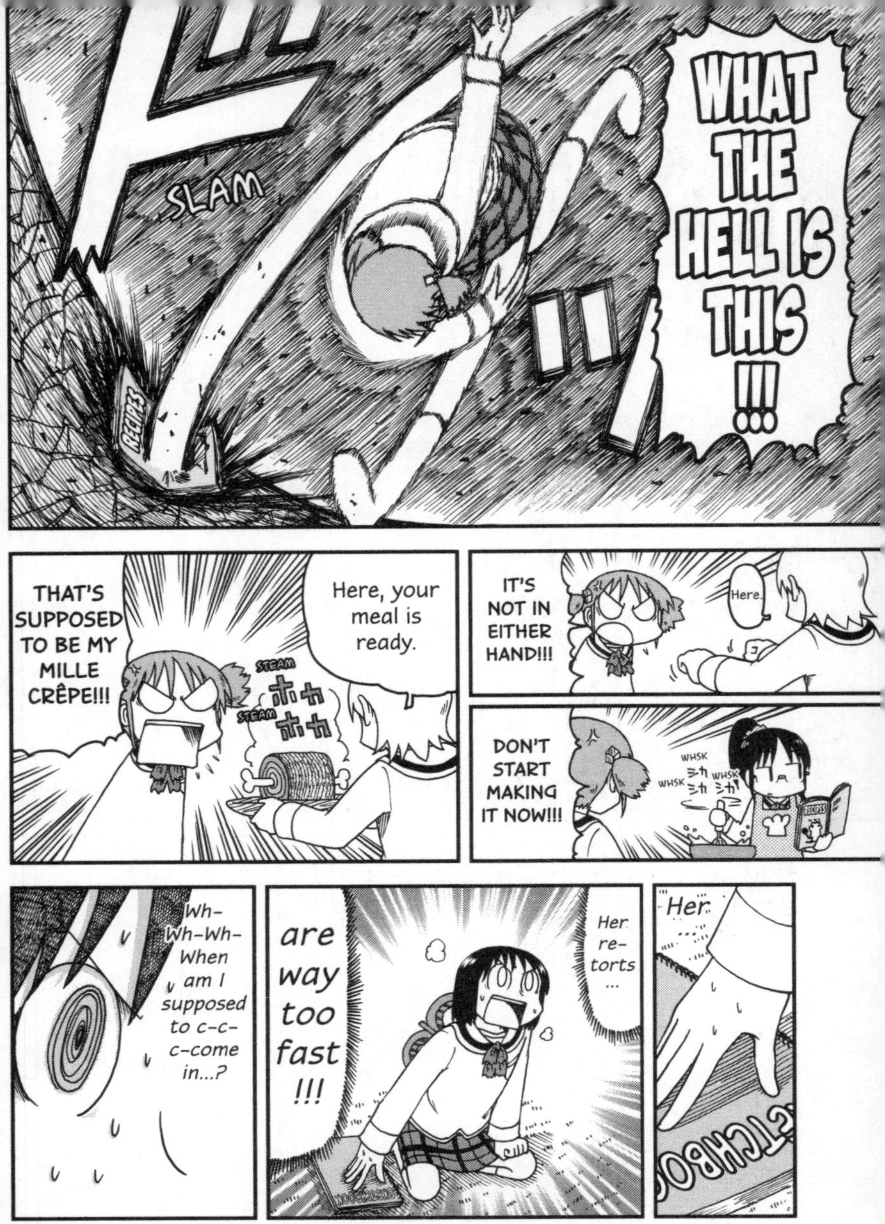
WHAT THE HELL IS THIS!!!
SLAM
RECIPES
Here.
IT'S NOT IN EITHER HAND!!!
DON'T START MAKING IT NOW!!!
WHSK WHSK WHSK
RECIPES
Here, your meal is ready.
THAT'S SUPPOSED TO BE MY MILLE CRÊPE!!!
STEAM
STEAM
Her...
Her retorts...
are way too fast!!!
Wh-Wh-Wh-When am I supposed to c-c-c-come in...?

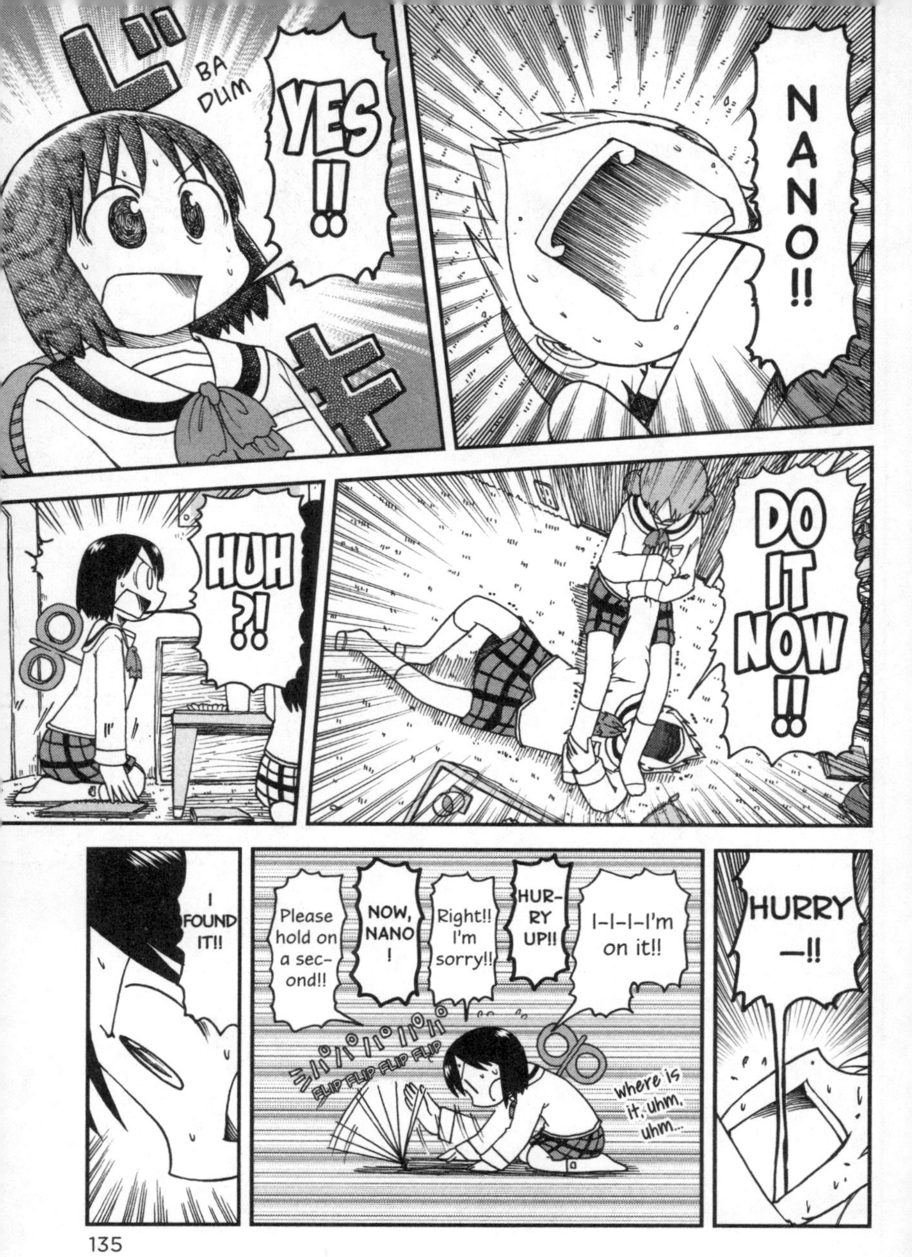
NANO!!
YES!!
BA DUM
DO IT NOW!!
HUH?!
HURRY—!!
I-I-I-I'm on it!!
HURRY UP!!
Right!! I'm sorry!!
NOW, NANO!
Please hold on a sec-ond!!
where is it, uhm, uhm...
FLIP FLIP FLIP FLIP
I FOUND IT!!

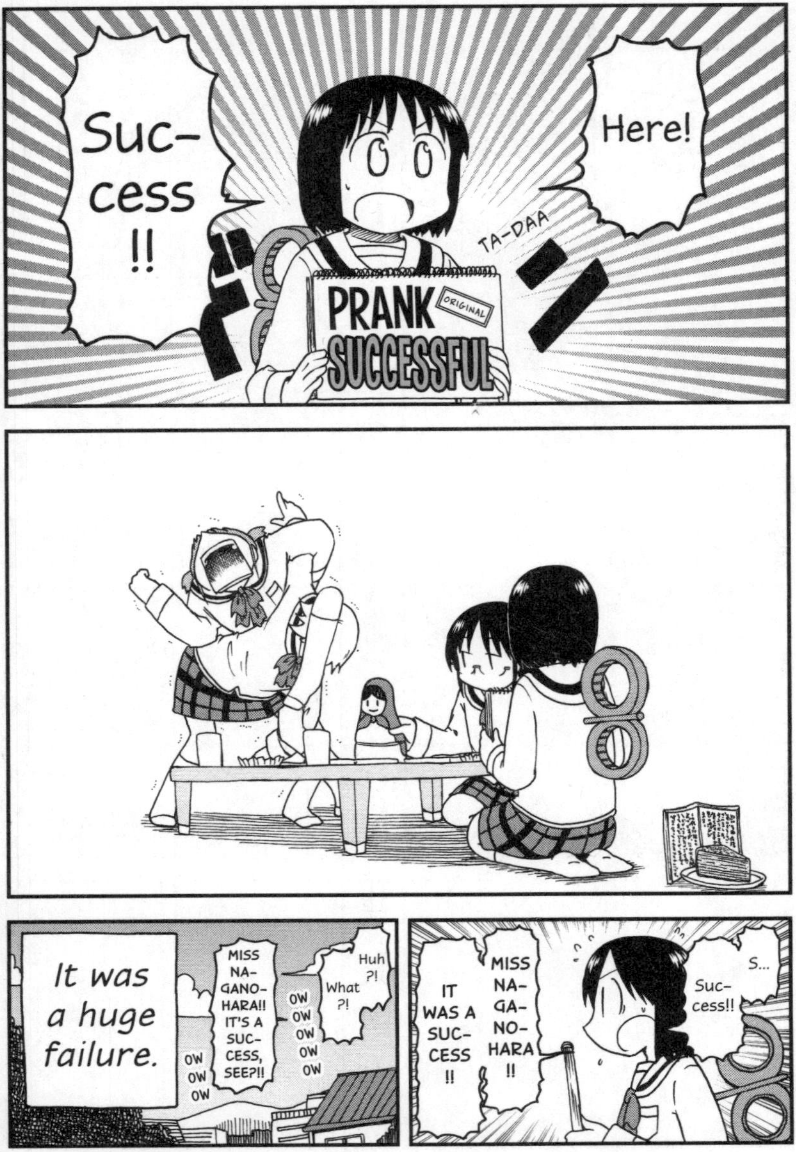
Here!
TA-DAA
PRANK
ORIGINAL
SUCCESSFUL
Suc-cess!!
S...
Suc-cess!!
MISS NA-GA-NO-HARA!!
IT WAS A SUC-CESS!!
Huh?!
What?!
MISS NA-GANO-HARA!! IT'S A SUC-CESS, SEE?!!
OW OW OW OW OW
OW OW OW
It was a huge failure.

chapter 189: end

big winner	flustered mama

title
chapter 190

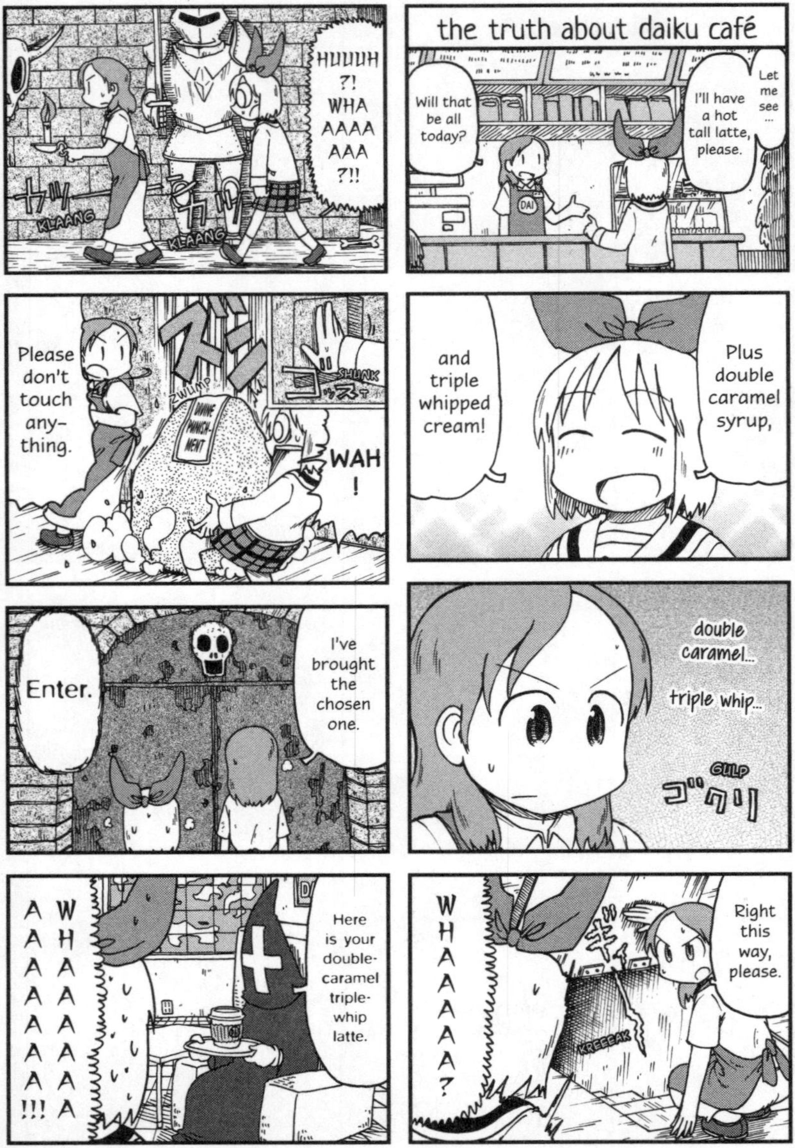

the truth about daiku café
Let me see ...
I'll have a hot tall latte, please.
Will that be all today?
Plus double caramel syrup,
and triple whipped cream!
double caramel...
triple whip...
GULP
ゴクリ
Right this way, please.
KREEEAK
WHAAAAAA?
HUUUH?! WHAAAAAAA?!!
KLAANG
KLAANG
WAH!
SHUNK
ZWUMP
DIVINE PUNISHMENT
Please don't touch anything.
I've brought the chosen one.
Enter.
Here is your double-caramel triple-whip latte.
WHAAAAAAAAA
AAAAAAAA!!!

82nd place prize

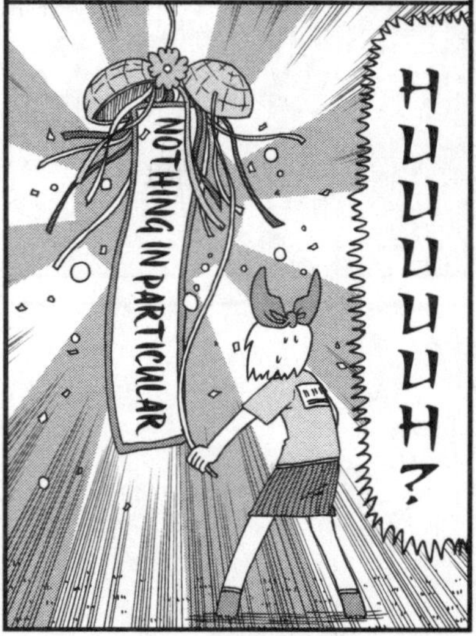
HUUUUUUH?
NOTHING IN PARTICULAR

will she break it? or will she be broken?

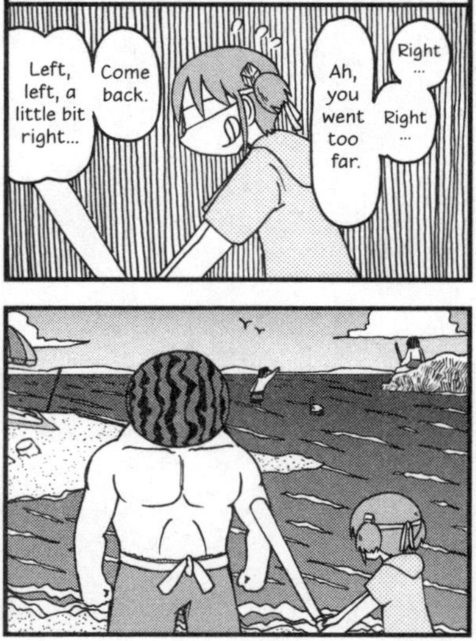
Right ...
Right ...
Ah, you went too far.
Come back.
Left, left, a little bit right...

flustered mama

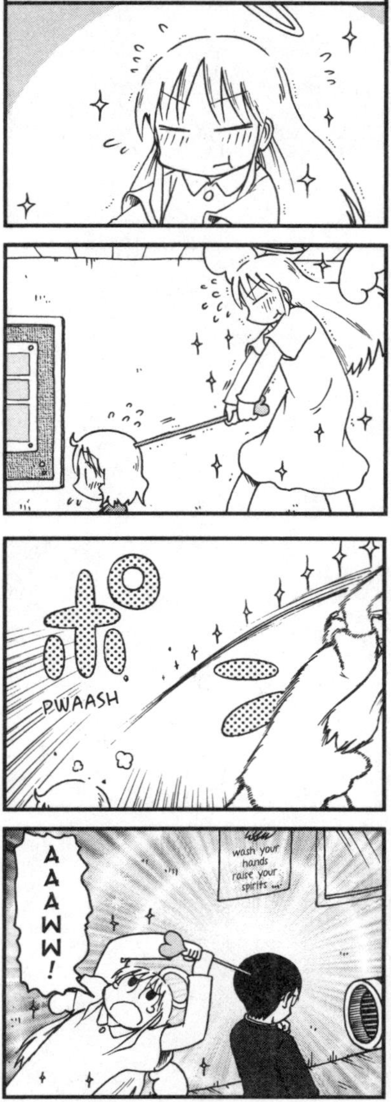
PWAASH
wash your hands raise your spirits ...
AAAAWW!

good morning

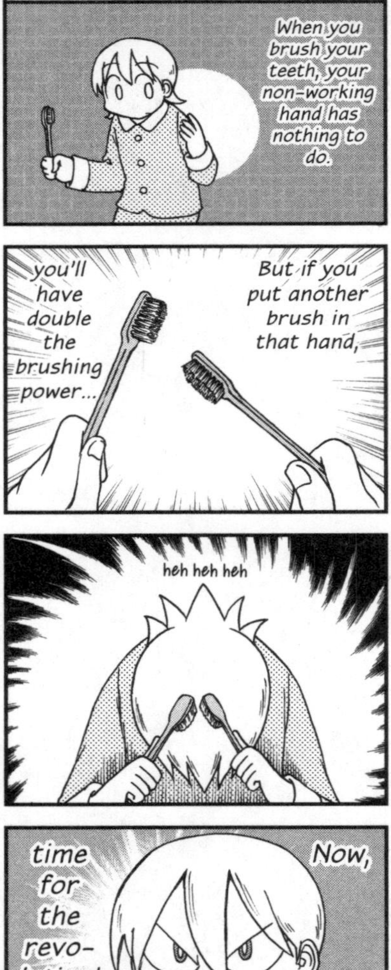

When you brush your teeth, your non-working hand has nothing to do.
But if you put another brush in that hand,
you'll have double the brushing power...
heh heh heh
Now,
time for the revolution!

principal vs. vice principal: ~with you~

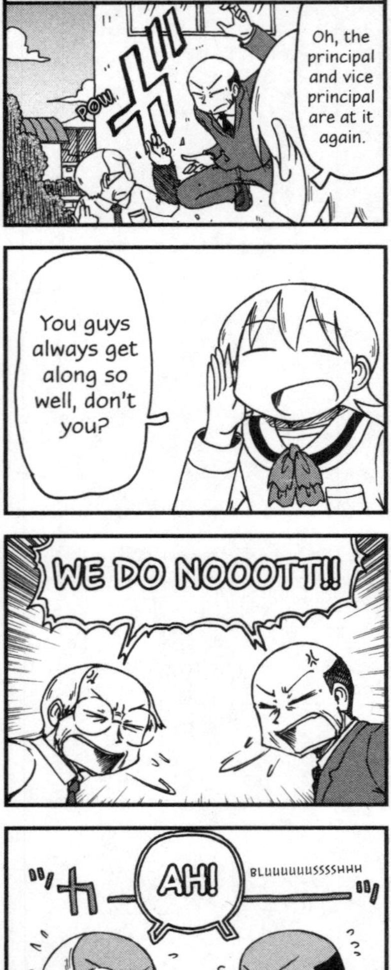

Oh, the principal and vice principal are at it again.
POW
You guys always get along so well, don't you?
WE DO NOOOTT!!
BLUUUUUUSSSSHHH
AH!
カ

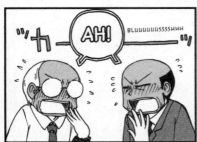

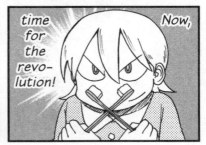

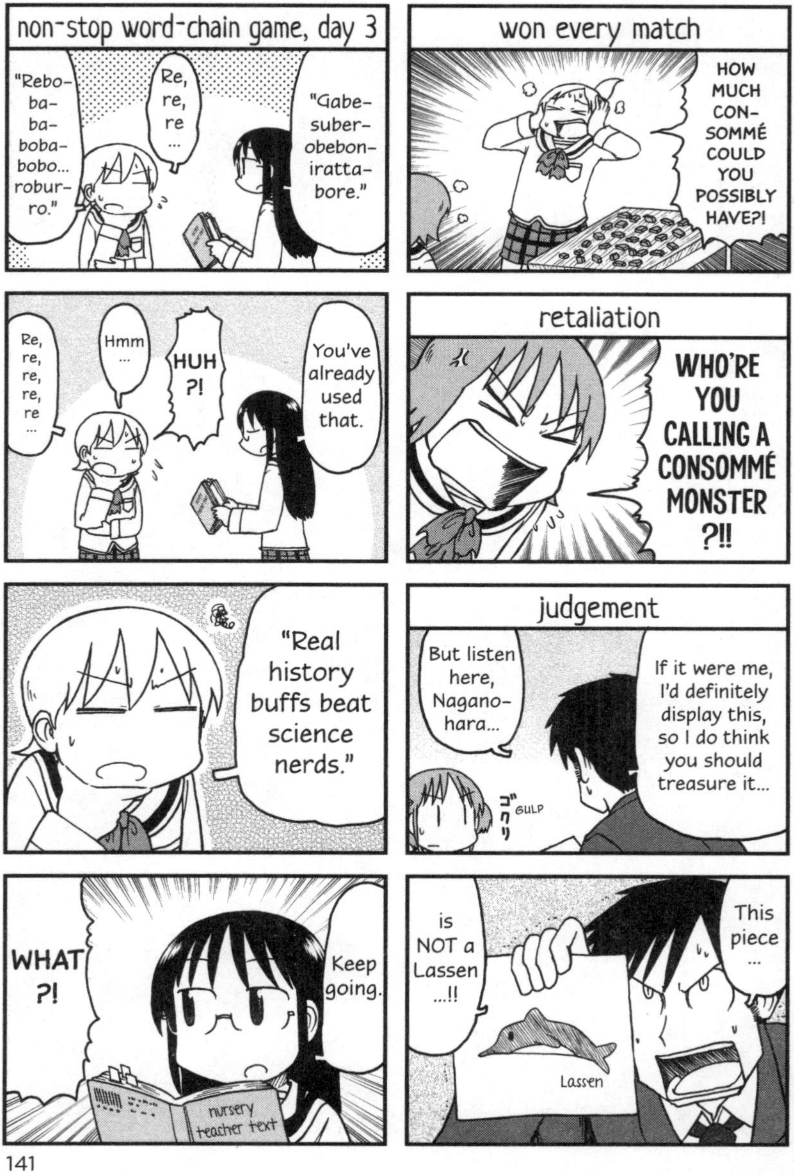
won every match
HOW MUCH CONSOMMÉ COULD YOU POSSIBLY HAVE?!
retaliation
WHO'RE YOU CALLING A CONSOMMÉ MONSTER ?!!
judgement
If it were me, I'd definitely display this, so I do think you should treasure it...
But listen here, Naganohara...
GULP
This piece ...
is NOT a Lassen ...!!
Lassen
non-stop word-chain game, day 3
"Gabe-suber-obebon-iratta-bore."
Re, re, re ...
"Rebo-ba-ba-boba-bobo...roburr-ro."
You've already used that.
HUH ?!
Hmm ...
Re, re, re, re, re ...
"Real history buffs beat science nerds."
Keep going.
WHAT ?!
nursery teacher text

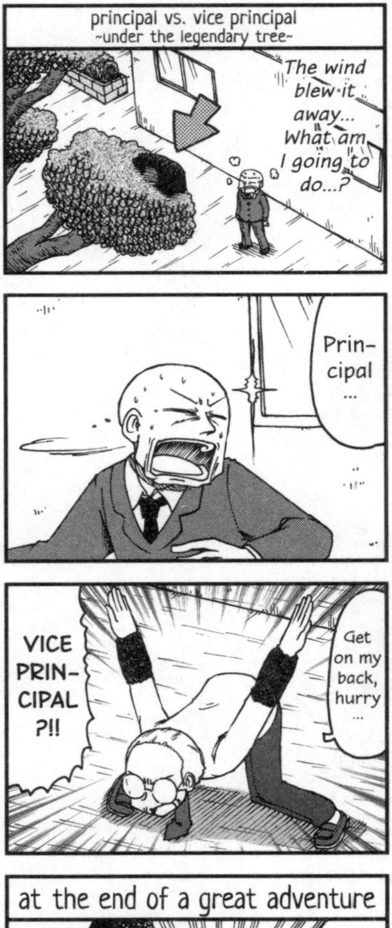
principal vs. vice principal
~under the legendary tree~
The wind blew it away... What am I going to do...?
Prin-cipal ...
Get on my back, hurry ...
VICE PRIN-CIPAL ?!!
at the end of a great adventure
If this is here, that must mean ...
WE'VE FINALLY GOTTEN BACK TO OUR OWN WORLD!!

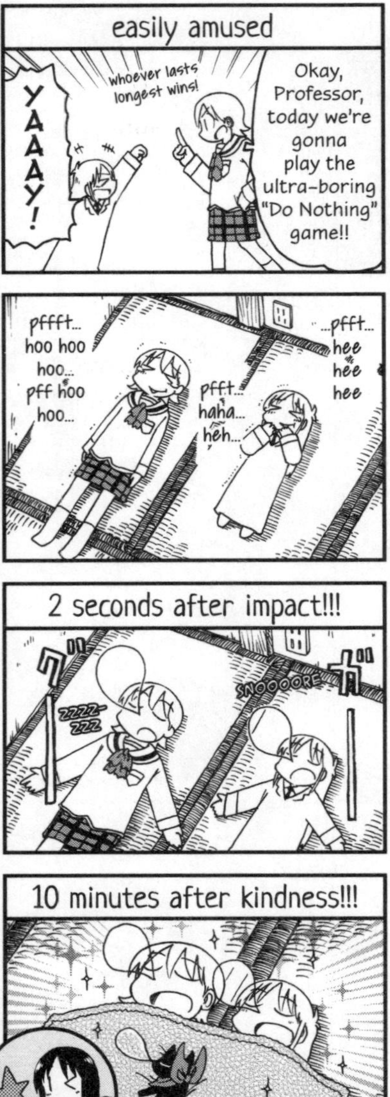
easily amused
Okay, Professor, today we're gonna play the ultra-boring "Do Nothing" game!!
whoever lasts longest wins!
YAAAY!
...pfft... hee hee hee
pfft... haha... heh...
pffft... hoo hoo hoo... pff hoo hoo...
2 seconds after impact!!!
SNOOOORE
zzzz-zzz
10 minutes after kindness!!!

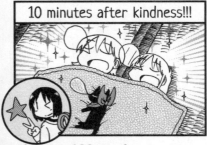

chapter 190: end

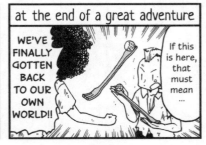

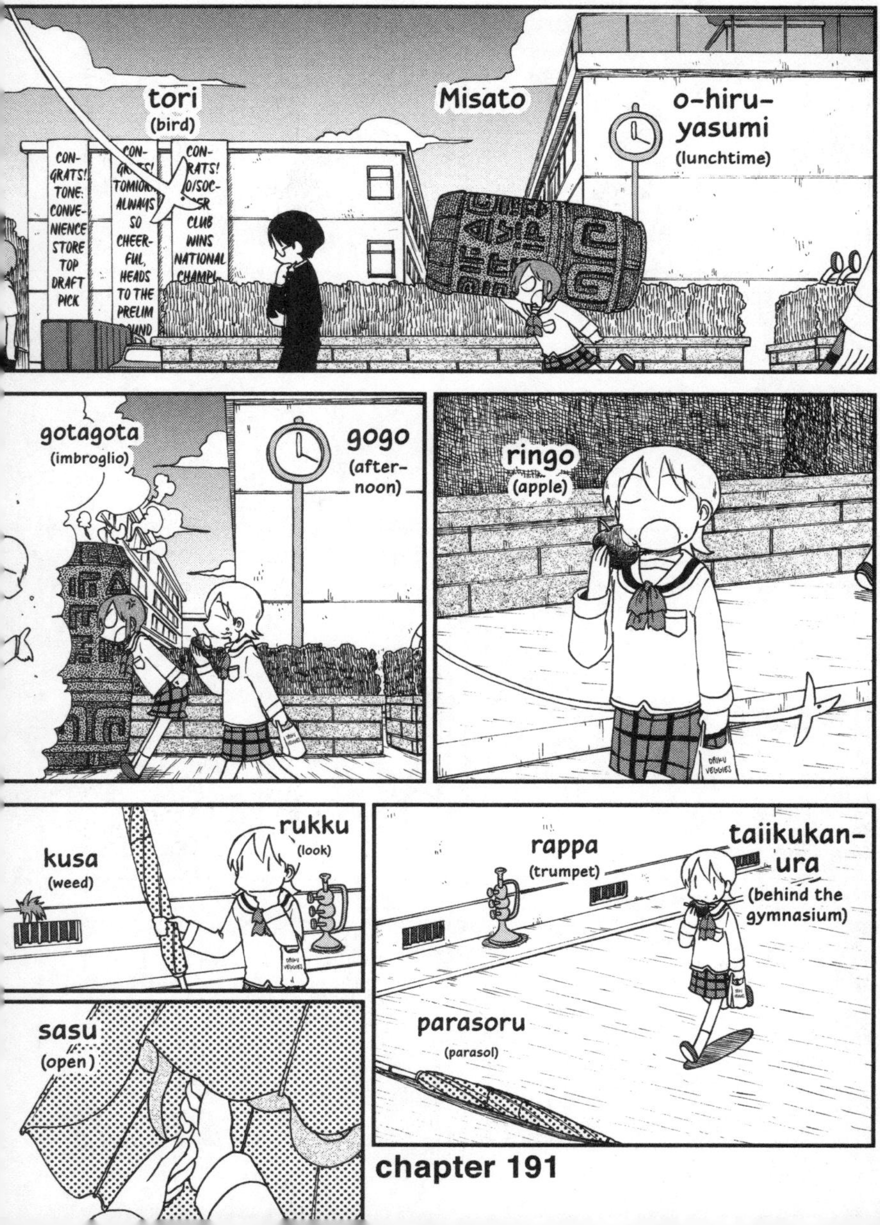
o-hiru-yasumi
(lunchtime)
Misato
tori
(bird)
CON- RATS! CLUB WINS NATIONAL
CON- TOMIOKA ALWAYS SO CHEERFUL, HEADS TO THE PRELIM
CON- GRATS! TONE: CONVENIENCE STORE TOP DRAFT PICK
ringo
(apple)
DAIKU VEGGIES
gogo
(afternoon)
gotagota
(imbroglio)
taiikukan-ura
(behind the gymnasium)
rappa
(trumpet)
parasoru
(parasol)
rukku
(look)
kusa
(weed)
sasu
(open)

chapter 191

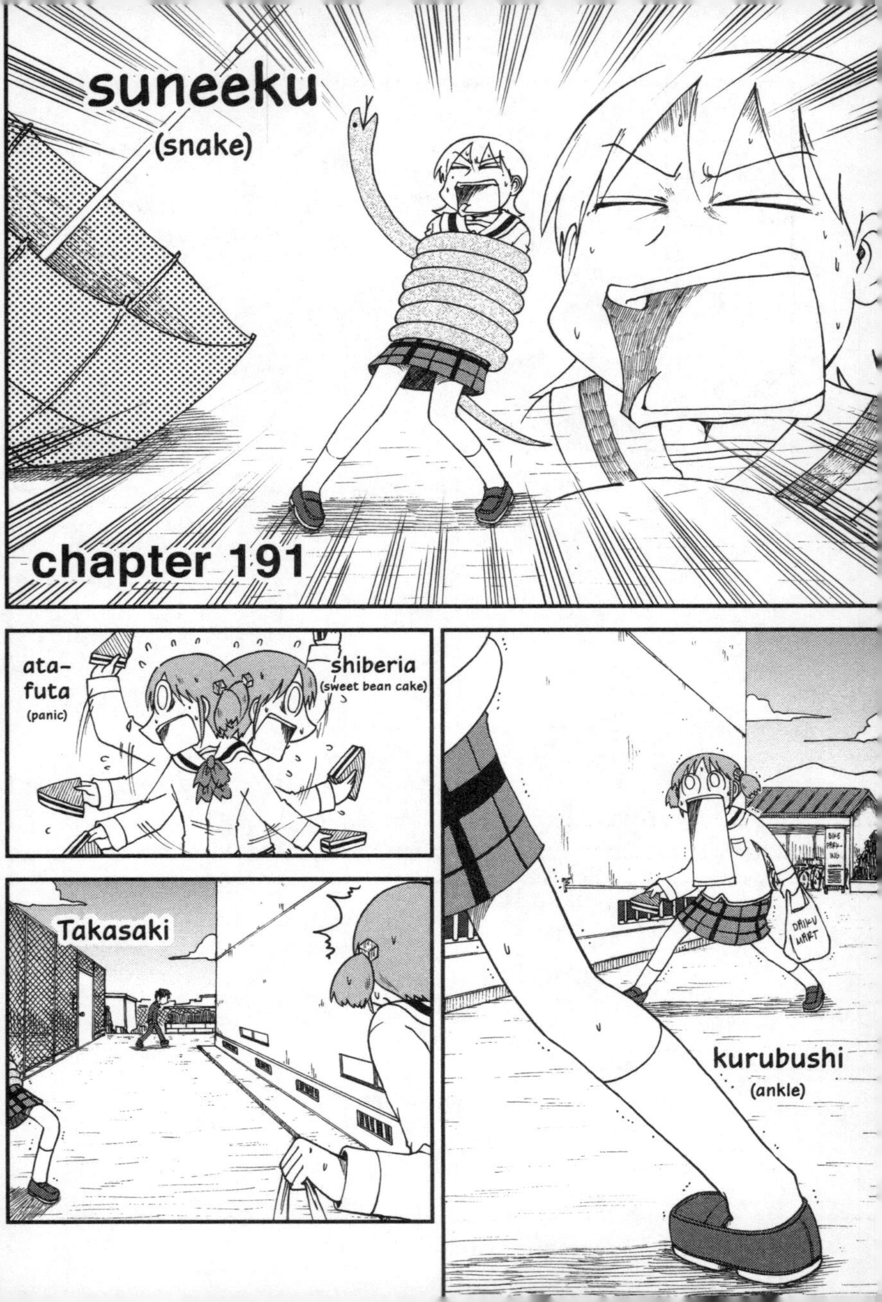
suneeku
(snake)
chapter 191
DAIKU MART
kurubushi
(ankle)
shiberia
(sweet bean cake)
ata-futa
(panic)
Takasaki

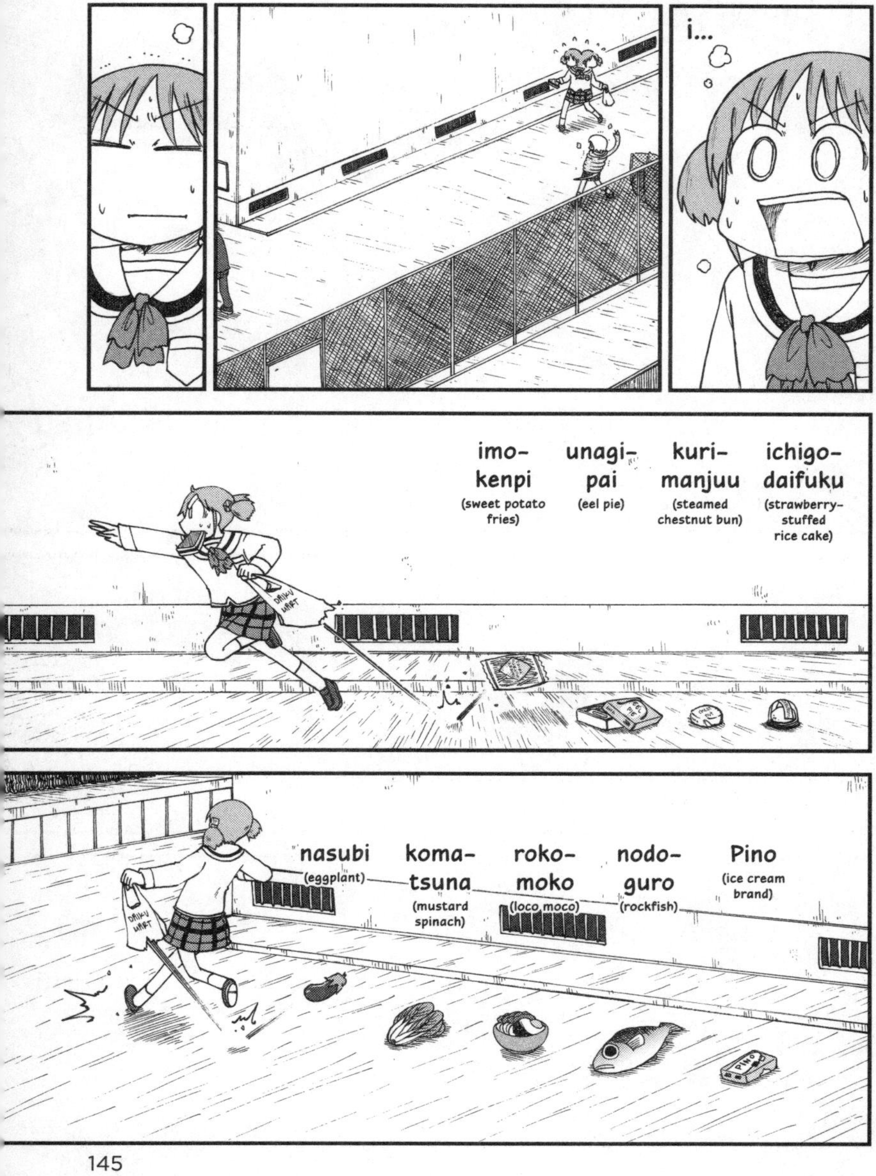
i...
imo-kenpi
(sweet potato fries)
unagi-pai
(eel pie)
kuri-manjuu
(steamed chestnut bun)
ichigo-daifuku
(strawberry-stuffed rice cake)
DAIKU MART
nasubi
(eggplant)
koma-tsuna
(mustard spinach)
roko-moko
(loco moco)
nodo-guro
(rockfish)
Pino
(ice cream brand)
PINO

bihe (snake)

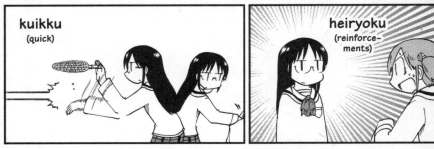

kuikku (quick)

heiryoku (reinforce-ments)

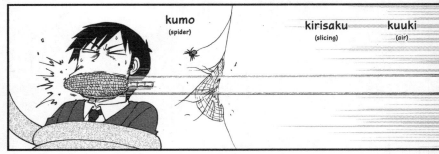

kumo (spider)

kirisaku (slicing)

kuuki (air)

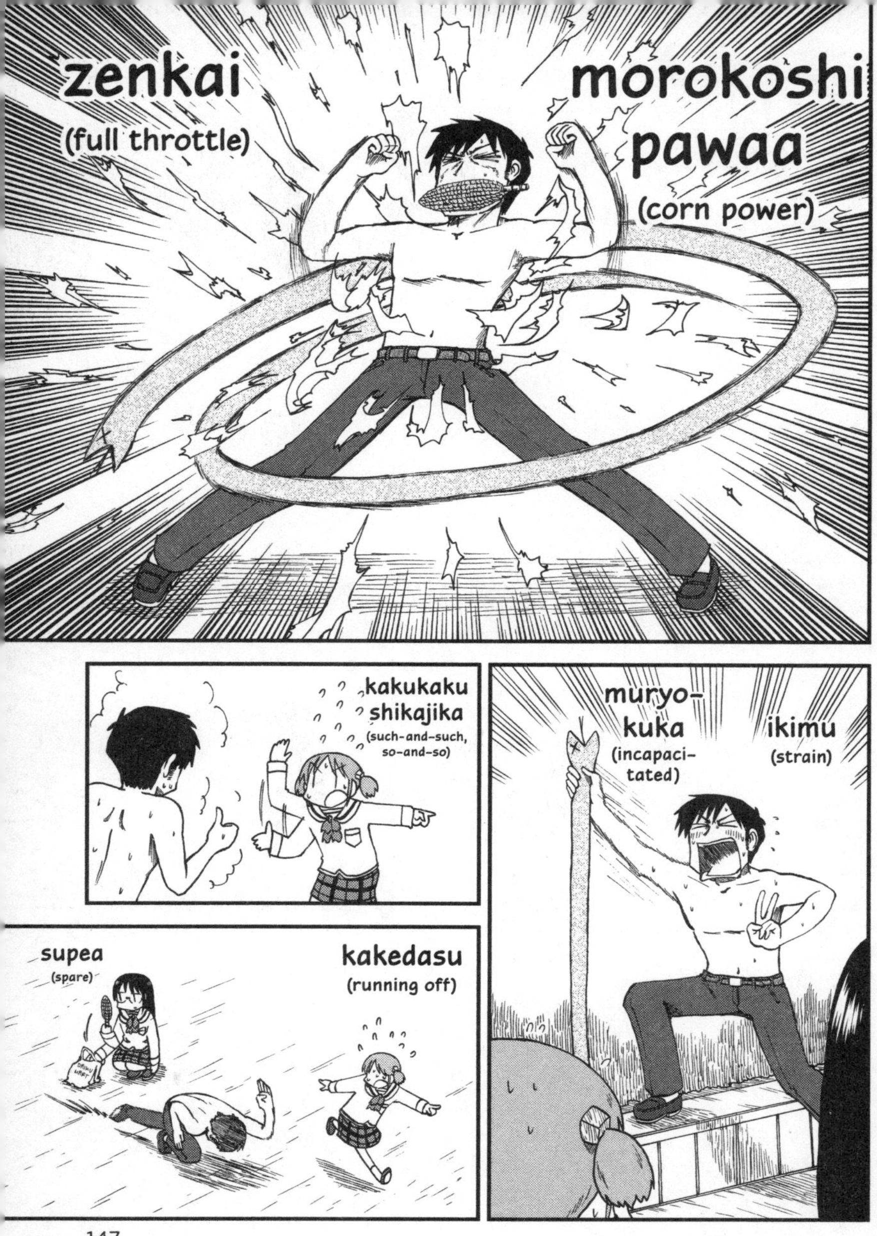
morokoshi pawaa
(corn power)
zenkai
(full throttle)
ikimu
(strain)
muryo-kuka
(incapaci-tated)
kakukaku shikajika
(such-and-such, so-and-so)
kakedasu
(running off)
supea
(spare)

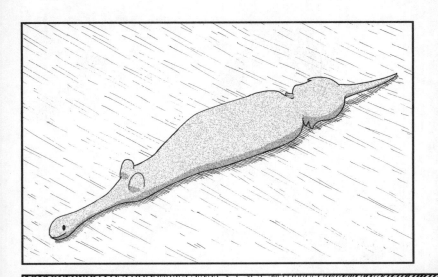

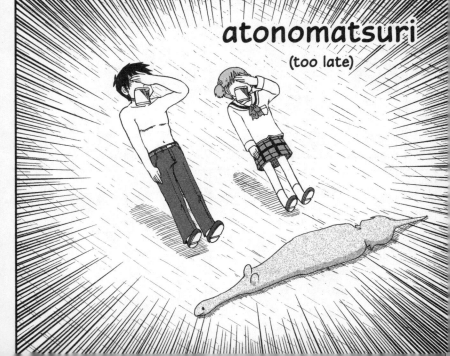

atonomatsuri
(too late)

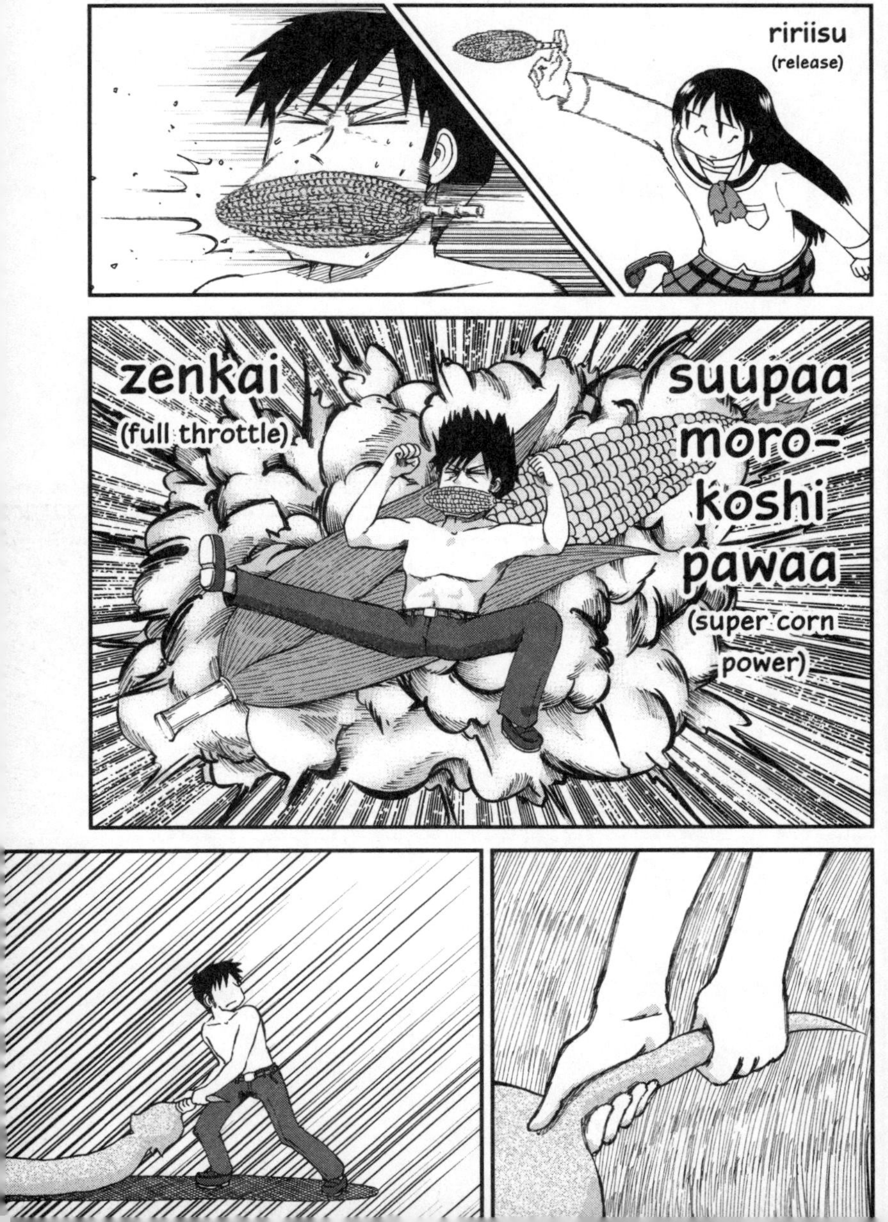
ririisu
(release)
suupaa moro-koshi pawaa
(super corn power)
zenkai
(full throttle)

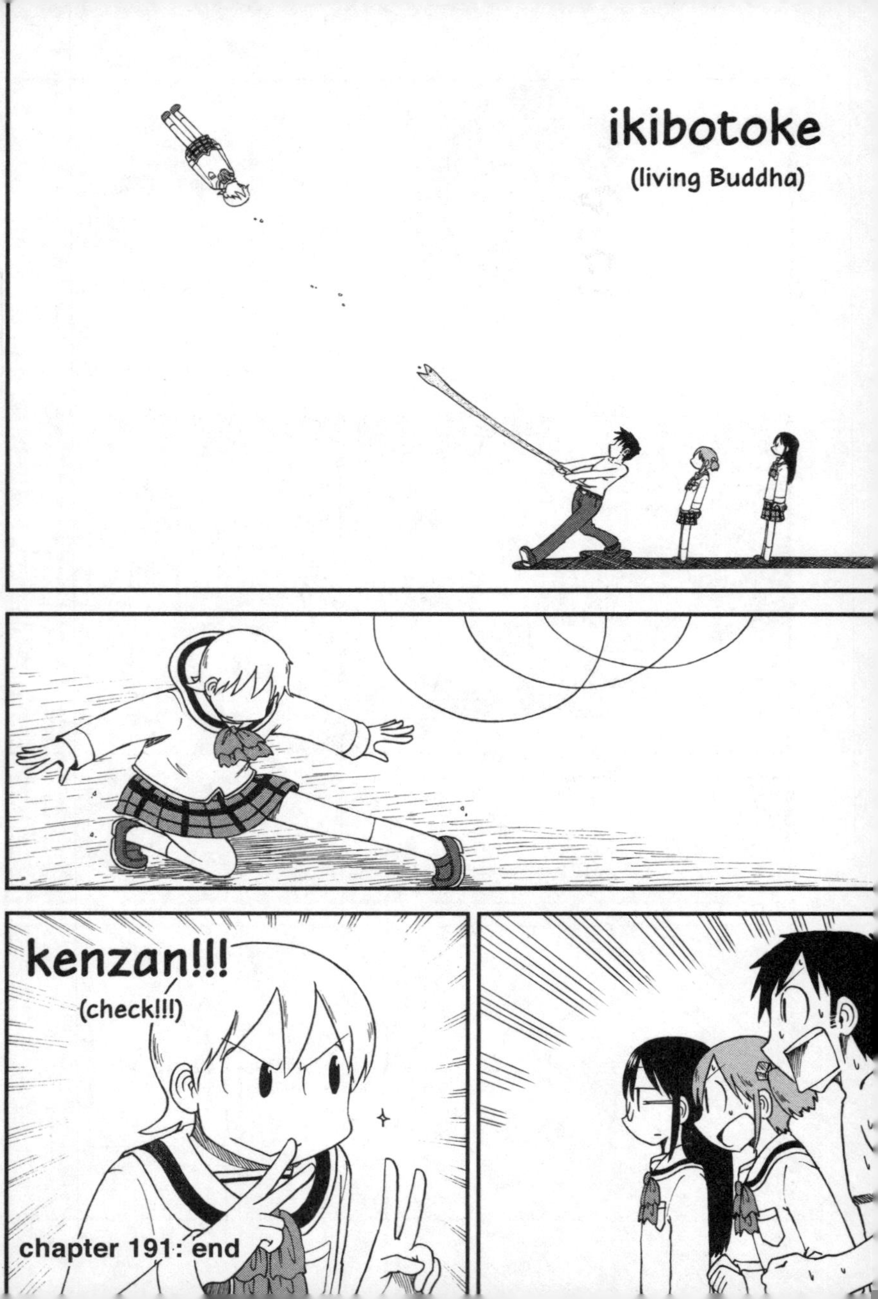
ikibotoke
(living Buddha)
kenzan!!!
(check!!!)
chapter 191: end

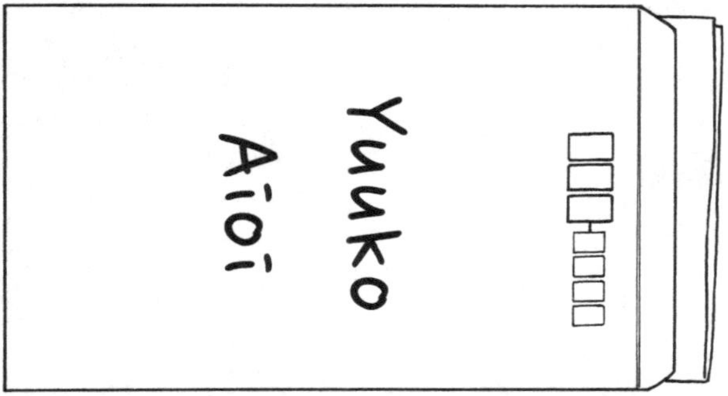
Yuuko Aioi

chapter 192

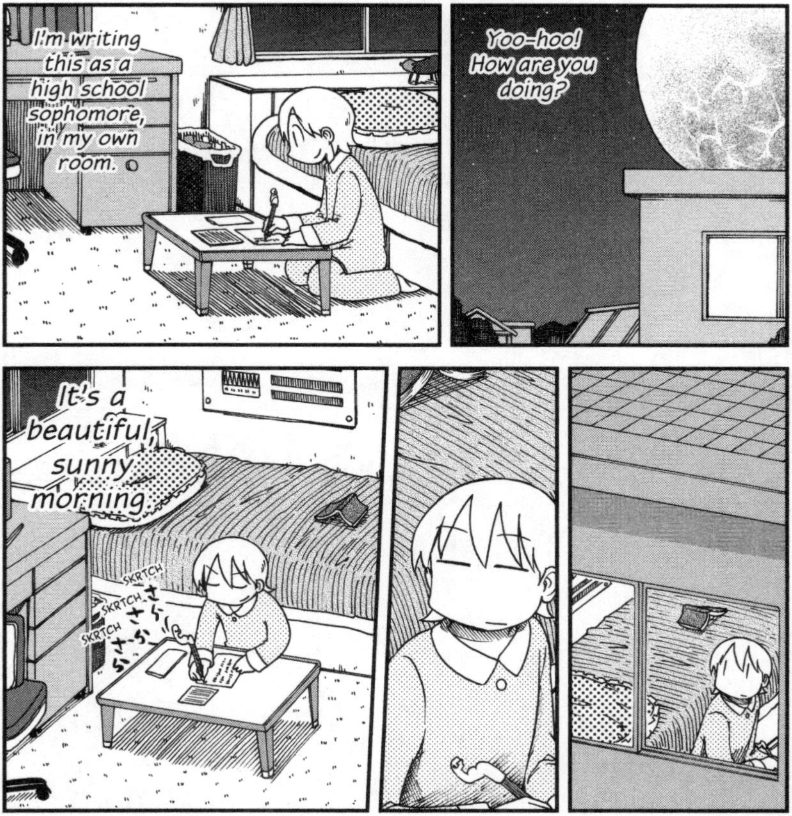
Yoo-hoo! How are you doing?
I'm writing this as a high school sophomore, in my own room.
It's a beautiful, sunny morning.
SKRTCH
SKRTCH
SKRTCH

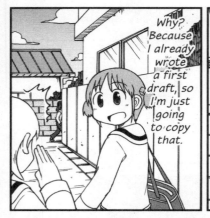

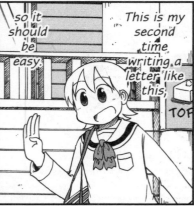

This is my second time writing a letter like this,
so it should be easy.
Why? Because I already wrote a first draft, so I'm just going to copy that.
Have you found a dream yet?
Are you working hard to make that a reality?
Yuuko Aioi
Have you grown into a proper adult and such?
HOUSE
Is everyone else doing well?

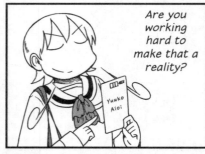

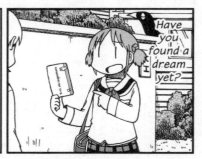

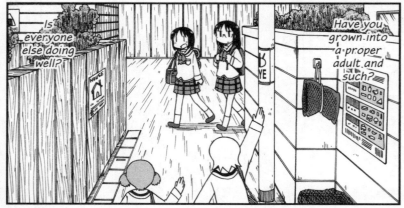

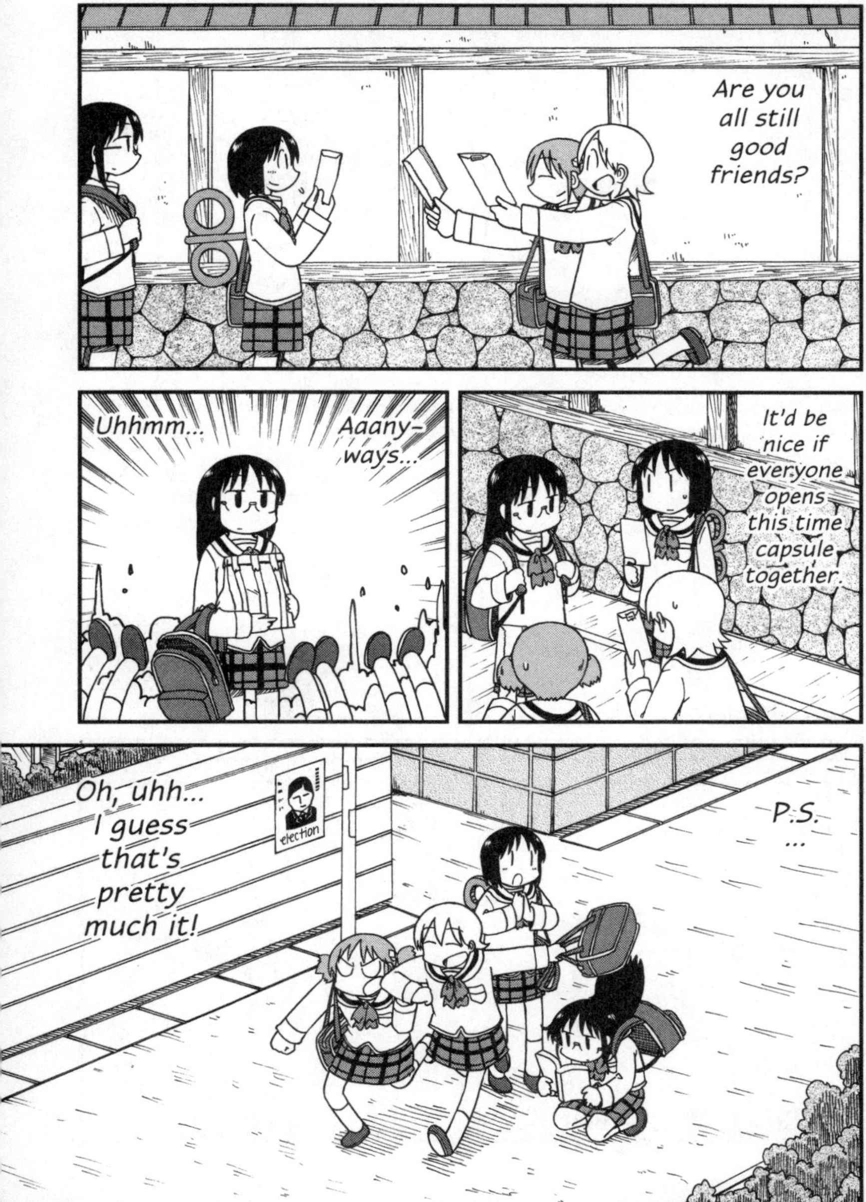
Are you all still good friends?
It'd be nice if everyone opens this time capsule together.
Aaany-ways...
Uhhmm...
P.S. ...
election
Oh, uhh... I guess that's pretty much it!

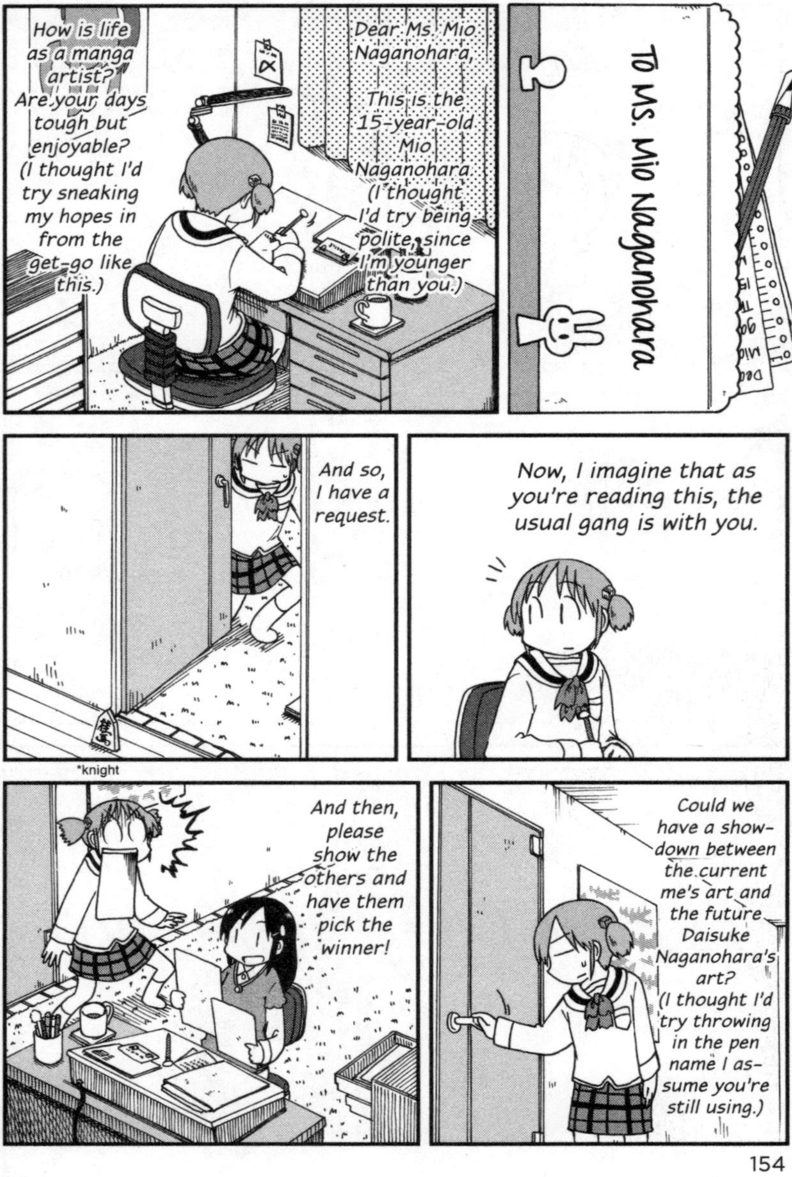
To Ms. Mio Naganohara
Dear Ms. Mio Naganohara,
This is the 15-year-old Mio Naganohara. (I thought I'd try being polite, since I'm younger than you.)
How is life as a manga artist? Are your days tough but enjoyable? (I thought I'd try sneaking my hopes in from the get-go like this.)
Now, I imagine that as you're reading this, the usual gang is with you.
And so, I have a request.
Could we have a show-down between the current me's art and the future Daisuke Naganohara's art? (I thought I'd try throwing in the pen name I as-sume you're still using.)
And then, please show the others and have them pick the winner!

*knight

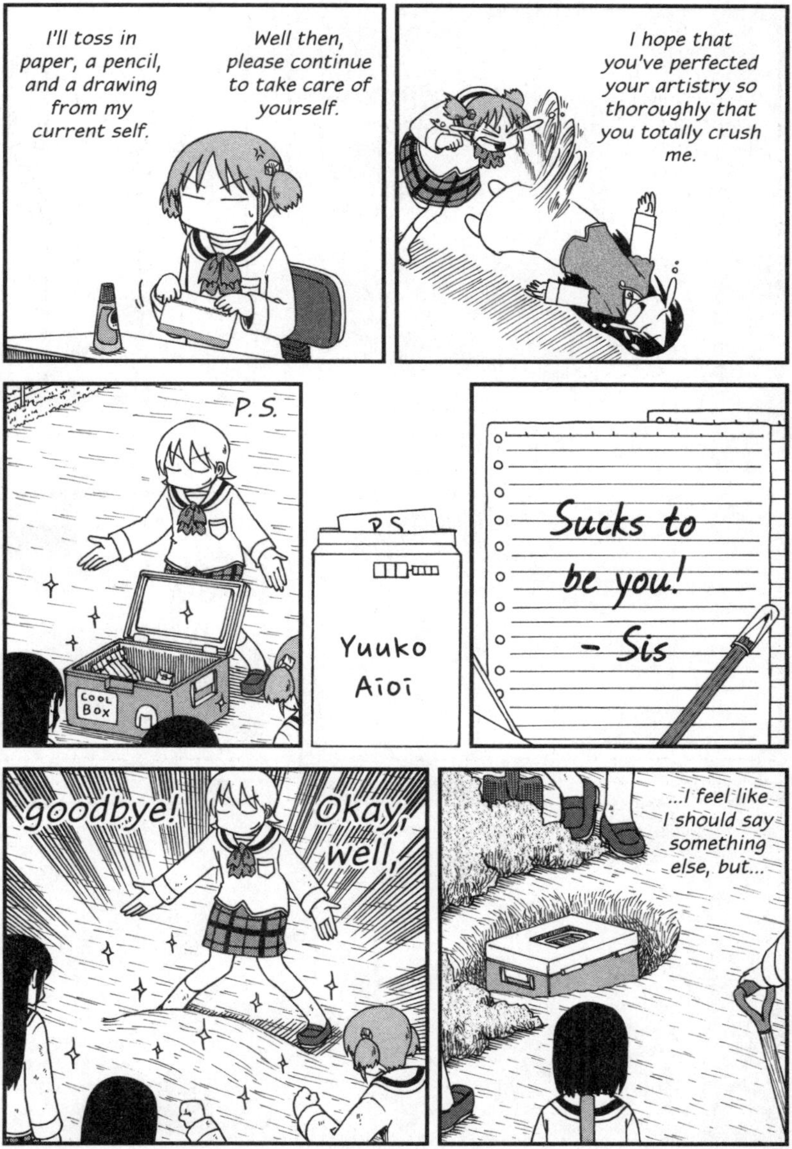
I hope that you've perfected your artistry so thoroughly that you totally crush me.
Well then, please continue to take care of yourself.
I'll toss in paper, a pencil, and a drawing from my current self.
Sucks to be you!
- Sis
P.S.
Yuuko Aioi
P.S.
COOL BOX
...I feel like I should say something else, but...
Okay, well,
goodbye!

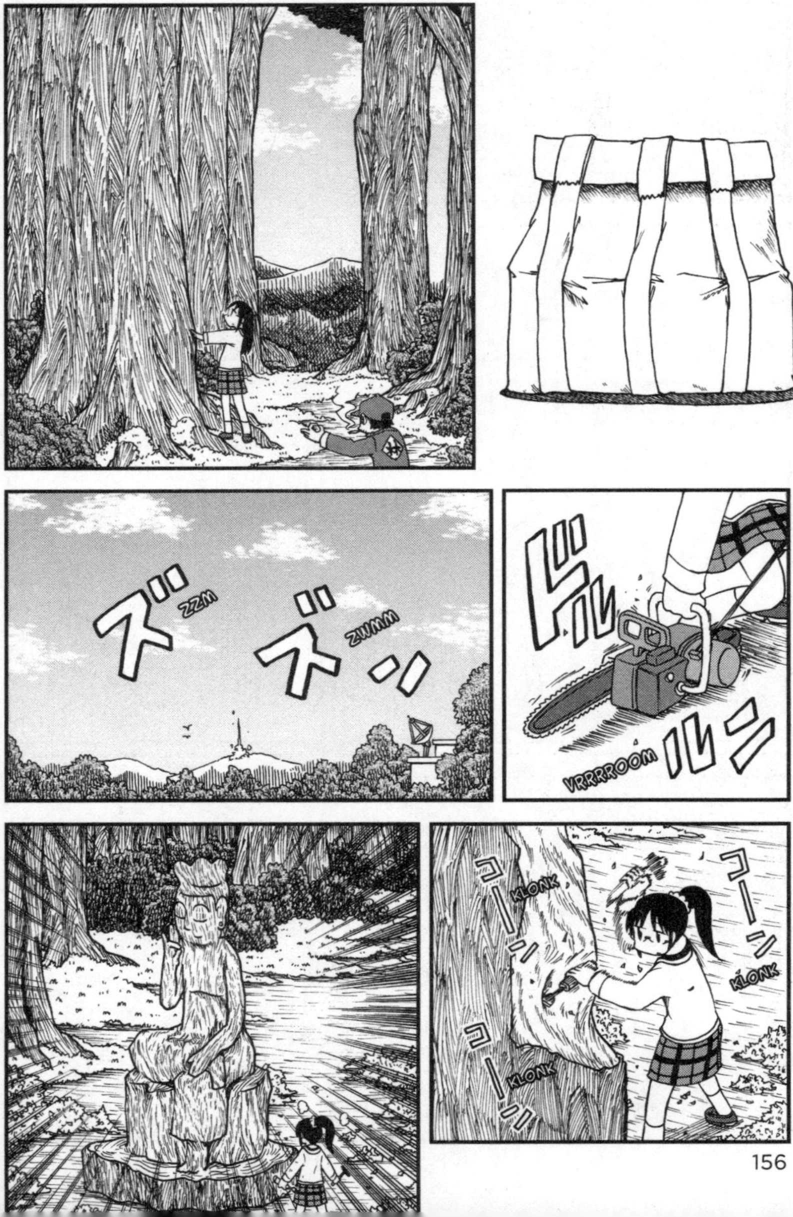

ドル
ルン
VRRRROOM
ズ
ZZM
ズッ
ZWMM
コーン
KLONK
コーン
KLONK
コーン
KLONK

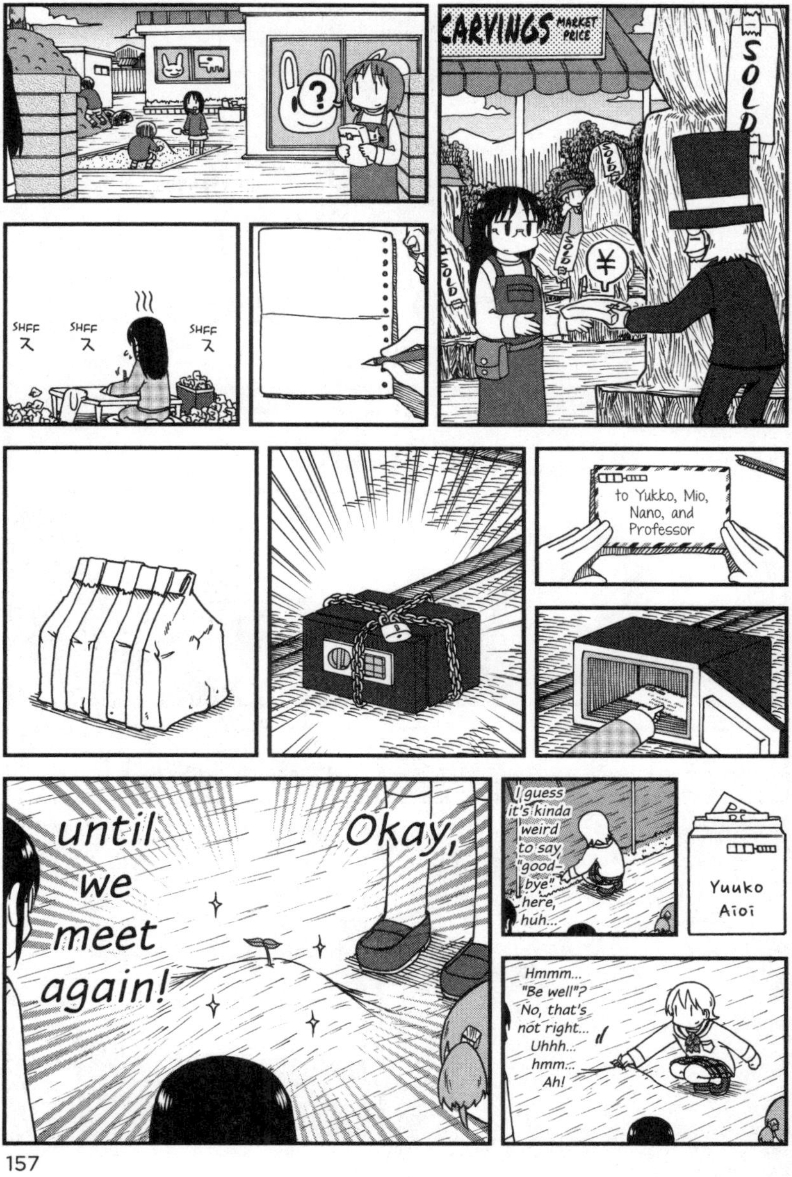
CARVINGS
MARKET PRICE
SOLD
SOLD
SOLD
SOLD
¥
?
SHFF ス
SHFF ス
SHFF ス
to Yukko, Mio, Nano, and Professor
Yuuko Aïoi
I guess it's kinda weird to say, "good-bye" here, huh...
Hmmm... "Be well"? No, that's not right... Uhhh... hmm... Ah!
Okay,
until we meet again!

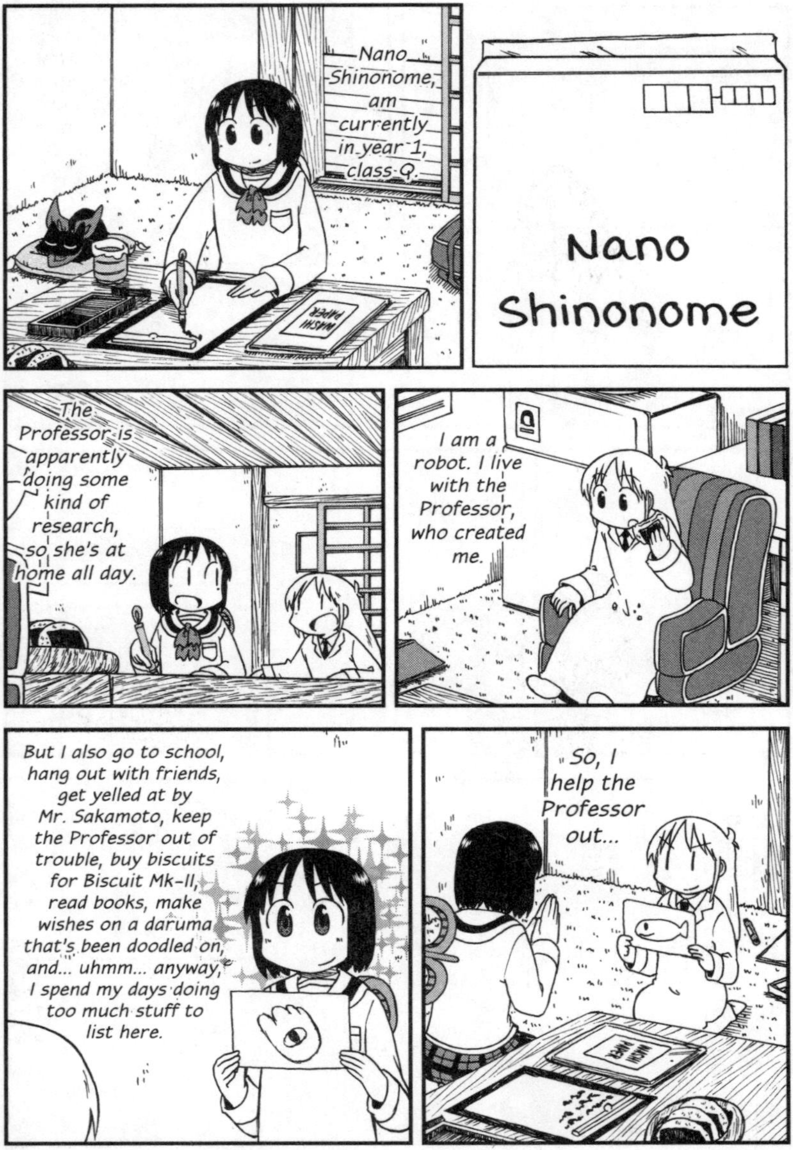
Nano Shinonome
Nano Shinonome, am currently in year 1, class Q.
I am a robot. I live with the Professor, who created me.
The Professor is apparently doing some kind of research, so she's at home all day.
So, I help the Professor out...
But I also go to school, hang out with friends, get yelled at by Mr. Sakamoto, keep the Professor out of trouble, buy biscuits for Biscuit Mk-II, read books, make wishes on a daruma that's been doodled on, and... uhmm... anyway, I spend my days doing too much stuff to list here.

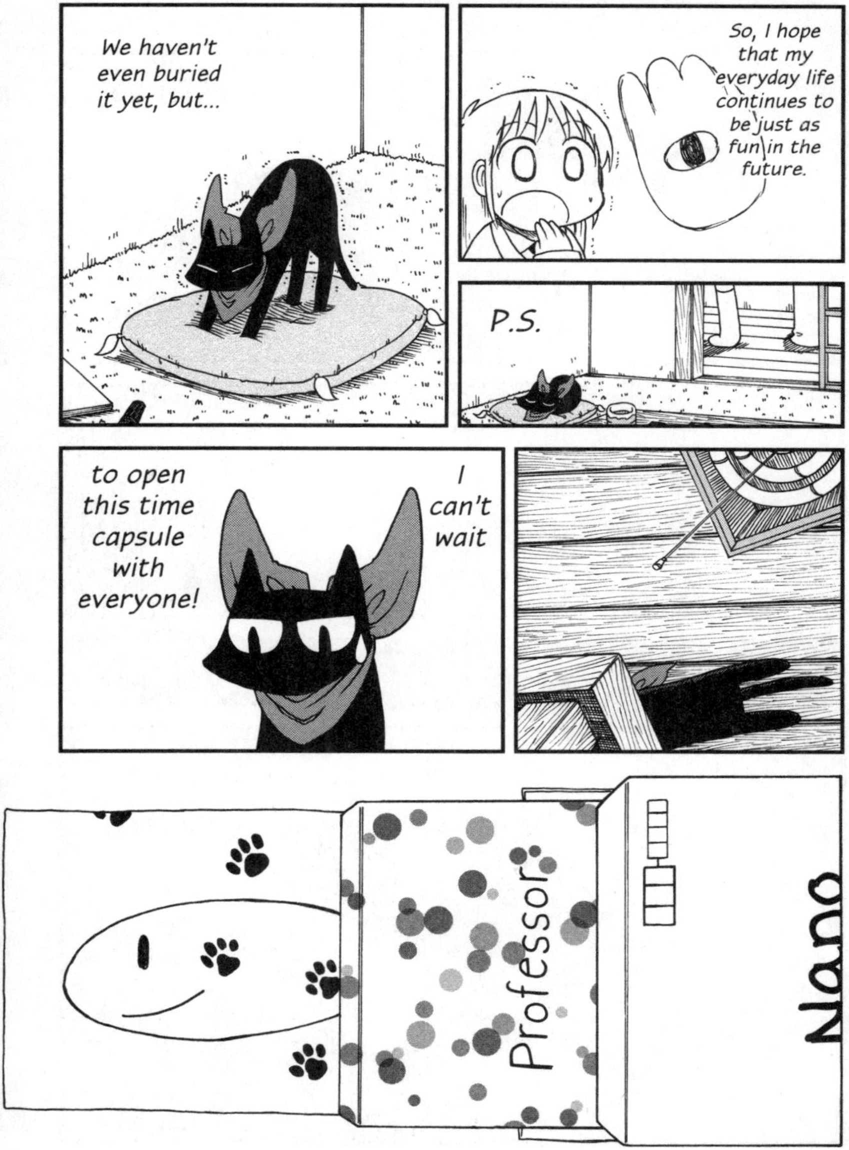
So, I hope that my everyday life continues to be just as fun in the future.
P.S.
We haven't even buried it yet, but...
I can't wait
to open this time capsule with everyone!
Nano
Professor

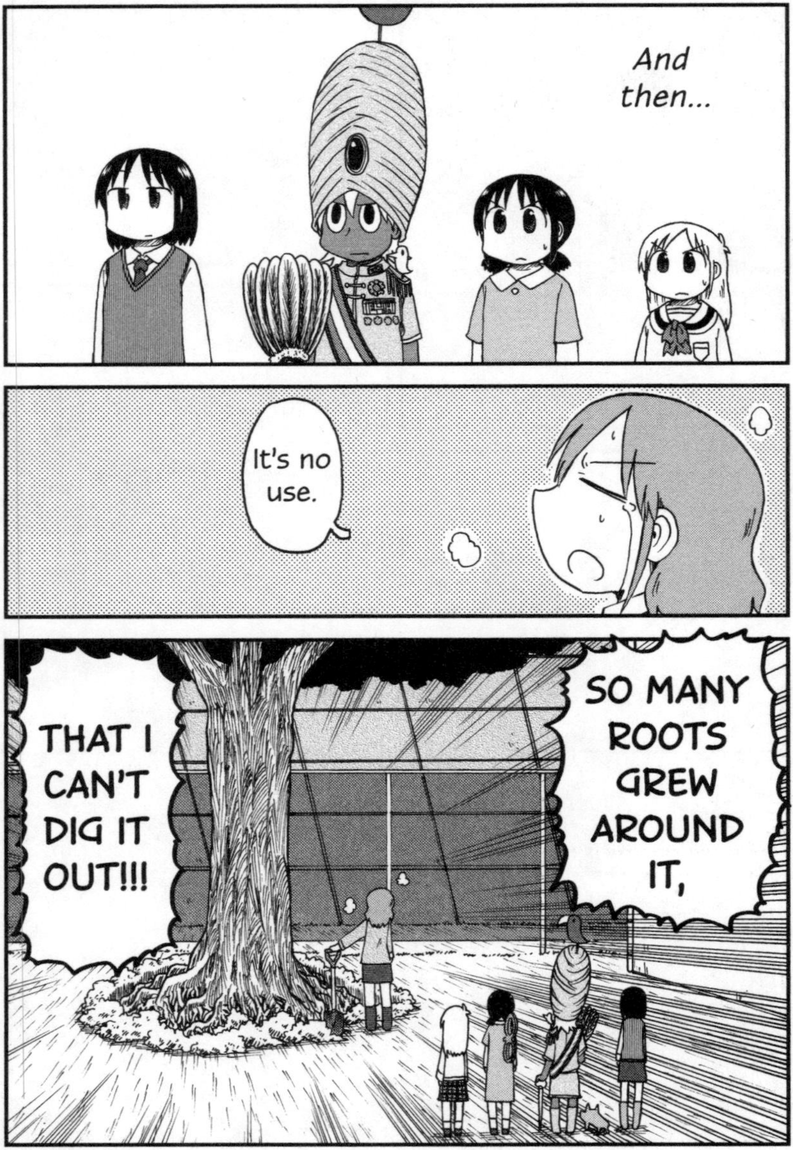
And then...
It's no use.
SO MANY ROOTS GREW AROUND IT,
THAT I CAN'T DIG IT OUT!!!

chapter 192: end

nichijou

Rock ... paper ...
scis-sors ...
Shoot!
Tie! One more time!
Tie!

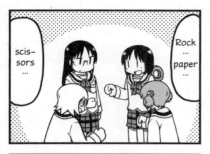

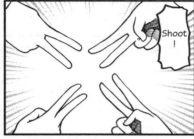

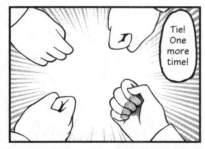

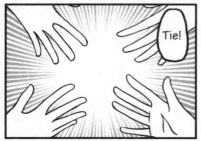

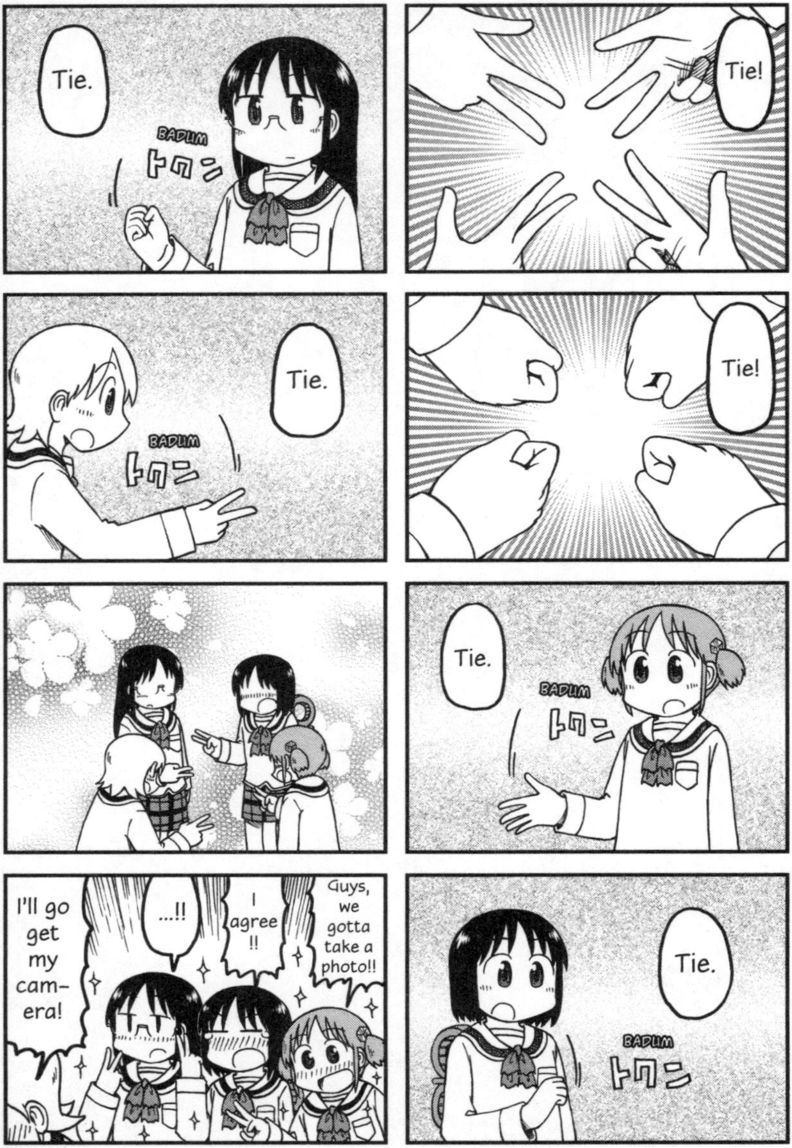
Tie!
Tie.
BADUM
トクン
Tie!
Tie.
BADUM
トクン
Tie.
BADUM
トクン
Tie.
BADUM
トクン
Guys, we gotta take a photo!!
I agree!!
...!!
I'll go get my cam-era!

nichijou: the end

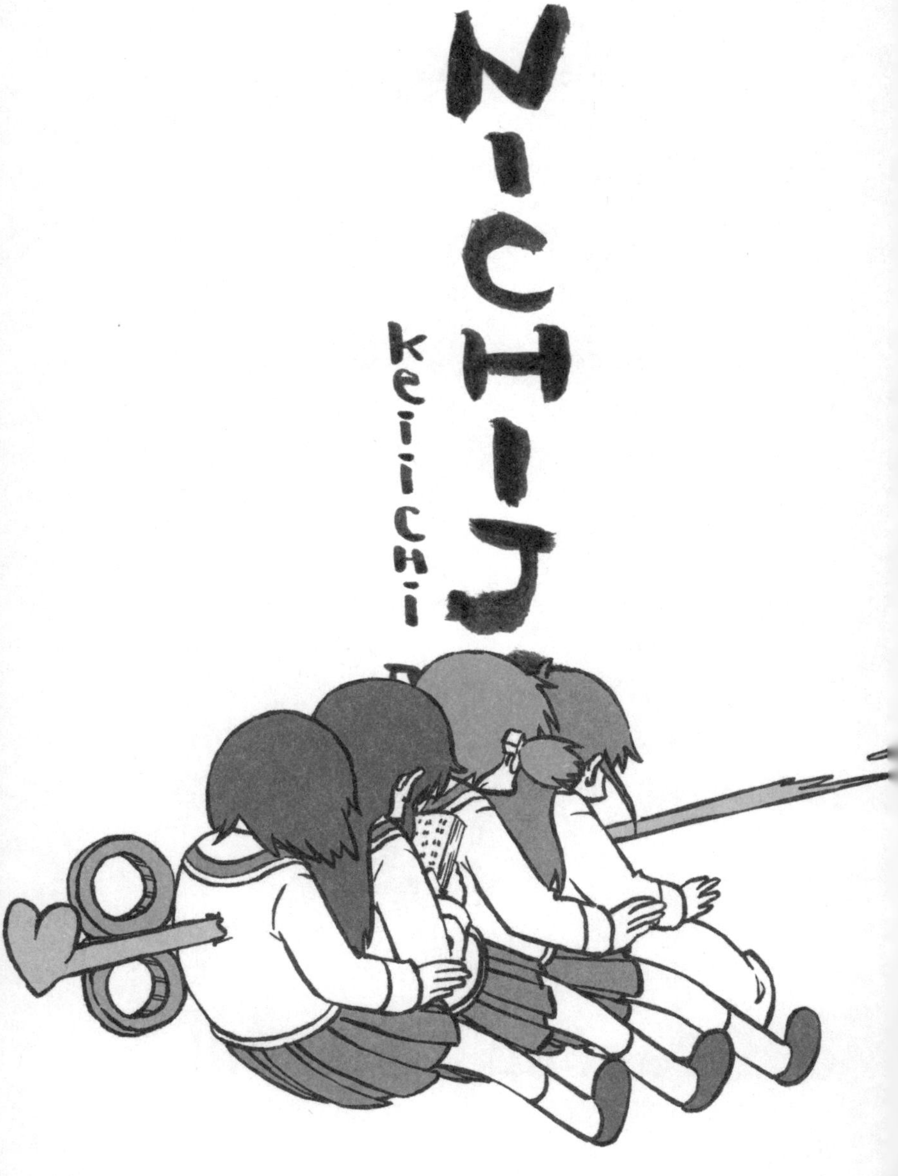
NICHIJ
keiiichi

The follow up to the hit manga series ***nichijou***, ***Helvetica Standard*** is a full color anthology of Keiichi Arawi's comic art and design work. Funny and heartwarming, ***Helvetica Standard*** is a humorous look at modern day Japanese design in comic form.

Helvetica Standard is a deep dive into the artistic and creative world of Keiichi Arawi. Part comic, part diary, part art and design book, ***Helvetica Standard*** is a deconstruction of the world of ***nichijou***.

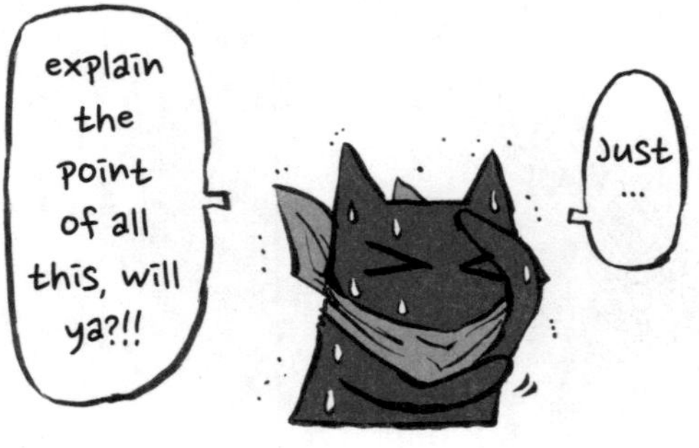
Just ...
explain the point of all this, will ya?!!

Coming This Fall!

Keiichi Arawi

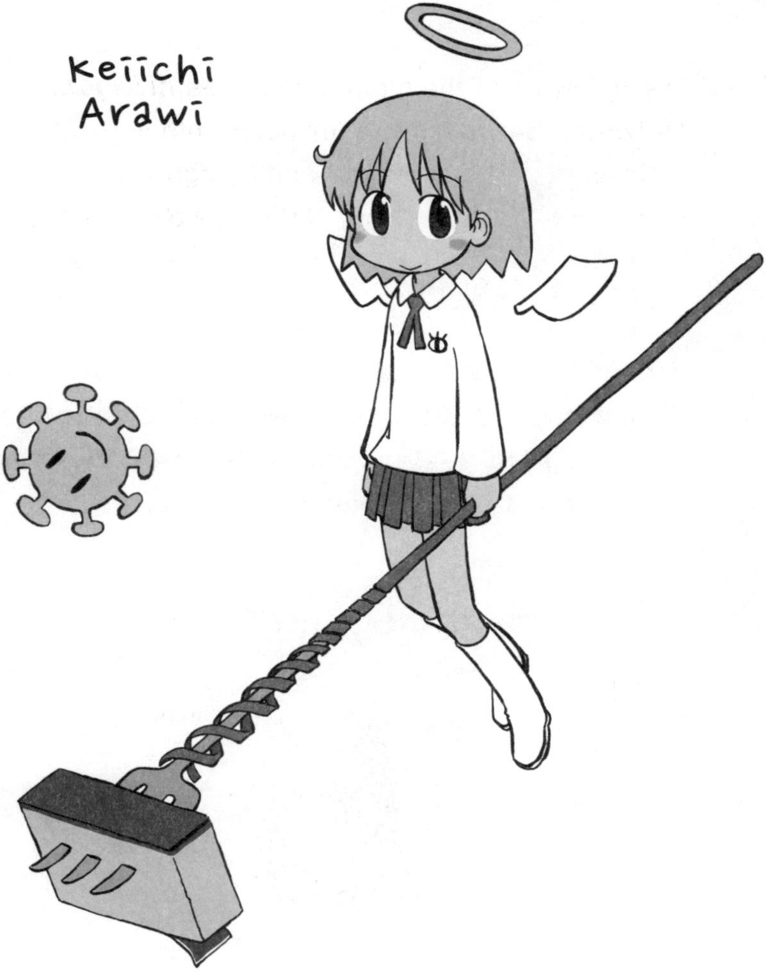

Helvetica Standard

The surrealist spiritual successor
to *nichijou*, *CITY* is Keiichi Arawi's latest
work that details the mildly bizarre lives
of the denizens of a certain city.

A penniless college student, Midori
Nagumo, has recently moved to town.
And as she runs, the city spins...

Coming Spring 2018!

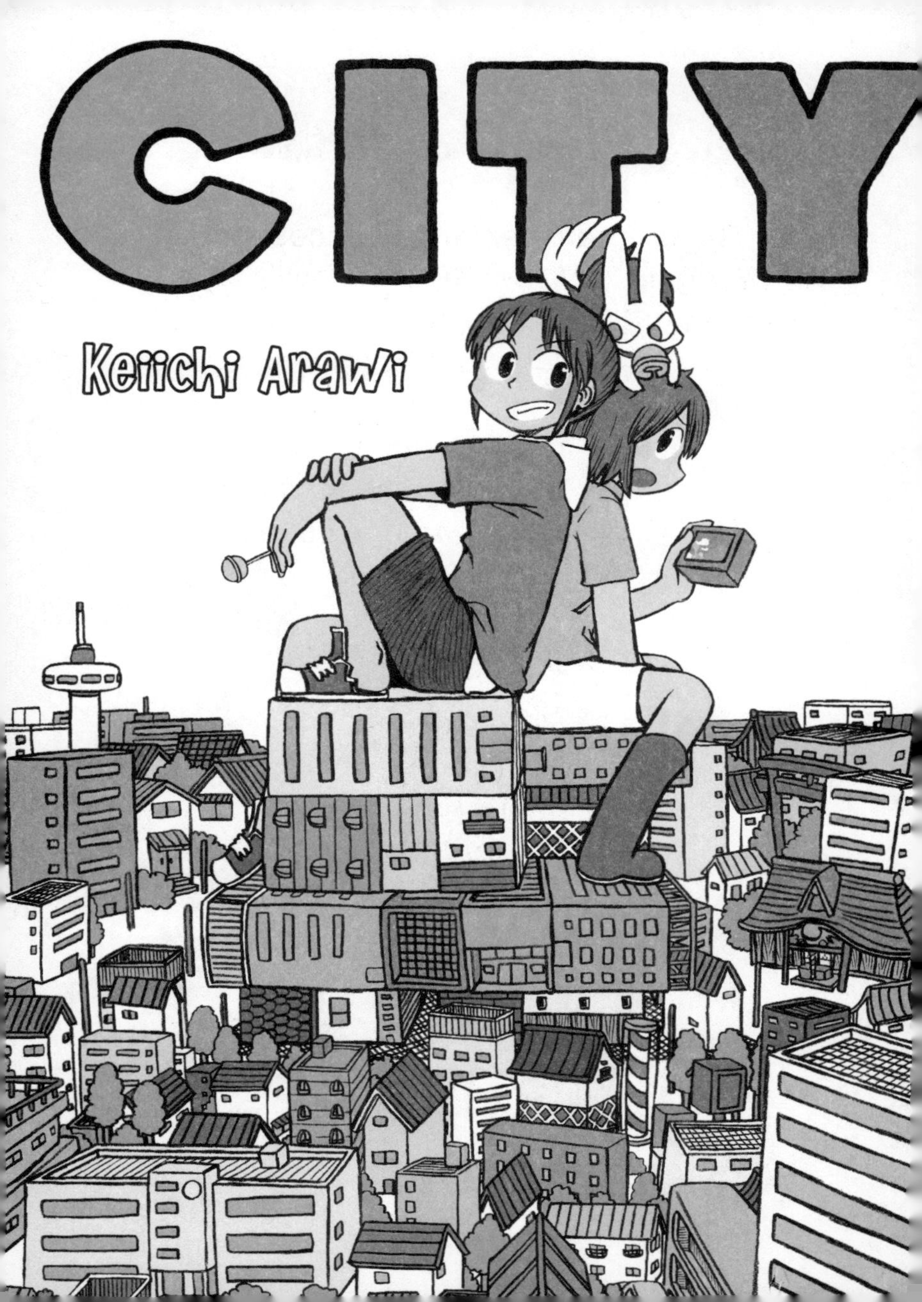
CITY
Keiichi Arawi

The Master of Killing Time

Toshinari Seki takes goofing off to new heights. Every day, on or around his school desk, he masterfully creates his own little worlds of wonder, often hidden to most of his classmates. Unfortunately for Rumi Yokoi, his neighbor at the back of the room, his many games, dioramas, and projects are often way too interesting to ignore; even when they are hurting her grades.

Volumes 1-9 available now!

WITHDRAWN

nichijou 10

my ordinary life

A Vertical Comics Edition

Translation: Jenny McKeon
Production: Grace Lu
            Hiroko Mizuno

© Keiichi ARAWI 2015
First published in Japan in 2015 by KADOKAWA CORPORATION, Tokyo.
English translation rights arranged with KADOKAWA CORPORATION, Tokyo
through TUTTLE-MORI AGENCY, INC., Tokyo.

Published by Vertical Comics, an imprint of Vertical, Inc., New York

Originally published in Japanese as *nichijou 10* by Kadokawa Corporation, 2015
nichijou first serialized in *Monthly Shonen Ace,* Kadokawa Corporation, 2006-2015

This is a work of fiction.

ISBN: 978-1-942993-69-8

Manufactured in Canada

First Edition

Vertical, Inc.
451 Park Avenue South
7th Floor
New York, NY 10016
www.vertical-comics.com

Vertical books are distributed through Penguin-Random House Publisher Services.

My Neighbor Seki

Tonari no Seki-kun

Takuma Morishige

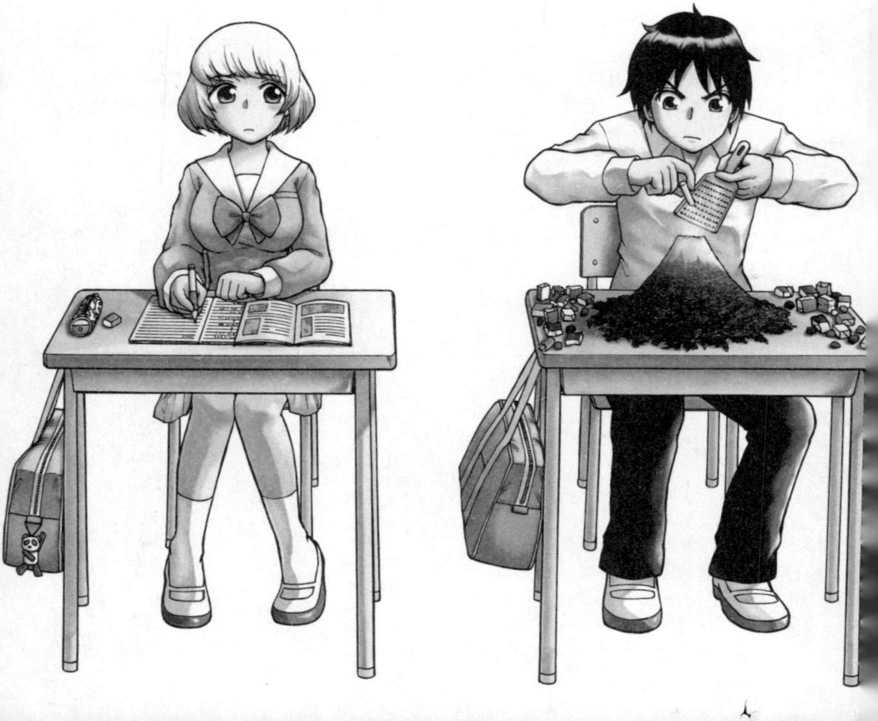